Baillière's
CLINICAL
HAEMATOLOGY
INTERNATIONAL PRACTICE AND RESEARCH

Baillière's

CLINICAL
HAEMATOLOGY

INTERNATIONAL PRACTICE AND RESEARCH

Volume 7/Number 1
March 1994

Cytokines and Growth Factors

M. K. BRENNER MB, PhD, FRCP, MRCPath
Guest Editor

Baillière Tindall
London Philadelphia Sydney Tokyo Toronto

This book is printed on acid-free paper.

Baillière Tindall   24–28 Oval Road,
W.B. Saunders   London NW1 7DX

The Curtis Center, Independence Square West,
Philadelphia, PA 19106–3399, USA

55 Horner Avenue
Toronto, Ontario M8Z 4X6, Canada

Harcourt Brace & Company (Australia) Pty Ltd,
30–52 Smidmore Street, Marrickville, NSW 2204, Australia

Harcourt Brace Japan, Inc.
Ichibancho Central Building, 22–1
Ichibancho, Chiyoda-ku, Tokyo 102, Japan

ISSN 0950-3536

ISBN 0–7020–1819–8 (single copy)

Baillière's Clinical Haematology is published four times each year by Baillière Tindall. Prices for Volume 7 (1994) are:

TERRITORY	ANNUAL SUBSCRIPTION	SINGLE ISSUE
Europe including UK	£87.00 (Institutional) post free £76.00 (Individual) post free	£27.50 post free
All other countries	Consult your local Harcourt Brace & Company office	

The editor of this publication is Catriona Byres, Baillière Tindall, 24–28 Oval Road, London NW1 7DX.

Baillière's Clinical Haematology is covered in Current Contents/Clinical Medicine, Index Medicus, the Science Citation Index, SciSearch and Research Alert.
Baillière's Clinical Haematology was published from 1972 to 1986 as *Clinics in Haematology*.

Typeset by Phoenix Photosetting, Chatham.
Printed and bound in Great Britain by University Printing House, Cambridge.

Contributors to this issue

WILLIAM ARCESE MD, Section of Haematology, Department of Human Biopathology, University La Sapienza, Via Benevento 6, I-00161 Rome, Italy.

GIUSEPPE AWISATI MD, PhD, Section of Haematology, Department of Human Biopathology, University La Sapienza, Via Benevento 6, I-00161 Rome, Italy.

MALCOLM K. BRENNER MB, PhD, FRCP, MRCPath, Director, Division of Bone Marrow Transplantation, St Jude Children's Research Hospital, 332 North Lauderdale, Memphis, TN 38101-0318, USA.

JACQUES P. CAEN MD, Professor of Hematology, Université Paris VII, Director of Institut des Vaisseux et du Sang, 8 Rue Guy-Patin, 75010 Paris, France.

JOHANNE D. CASHMAN MSc, PhD, Postdoctoral Fellow, Terry Fox Laboratory, 601 W10 Ave, Vancouver, British Columbia, V5Z IL3, Canada.

CAROLE M. COZE MD, Assistant Chef-de Clinique, Service d'oncologie pediatrique, Hôpital d'Enfants de la Timone, 13385 Marseille Cedex 5, France.

CONNIE J. EAVES PhD, Deputy Director, Terry Fox Laboratory, Professor of Medical Genetics, University of British Columbia, B. C. Cancer Research Center, 601 W10 Ave, Vancouver, British Columbia, V5Z IL3, Canada.

ZHONG C. HAN MD, PhD, Head, Laboratory of Cellular and Molecular Biology, Institut des Vaisseaux et du Sang, 8 Rue Guy-Patin, 75010 Paris, France, Research Professor, Shanghai Institute of Cell Biology, Shanghai, China.

HELEN E. HESLOP MD, FRACP, MRCPA, Assistant Member, Department of Hematology/Oncology, St Jude Children's Research Hospital, 332 North Lauderdale, Memphis, TN 38105, Assistant Professor, University of Tennessee, College of Medicine, Memphis TN 38163, USA.

DONNA E. HOGGE MD, PhD, FRCP(C), Senior Scientist, Terry Fox Laboratory, Clinical Associate Professor, University of British Columbia, B. C. Cancer Research Center, 601 W10 Ave, Vancouver, British Columbia, V5Z IL3, Canada.

R. KEITH HUMPHRIES MD, PhD, Associate Professor, Department of Medicine, University of British Columbia, Senior Scientist, Terry Fox Laboratory, B. C. Cancer Agency, 601 W10 Ave, Vancouver, British Columbia, V5Z IL3, Canada.

JAMES N. IHLE PhD, Chairman, Department of Biochemistry, St Jude Children's Research Hospital, 332 North Lauderdale, Memphis, TN 38105, USA.

PETER M. LANSDORP MD, PhD, Director, Cryogenic Laboratory, British Columbia Cancer Agency, 601 W10 Ave, Vancouver, British Columbia, V5Z IL3, Canada.

FRANCO MANDELLI MD, Professor of Haematology, Section of Haematology, Department of Human Biopathology, University La Sapienza, Via Benevento 6, I-00161, Rome, Italy.

PHILIP L. McCARTHY Jr. MD, Assistant Professor of Medicine, Baylor College of Medicine/The Methodist Hospital, MS902, 6565 Fanin St, Houston TX 77030, USA.

FREDERICK W. QUELLE PhD, Department of Biochemistry, St Jude Children's Research Hospital, 332 North Lauderdale, Memphis, TN 38105, USA.

HEATHER J. SUTHERLAND MD, PhD, FRCP(C), Terry Fox Laboratory, Clinical Assistant Professor, Department of Medicine, University of British Columbia, 601 W10 Ave, Vancouver, British Columbia, V5Z IL3, Canada.

B. TANG PhD, Department of Biochemistry, St Jude Children's Research Hospital, 332 North Lauderdale, Memphis TN 38105, USA.

BRUCE A. WITTHUHN PhD, Department of Biochemistry, St Jude Children's Research Hospital, 332 North Lauderdale, Memphis, TN 38105, USA.

TAOLIN YI PhD, Cleveland Clinic, Department of Cancer Biology, 9500 Euclid Avenue, Cleveland OH 44195-5069, USA.

Table of contents

PREVIOUS ISSUES

Vol. 4, No. 4 1991
Molecular Immunohaematology
A. E. G. KR. VON DEM BORNE

Vol. 5, No. 1 1992
Epidemiology of Haematological Disease: Part I
A. F. FLEMING

Vol. 5, No. 2 1992
Epidemiology of Haematological Disease: Part II
A. F. FLEMING

Vol. 5, No. 3 1992
Growth Factors in Haemopoiesis
B. I. LORD & T. M. DEXTER

Vol. 5, No. 4 1992
The Molecular Genetics of Haematological Malignancy
B. D. YOUNG

Vol. 6, No. 1 1993
The Haemoglobinopathies
D. R. HIGGS & D. J. WEATHERALL

Vol. 6, No. 2 1993
Red Cell Membrane and Red Cell Antigens
M. J. A. TANNER & D. J. ANSTEE

Vol. 6, No. 3 1993
Blood Constituents and the Vessel Wall
J. P. CAEN & G. TOBELEM

Vol. 6, No. 4 1993
Chronic Lymphocytic Leukaemia and Related Disorders
C. ROZMAN

FORTHCOMING ISSUES

Vol. 7, No. 2 1994
Acute Lymphoblastic Leukaemia
D. HOELZER

Vol. 7, No. 3 1994
Thrombophilia
T. W. MEADE

Foreword

The first phase of cytokine development came 15 years ago, with the discovery and purification of the first interleukins. The following decade saw the cloning of a multiplicity of cytokines and their introduction into clinical use as single agents. This second phase produced some notable successes. Alpha-interferon proved a useful therapeutic agent for chronic myelogenous and hairy cell leukaemias, while granulocyte and granulocyte-macrophage colony stimulating factors had a substantial impact on cancer chemotherapy and bone marrow transplantation. While IL-2 produced less dramatic effects than had earlier been hoped, the drug now has an established place in the therapy of renal cell carcinoma and malignant melanoma and may be valuable as adjuvant therapy in the haematological malignancies. These successes, however, may be trivial compared to the potential uses of cytokines currently being explored in the third phase of study. This most recent phase is based on an improved understanding of the molecular mechanisms by which cytokines produce their effect, on an appreciation of the way in which cytokines in sequence or in combination can produce effects distinct from the actions of single agents, and on an understanding of the homeostatic mechanisms which regulate cytokine activity. Finally, the development of gene transfer techniques is allowing us to explore entirely new ways of administering cytokines, in which they may be secreted by novel cell types, in different concentrations and in otherwise inaccessible sites. It is on this current phase of activity that the chapters in this book focus.

Dr Coze opens the volume with a ready reference glossary of the cytokines which follow. Dr James Ihle and colleagues provide information on the cytokine receptors and signal transduction molecules in haemato-poietic cells which may be targets for future therapeutic intervention. Dr Hogge and colleagues describe growth factors acting early in haemopoiesis, while Drs Han and Caen discuss cytokines acting on committed haemo-poietic progenitor cells. Used in combination, these cytokines represent a powerful means for producing expansion and differentiation of even the earliest haemopoietic multipotent progenitor cells and such use will continue to influence the practice of oncology and bone marrow transplantation. Dr Mandelli and colleagues describe how the interferons are used clinically and how future applications are developing, while I discuss present and future uses of the immunomodulatory cytokines. In Dr McCarthy's chapter, cytokine inhibitors are described and their critical role in modulating the effects of stimulatory cytokines are examined, while Dr Heslop illustrates how the combination of cytokines and gene therapy provides novel therapeutic opportunities.

The contributors to this volume have all tried to balance known facts and applications with somewhat more speculative projections. We hope these speculations are neither outdated nor disproven by the time this volume appears in print!

M. K. BRENNER

1

Glossary of cytokines

CAROLE M. COZE

INTRODUCTION

This chapter is intended as a ready-reference and aide-memoire, and provides outline descriptions of many of the cytokines of current interest in haematological practice.

INTERLEUKIN-1

Synonyms

Haemopoietin-1, endogenous pyrogen, lymphocyte activating factor, osteo-clast activating factor, leukocytic endogenous mediator, mononuclear (cell) factor, catabolin, melanoma growth inhibitory factor, tumour inhibitory factor-2, lymphocyte proliferation promoting factor of neutrophils.

Molecular structure

There are three distinct molecules in the system:

1. Two agonist polypeptides, IL-1α and IL-1β, which are products of different genes located on chromosome 2q12–21 and share only 25% structural homology. However, they bind to the same receptors (IL-1RI, IL-1RII).
2. A natural receptor antagonist (IL-1ra).

Synthesis

Both agonist polypeptides are synthesized as 31 kDa precursors (proIL-1) cleaved to yield physiologically active mature proteins (17 kDa). In response to exogenous stimuli such as antigen or endotoxin, blood monocytes and tissue macrophages are the first source of IL-1, although a wide variety of nucleated cells may also be induced to synthesize the cytokine.

Receptors

There are two distinct receptors, both belonging to the immunoglobulin superfamily. IL-1α generally binds better to IL-1RI (80 kDa, $K_d = 0.05–$

0.5 nM for IL-1α and 0.5–10 nM for IL-1β) and IL-1β to IL-1RII (68 kDa, $K_d = 0.3$–30 nM for IL-1α and 4–5 nM for IL-1β), each cytokine may bind to both receptors.

Actions

1. IL-1 is a major component of the acute-phase response, producing fever, sleepiness, anorexia, myalgia, arthralgia, hypotension (toxic shock syndrome at higher doses), neutrophilia, increased ACTH and vasopressin levels. IL-1 also induces synthesis of hepatic acute-phase proteins, stimulates secretion of other cytokines and increases expression of cell surface adhesion molecules.
2. IL-1 synergizes with other cytokines such as TNF-α and IL-6 to activate B and T lymphocytes.
3. IL-1 induces production of multiple haematopoietic growth factors, including G-CSF, GM-CSF, M-CSF and IL-3 and may also directly induce early progenitor cells to enter the cell cycle. Paradoxically it may also protect these cells from cytotoxic agents or radiation.

INTERLEUKIN-2 (IL-2)

Synonyms

T-cell growth factor.

Molecular structure

The human IL-2 gene is located on chromosome 4q 26–28 and produces a 15–16 kDa glycoprotein.

Synthesis

Mainly produced by T(h1) helper cells after the T-cell receptor (TCR) complex has engaged a major histocompatibility complex (MHC)/antigen complex on antigen-presenting cells.

Receptors

The high-affinity receptor ($K_d = 10$–50 pM, rapid association/slow dissociation) is a heterotrimer, the components of which belong to the haematopoietin receptor superfamily, defined by the presence of four conserved cysteine residues and a common double tryptophan–serine (WSXWS). The components are:

1. IL-2Rα (CD25, TAC, 55 kDa, low affinity receptor: $K_d = 10$–20 nM, rapid association/dissociation, no signal transduction);
2. IL-2Rβ (75 kDa);
3. IL-2Rγ (68 kDa).

The β and γ receptors associate to form the intermediate affinity receptor ($K_d = 0.5$–1 nM, slow association/dissociation). This heterodimer appears responsible for signal transduction. A soluble IL-2R has also been described which inhibits IL-2 activity.

Actions

Binding of IL-2 to its receptor generally induces a rapid clonal expansion of antigen-specific T cells and synthesis of multiple cytokines. Other lymphoid cells (B, NK, LAK), as well as monocytes and macrophages are additional target cells.

INTERLEUKIN-3 (IL-3)

Synonyms

Mast cell growth factor, Thy-1 inducing factor, WEHI-3 growth factor, multi-CSF, CSF-2a, CSF-2b, eosinophilic CSF, megakaryocyte CSF, erythroid CSF, burst promoting activity, neutrophils/granulocytes CSF, P-cell stimulating factor, haemopoietin-2.

Molecular structure

The IL-3 gene is part of a cluster of cytokine genes (IL-4, IL-5, GM-CSF) located within 500 kilobases on chromosome 5q23–31. The IL-3 gene product is a highly glycosylated monomeric protein (28 kDa) displaying species-specific activity.

Synthesis

IL-3 is mainly synthesized by activated T-cell lymphocytes and plays a key role in the response of the haematopoietic system to stress.

Receptors

The IL-3 receptor (IL-3R) is heteromultimeric, including at least two different subunits, both belonging to the haematopoietin receptor super-family:

1. IL-3R$_\alpha$ (70 kDa, low affinity: $K_d = 10$–100 nM) which is IL-3-specific.
2. IL-3R$_\beta$ (120 kDa, homologous to IL-5R and GM-CSFR β subunit). This sub-unit has no independent binding capacity.

The high affinity receptor ($K_d = 50$–200 pM) is constituted by the association of the α and β subunits.

Actions

IL-3 stimulates the proliferation and differentiation of early haematopoietic progenitor cells and lineage-committed precursors. It synergizes with other colony stimulating factors. Its role in steady-state haematopoiesis and lymphocyte development remains controversial.

INTERLEUKIN-4 (IL-4)

Synonyms

B-cell differentiation factor, B-cell growth factor 1, B-cell stimulatory factor-1.

Molecular structure

The IL-4 gene maps within the cytokine locus on human chromosome 5. The gene product is a glycosylated protein of approximately 19 kDa showing species-specific activity.

Synthesis

Helper T lymphocytes are the main source of IL-4, although mast cells, bone marrow stromal cells and other origins have been described.

Receptors

The IL-4 receptor (IL-4R) is a single high affinity chain (130 kDa, $K_d = 40$–120 pM) which shows homology with the haematopoietin receptor super-family. Receptors are expressed on almost all nucleated cell types and a soluble form of receptor may act as a physiological inhibitor of IL-4 activity.

Actions

IL-4 is a pleiotropic cytokine and is involved in the following activities:

1. T- and B-cell ontogeny, stimulation of B-cell proliferation, differentiation and antigen presentation. Modulation of T-cell growth and effector function.
2. Induction of NK- and LAK-cell proliferation and activity but inhibition of cytotoxic T-cell activity.
3. Enhancement of monocyte/macrophage antigen processing and presentation.
4. Stimulation of fibroblasts and endothelial cells.

INTERLEUKIN-5 (IL-5)

Synonyms

T-cell replacing factor, B-cell growth factor 2, eosinophil differentiation factor, eosinophilic CSF.

Molecular structure

The IL-5 gene is located within the cytokine cluster on human chromosome 5. The product is a heavily glycosylated protein (40–45 kDa) which displays an unusual homodimeric disulphide-linked structure.

Sources

Antigen-activated (T) lymphocytes.

Receptors

The IL-5 receptor is a heterodimer which belongs to the haematopoietin receptor superfamily.

1. IL-5R$_\alpha$ is the low affinity component ($K_d = 2$–30 nM, 60 kDa) which cannot transduce a signal.
2. IL-5R$_\beta$ (120 kDa) is entirely non-binding and is structurally similar to the IL-3R and GM-CSFR β subunit. This subunit may be responsible for signal transduction.

The two subunits associate to generate the high affinity receptor (10–100 pM). Soluble IL-5R may act as a physiological antagonist.

Activities

Restricted to the eosinophilic and basophilic lineages, stimulating progenitor growth and differentiation and increasing chemotaxis.

INTERLEUKIN-6 (IL-6)

Synonyms

B-cell stimulatory factor 2, monocyte-derived hepatocyte stimulatory factor, interferon-β2, hybridoma/plasmacytoma growth factor, monocyte granulocyte inducer type 2, 26 kDa protein.

Molecular structure

The IL-6 gene is located on human chromosome 7p21–22. The product has a molecular mass of 21–28 kDa.

Source

IL-6 is an acute-phase response protein. It may be produced by T cells, monocytes/macrophages, fibroblasts and hepatocytes in response to stimuli which include antigens, other cytokines and lipopolysaccharides.

Receptors

The IL-6 receptor is a heterodimeric glycoprotein.

1. IL-6R is 60 kDa ($K_d = 1–10$ nM) and provides binding specificity.
2. gp130 which is non-binding but transduces the signal. This component contains both a non-binding Ig-like domain and a second domain containing the common motif for the haematopoietic receptor superfamily.

The two subunits associate to generate the high affinity receptor (40–70 pM) and both membrane-bound and soluble forms have been described.

Actions

IL-6 produces T-cell growth, differentiation and activation of effector function. IL-6 is essential because it stimulates immunoglobulin production and acts synergistically with other CSFs to induce proliferation of haematopoietic progenitor cells including those of the megakaryocytic lineage. IL-6 is also a potent inducer of other acute-phase proteins.

INTERLEUKIN-7 (IL-7)

Synonyms

Pre B-cell growth factor, lymphopoietin-1.

Molecular structure

The IL-7 gene is located on human chromosome 8q12–13. The product is a 25 kDa glycoprotein.

Synthesis

IL-7 was obtained from bone marrow stromal cell lines and from hepatocellular carcinoma lines. Bone marrow stroma is the presumed major source in vivo.

Receptors

IL-7R is a heterodimer, both components belonging to the haemopoietin receptor superfamily.

1. Low affinity of 65 kDa light chain ($K_d = 10–100$ nM).
2. High affinity 75 kDa heavy chain ($K_d = 10–100$ pM).

A soluble IL-7R has also been described.

Activities

IL-7 plays a major role in the control of T and B lymphopoiesis, inducing progenitor proliferation and differentiation. It also induces the generation of both CTL and LAK cells and may synergize with other cytokines (e.g. IL-2 and IL-12) in this action. Effects on mature B cells remain controversial.

INTERLEUKIN-8 (IL-8)

Synonyms

Neutrophil-activating protein-1 (NAP-1), monocyte-derived neutrophil chemotactic factor, monocyte-derived neutrophil activating peptide, T-lymphocyte chemotactic factor, leukocyte adhesion inhibitor, granulocyte chemotactic protein.

Molecular characteristics

The IL-8 gene is part of a gene superfamily (chemokines α) on human chromosome 4q12–21. It is a 6–8 kDa polypeptide which forms a hydrogen-bonded homodimer and shares structural as well as functional homology with the other inflammatory and growth regulatory proteins in the chemokines α superfamily (e.g. NAP-2, GRO).

Synthesis

IL-8 is produced by peripheral blood mononuclear cells, endothelial cells and fibroblasts. Other cells may also contribute. Production occurs after stimulation with mitogens, other cytokines, or viral/bacterial antigens.

Receptors

Two distinct high affinity IL-8Rs (IL-8RA and IL-8RB) have been described, both of which belong to the G-protein coupled receptor super-family.
1. IL-8RA (p44, $K_d = 0.2–4$ nM).
2. IL-8RB (p70, $K_d = 0.2–4$ nM).
These receptors also bind other IL-8-related molecules in the chemokines α family with variable affinity with high (IL-8RB) or low affinity (IL-8RA).

Activities

IL-8 is a potent neutrophil chemoattractant. It has additional pro-inflammatory effects including increased neutrophil degranulation and chemotactivity for basophils and lymphocytes.

INTERLEUKIN-9 (IL-9)

Synonyms

Megakaryocytoma growth promoting factor, p40, T-cell growth factor-II, mast cell enhancing activity.

Molecular structure

The IL-9 gene is located within the cytokine cluster on chromosome 5. The product is a heavily glycosylated protein (30–40 kDa) showing partial cross-species reactivity.

Synthesis

The IL-9 gene is expressed upon stimulation of peripheral blood mononuclear cells with mitogens or cytokines.

Receptors

The IL-9R is a 52 kDa protein belonging to the haematopoietin receptor superfamily. Both membrane-bound and soluble forms of the receptor have been described.

Activities

IL-9 stimulates the growth of mast cells and erythroid progenitor cells in the presence of erythropoietin.

INTERLEUKIN-10 (IL-10)

Synonyms

Cytokine synthesis inhibitory factor.

Molecular structure

The IL-10 gene is located on human chromosome 1. The product is an 18 kDa monomer with no N-glycosylation, which shows striking homology with BCRF1 (vIL-10), an Epstein–Barr virus (EBV) gene.

Source

IL-10 is produced by type 2 helper T cells as well as B cells, monocytes/macrophages and keratinocytes.

Receptors

Not yet identified.

Activities

IL-10 inhibits cytokine secretion by T cells and monocytes and down-regulates MHC class II antigen expression on antigen presenting cells. This inhibitory role is coupled with stimulation of B-lymphocyte proliferation and differentiation, and enhancement of mast cell growth.

INTERLEUKIN-11 (IL-11)

Synonyms

Adipogenesis inhibitory factor.

Molecular structure

The IL-11 gene is located on human chromosome 1q13.3–13. The product is a non-glycosylated 23 kDa protein.

Source

IL-11 has been isolated from a bone marrow-derived stromal cell line as well as from human fetal lung fibroblasts.

Receptor

A single 151 kDa receptor has been identified ($K_d = 0.35$ nM) which is closely linked to a functional tyrosine kinase pathway.

Activities

1. IL-11 stimulates early multipotent haematopoietic progenitor cells as well as those committed to erythropoietic or megakaryocytic lineage.
2. In the immune system, IL-11 promotes T-cell-dependant B-cell immunoglobulin secretion.
3. In fibroblasts and adipocytes, IL-11 is a potent inhibitor of adipogenesis.

INTERLEUKIN-12 (IL-12)

Synonyms

Natural killer stimulatory factor (NKSF), cytotoxic lymphocyte maturation factor.

Molecular structure

The IL-12 gene has not been localized, but the product is a 70 kDa heterodimer consisting of p40 and p35 chains linked by disulphide bonds. The p40 subunit is homologous to the IL-6R extracellular domain.

Source

IL-12 was originally purified and cloned from a human B-lymphoblastoid cell line but physiologically the dominant source is macrophages and B cells.

Receptors

IL-12 binds to a cellular receptor of 110 kDa (K_d = 100–600 pM).

Activities

IL-12 acts as a growth factor for T and NK cells and enhances NK/LAK activity (synergistic with suboptimal amounts of IL-2). IL-12 also stimulates IFN-γ production by T cells.

INTERLEUKIN-13 (IL-13)

Molecular structure

The human IL-13 gene is located on chromosome 5, adjacent to the genes for IL-3, IL-4, IL-5 and GM-CSF, suggesting it is another member of this cytokine family. A 10 kDa, largely non-glycosylated, protein is produced.

Synthesis

Mainly produced by activated type 2 helper T cells.

Receptors

Not yet identified, though competitive studies suggest they will be similar to IL-4 receptors.

Activities

1. Stimulates activated B cells to proliferate and produce IgM, IgG($_4$) and IgE. May be involved in regulating immunoglobulin class switching.
2. Upregulate monocyte Class II MHC antigen expression and expression of low affinity IgE receptor (CD23).

GRANULOCYTE-COLONY STIMULATING FACTOR (G-CSF)

Molecular structure

The G-CSF gene is located on human chromosome 17q21–22. The product is a single glycosylated polypeptide chain (19–25 kDa) which shows significant amino acid sequence homology with IL-6.

Source

G-CSF is mainly produced by monocytes and macrophages upon activation with endotoxin, TNF-α or IFN-γ.

Receptors

The G-CSF receptor exists as a monomeric form of 130 kDa which is low affinity (2–4 nM) and an oligomer of high affinity (120–360 pM). The extracellular portion of the receptor has an immunoglobulin-like domain, a domain homologous to the haematopoietin receptor and three fibronectin type II domains. A G-CSFR isoform (differing in the intracytoplasmic domain) as well as a soluble G-CSFR have been described.

Activities

G-CSF is a stimulator of the neutrophilic granulocyte lineage. It stimulates proliferation and differentiation of cells from committed progenitors to mature neutrophils and enhances the survival and functional activity of these mature cells.

GRANULOCYTE–MACROPHAGE-COLONY STIMULATING FACTOR (GM-CSF)

Molecular structure

The GM-CSF gene is located within the cytokine cluster on human chromosome 5. The product is a glycosylated protein of 22 kDa.

Source

GM-CSF is secreted by a variety of cells, but steady state expression is low, GM-CSF being secreted mainly by macrophages, endothelial cells and activated T cells in response to endotoxin stimulation.

Receptors

The high affinity receptor (30–60 pM) is formed by the association of two subunits both belonging to the haematopoietin receptor superfamily.

1. An α chain of 85 kDa ($K_d = 2$–8 nM) which binds GM-CSF but cannot transduce a signal.
2. A β chain of 120 kDa (homologous to the IL-3R and IL-5R β chains) which does not bind GM-CSF but associates with the α chain and transduces the signal. A soluble receptor form has been described.

Activities

1. GM-CSF induces growth and differentiation of both multilineage haematopoietic progenitor cells and committed progenitor cells of the granulocyte/macrophage lineage.
2. GM-CSF enhances the function of mature neutrophils, eosinophils and monocytes/macrophages.
3. GM-CSF is a potent stimulatory factor for endothelial cells.

MACROPHAGE-COLONY STIMULATING FACTOR (M-CSF)

Synonym

Colony stimulating factor-1.

Molecular structure

The M-CSF gene is located within the cytokine cluster on human chromosome 5. The product is a heavily glycosylated protein (40–70 kDa) which forms a disulphide-linked homodimer. Both soluble and membrane-bound M-CSF have been described.

Source

M-CSF is produced by a wide variety of cells including fibroblasts, activated macrophages, endothelial cells, bone marrow stromal cells and endometrial cells.

Receptor

The M-CSF receptor is a single chain high affinity receptor of 160 kDa ($K_d = 0.2$–0.4 nM). M-CSF-R is the product of c-*fms* proto-oncogene, located in the cytokine gene cluster on chromosome 5. The receptor contains five immunoglobulin-like motifs in its extracellular domain and belongs to the tyrosine kinase receptor superfamily.

Activities

1. M-CSF stimulates the growth of committed progenitor cells and enhances the function of mature macrophages (cytotoxicity, antibody-dependant cell-mediated cytotoxicity, cytokine release).
2. M-CSF may contribute to placental formation and differentiation.

STEM CELL FACTOR (SCF)

Synonyms

Mast cell growth factor, c-kit ligand, Steel factor.

Molecular structure

The SCF gene is located on 12q22–24. The product is a heavily glycosylated protein (20–35 kDa) which is found either in solution as a non-covalently-associated homodimer or as a transmembrane protein, both displaying biological activities.

Source

Bone marrow stroma cells and fibroblasts are the major sources of SCF suggesting an environmental effect.

Receptor

SCF-R is a transmembrane glycoprotein of 145 kDa ($K^d = 0.1$–1 pM) encoded by the c-*kit* proto-oncogene. It belongs to the tyrosine kinase receptor superfamily.

Activities

SCF enhances the proliferation of both early and lineage-committed progenitor cells. It also enhances the growth of mast cells. Many of its activities synergize with other factors active on haematopoietic progenitor cells. SCF also plays a key role in migration and proliferation of embryonic stem cells, primordial germ cells and melanocytes.

TUMOUR NECROSIS FACTORS (TNF-α and TNF-β)

Synonyms

Cachectin (TNF-α); lymphotoxin (TNF-β).

Molecular structure

The genes for both TNFs are located within 2 kb of each other on human chromosome 6 within the MHC locus. However, the products of each gene show only 35% homology at the amino acid level.

The TNF-α product is a 17 kDa non *N*-glycosylated protein, produced in soluble as well as membrane-bound forms. The TNF-β product is a 25 kDa glycosylated protein.

Receptors

Both TNF-α and TNF-β bind with apparently identical affinity to the same receptors, which are ubiquitous in distribution.

Two different high affinity receptors have been described. Both may form oligomers.

1. TNFR-I is present in both membrane bound and soluble forms. The monomer is a p55, with a K_d of 1–10 nM. The oligomer has a K_d of 300–500 pM.
2. TNFR-II. The monomer is a p75 with a K_d of 1–10 nM and the oligomer has a K_d of 50–100 pM.

Activation of both receptors results in the formation of a trimeric structure displaying higher affinity. TNFR-I and -II share 40% homology in their extracellular domain, but display no homology in the intracellular domain. Both receptors belong to the tyrosine kinase receptors superfamily. Soluble TNFRs may have antagonist action.

Source

TNF-α is secreted by a wide variety of cells (fibroblasts, monocytes/macrophages, T and B cells). TNF-β is produced predominantly by (T) lymphocytes. TNF secretion is induced by a variety of stimuli including antigen, endotoxin and mitogens.

Activities

TNF is perhaps the most pleiotropic of cytokines. Only activities on haematological immunological cells are summarized.

1. Induction of haemorrhagic necrosis of transplantable tumours mediated partly by increasing the haemostatic properties of endothelial cells.
2. Increasing expression of HLA class I and II, and thereby facilitating antigen presentation.
3. Induction of other cytokine gene expression.
4. Recruitment and activation of cellular components of the inflammatory response (lymphocytes, monocytes and neutrophils).
5. Increased cytotoxicity of T, NK and LAK cells.

INTERFERONS (IFNs)

Molecular structure

Three main groups of interferons have been described: IFN-α, IFN-β (type-I IFN) and IFN-γ (type-II IFN), all being species-specific. IFN-α is a 18–20 kDa non-glycosylated protein, whereas IFN-β (20 kDa) and IFN-γ (20–25 kDa) are both glycosylated. INF-α and -β genes are clustered on human chromosome 9pter–q12 and contain no introns; there is one single gene for IFN-β whereas IFN-α is a family of more than 25 different non-allelic genes as well as pseudogenes. IFN-γ is a single intronic gene located on human chromosome 12p12–qter.

Source

Steady state expression of IFN genes is very low. Although almost every cell type can produce IFN-α and -β upon stimulation, the main source of IFN-α is leukocytes and of IFN-β fibroblasts; viruses are the most potent natural inducers but bacterial endotoxins and other cytokines have also been shown inducing IFN-α and -β synthesis). In contrast, production of IFN-γ is a specialized function of all subsets of T cells upon activation with antigen or mitogens.

Receptors

Two IFN receptors have been described: type I (IFNAR, 95–110 kDa, $K_d = 10$–100 pM) competitively binds IFN-α and IFN-β, whereas type II (90–95 kDa) binds specifically to IFN-γ. Soluble forms of both receptors have been described.

Activities

Apart from the major antiviral role of IFNs a wide range of other immunological activities have been described: modulation of MHC antigens (mainly class II for IFN-γ, class I for IFN-α and IFN-β), stimulation of all monocyte/macrophage function (IFN-γ), modulation of B, T and NK cell activities, inhibition of tumour growth and induction of differentiation.

2

Cytokine receptors and signal transduction

JAMES N. IHLE
BRUCE WITTHUHN
BO TANG
TAOLIN YI
FREDERICK W. QUELLE

Haematopoiesis is regulated through the interaction of a variety of haemato-poietic growth factors with their cognate receptors (Clark and Kamen, 1987; Metcalf, 1989; Nicola, 1989; Arai et al, 1990; Ihle, 1990, 1992; Miyajima et al, 1992). During the past several years a variety of growth factors that regulate various aspects of the proliferation, differentiation or function of haematopoietic cells have been identified and molecularly cloned. Many of the haematopoietic growth factors exhibit pleiotropic effects on different cell populations and considerable redundancy exists among the growth factors. These properties initially suggested that growth factors may activate overlapping signal transducing pathways in a particular cell type and that cells at different stages of differentiation may differ in the signalling events that are induced by a particular growth factor. The elucidation of the structure of the receptors and the signalling pathways utilized have, in part, begun to provide mechanistic explanations for the often bewildering biological effects.

The receptors for most of the haematopoietic growth factors have also been cloned within the last few years. The receptors for stem cell growth factor (SCF) and for colony stimulating factor-1 (CSF-1) are protein tyrosine kinase containing receptors with structural similarity to the platelet-derived growth factor (PDGF) receptor. However, the receptors for the majority of the haematopoietic growth factors are members of a cytokine receptor superfamily. This family of receptors is characterized by conserved elements in the extracellular domains as discussed below. In contrast to the tyrosine kinase-containing receptors, the cytoplasmic domains of the cytokine receptors do not contain extensive similarity and specifically do not contain a conserved motif that might be associated with a common signal transducing domain. Only recently has it become evident that in spite of the lack of similarity in the intracellular domains, many of the cytokine receptors activate the same signalling pathways.

This review focuses on the receptors and signalling pathways utilized by receptors of the cytokine superfamily. Since it is not possible to cover all the specific receptors, only concepts that are common to a number of the receptors will be considered. For examples, we draw upon our experience with the receptors for IL-3, GM-CSF, EPO, G-CSF and IL-2, although many of the concepts initially established for any one of these receptors have been shown to apply to a number of the members of the cytokine receptor superfamily.

STRUCTURE OF CYTOKINE RECEPTORS

The structures of the cytokine receptors have been deduced from molecular cloning of the genes. From the sequences of the first cytokine receptors it became apparent that there were conserved motifs in the extracellular domains suggesting that the cytokine receptors might belong to a receptor superfamily. The conserved motifs included a distinctive, spatially conserved position of four cysteine residues and the presence of a conserved motif, Trp–Ser–X–Trp–Ser (WSXWS), where X can represent any amino acid. However, as illustrated in Figure 1, the cysteine and WSXWS motifs can vary in position within the extracellular domains. For example, the β subunit of the IL-3 receptor contains two sets of motifs. Although most of the receptors have a WSXWS motif near the transmembrane domain, the signalling transducing subunit of the IL-6 receptor and the G-CSF have an insert containing fibronectin type III repeats between the transmembrane domain and the WSXWS motif.

With the cloning and characterization of many of the receptors, it became apparent that high affinity binding of many haematopoietic growth factors required receptors consisting of multiple subunits. It was initially demonstrated that high affinity IL-2 binding required two subunits (Leonard et al, 1984; Hatakeyama et al, 1989b) and more recently a third subunit has been identified (Takeshita et al, 1992). Interestingly, the α (TAC) receptor subunit is dispensable for biological activity (Asao et al, 1993) and, unlike the β and γ subunits, the α subunit does not have the structural motifs associated with the cytokine receptor subfamily. The receptors for IL-3, GM-CSF and IL-5 share a common β subunit (Hayashida et al, 1990; Itoh et al, 1990; Miyajima et al, 1992) and have distinct α subunits (Gearing et al, 1989; Takaki et al, 1990; Kitamura et al, 1991; Tavernier et al, 1991; Hara and Miyajima, 1992; Park et al, 1992). In humans, low affinity binding is seen with the individual α subunits, while the β subunit is unable to bind any of the growth factors. High affinity binding requires both subunits. Similarly, a number of growth factors share a common receptor-associated signal transducing molecule initially termed gp130. The requirement for gp130 was first demonstrated in studies of the IL-6 receptor (Yamasaki et al, 1988; Taga et al, 1989; Hibi et al, 1990) but gp130 has subsequently been shown also to be required for the response to leukaemia inhibitory factor (LIF), oncostatin M and ciliary neurotrophic factor (CNTR) (Davis et al, 1991; Gearing et al, 1992; Ip et al, 1992).

In contrast to the situation in humans, in mice there are two very closely related genes encoding the β subunit (Gorman et al, 1990). One of the genes (AIC2A) is specific for IL-3 while the other gene (AIC2B) can associate with the α subunit specific for IL-3, GM-CSF and IL-5. The two genes are tightly linked on mouse chromosome 15 (Gorman et al, 1992) and the exon/intron structure and flanking sequences are identical. It is likely, therefore, that subsequent to the evolutionary divergence of mice and men, there was a gene duplication of the β subunit gene.

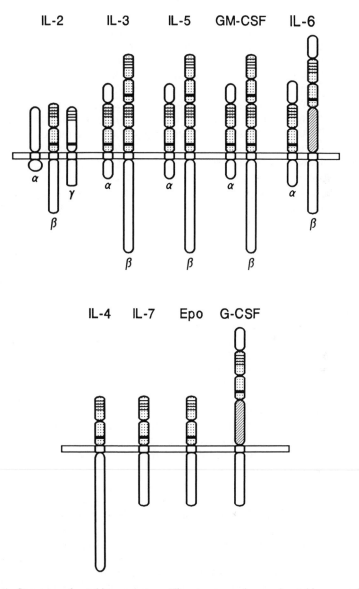

Figure 1. Structure of cytokine receptors. The structure of several cytokines are shown schematically. The WSXWS (heavy line) motif is shown as well as the position of the four conserved cysteine residues (lines).

Comparison of the haematopoietic growth factor receptors with other receptors has suggested that the superfamily may extend to include the receptors for growth hormone and prolactin (Bazan, 1989, 1990). In addition, the receptors for interferon (IFN) α and γ have similarity in structure and internal symmetry in the extracellular domains. Based on these comparisons, it has been hypothesized that the IFN and haemato-poietic growth factor receptors evolved from a common progenitor. As indicated below, this hypothesis is supported by the commonality of the signalling molecules utilized by members of this superfamily.

A comparison of the haematopoietic receptor extracellular domains has allowed the prediction of a common structure (Bazan, 1990). The 200 amino acid region containing the cysteines and the WSXWS motifs can be sub-divided into two domains of approximately 100 amino acids. Each of these domains was envisioned to consist of seven antiparallel β sheets which formed a barrel-like structure. Many aspects of this model have been supported from recent studies (De Vos et al, 1992) which established the structure of the growth hormone receptor by X-ray crystallography. This structure now serves as a general model for the haematopoietic receptor superfamily. The results showed that two 100 amino acid domains formed a compact structure containing two antiparallel β sheets of four and three strands. The four conserved Cys residues form disulphide bonds that stabilize the structure of the most distal subdomain. The growth hormone receptor does not contain the WSXWS motif but has the sequence YGFS in a comparable position. This sequence is not within the ligand-binding interfaces and thus the potential role of the WSXWS motif could not be deduced. However in the receptor for EPO, the WSXWS motif is required for efficient folding and exiting from the endoplasmic reticulum (Chiba et al, 1992; Yoshimura et al, 1992; Miura and Ihle, 1993).

The structure of the complex of growth hormone with its receptor also demonstrated that ligand binding causes receptor dimerization. Interest-ingly, a single growth hormone molecule, which is a non-symmetrical molecule, binds two receptors at the same binding sites on the receptors. However, the contact surface on one receptor is larger than on the other. Based on this and other biochemical evidence it is proposed that binding first occurs between the hormone and a receptor at the larger contact site. This stable structure then recruits a second receptor into the complex. It is further hypothesized that it is the formation of the dimer that initiates the intra-cellular signalling events.

DIMERIZATION IN BIOLOGICAL RESPONSE INITIATION

Following ligand binding, cytokine receptors initiate a variety of cellular responses by altering intracellular biochemical events. How is the binding of ligand in the extracellular domain coupled to changes in the intracellular domains to initiate a biochemical reaction? There are several possibilities for various cytokine receptors, although, all implicate homodimerization or heterodimerization. For example, following binding of IL-6 to the IL-6 receptor α subunit, there is a rapid association of the complex with the β, gp130 subunit (Taga et al, 1989). In this case, signal transduction does not require the cytoplasmic domain or transmembrane domain of the α subunit. Thus either binding of the α/IL-6 complex changes the conformation of the gp130 or the α/IL-6 complex may initiate an oligomerization of gp130 molecules. Recent studies (Murakami et al, 1993) support the concept that a critical event in IL-6 signalling is disulphide-linked homodimerization of gp130 and the subsequent recruitment of a tyrosine protein kinase. Similarly, binding of CNTR to its receptor induces the formation of a disulphide-linked heterodimer composed of the LIF receptor β chain and gp130 which then results in tyrosine phosphorylation of gp130 (Davis et al, 1993). Similarly LIF binding induces heterodimerization of the LIF β subunit with gp130 to initiate a comparable response.

The situation is somewhat different for the IL-3/GM-CSF/IL-5 cytokine group. In these cases ligand binds to the α subunit and this complex then binds the common β subunit. However, unlike the situation with IL-6, the cytoplasmic domain of the α subunits is essential for initiation of a biological response (Polotskaya et al, 1993). Thus one can hypothesize that in this case, ligand binding stabilizes the heterodimer and brings together the cyto-plasmic domains. The novel structure formed by the association of the α/β cytoplasmic domains may then allow the initiation of a response.

Like growth hormone receptor, there is considerable evidence to support a role for homodimerization of the erythropoietin (EPO) receptor in initiation of a response. For example, an interesting mutation was detected during the construction of retroviral expression vectors for the receptor (Yoshimura et al, 1990b) which conferred on the mutant the ability to abrogate the growth factor requirements of IL-3-dependent cells. The mutation involved substitution of Arg^{129} by a Cys residue in the extracellular domain. This mutation causes the EPO receptor to become constitutively active and oncogenic in vivo (Longmore and Lodish, 1991). Importantly, receptor activation is not seen when Arg^{129} is replaced with a Ser, Glu or a Pro residue. Since the Cys^{129} mutant forms disulphide-linked oligomers, the results are consistent with a requirement for receptor dimerization.

The concept that activation of the EPO receptor occurs following dimerization is further supported by studies with the Cys^{129} mutant (Zon et al, 1992). In particular, carboxyl truncations can inactivate both the wild type receptor and the receptor containing the Cys^{129} mutation. Co-expression of the inactive, truncated Cys^{129} mutant with the wild type receptor in IL-3-dependent cells results in EPO-independent growth. Thus, the mutant receptor can be hypothesized to facilitate association of wild type receptors in the absence of ligand and thereby activate signal transduction.

The receptor for EPO is unique among haematopoietic growth factors in its ability to be activated by the interaction with a retroviral gene product, gp55, of the Friend spleen focus-forming virus (SFFV). SFFV was isolated as a variant of the Friend murine leukaemia virus which had the unique ability to rapidly induce erythroleukaemias (Ben-David and Bernstein, 1991). The oncogenic gene encodes a modified viral glycoprotein consisting of the fusion of the carboxyl region of an ecotropic viral glycoprotein with the amino terminal region of the envelope glycoprotein of a xenotropic, mink cell focus-forming (MCF) virus. Gp55 can confer EPO-independent growth on cells in a manner that is dependent upon its ability to associate with the EPO receptor (Hoatlin et al, 1990; Li et al, 1990; Yoshimura et al, 1990a). Recent studies have further indicated that gp55 preferentially binds to the high-mannose, endoglycosidase-H-sensitive form of the receptor for EPO (Yoshimura et al, 1990a).

The association of gp55 and the receptor for EPO depends upon regions within the amino terminus and transmembrane domain of gp55. In particular, gp55, lacking the transmembrane domain, is non-leukaemogenic (Srinivas et al, 1991). The receptor transmembrane domain was shown also to be required by using a series of chimeric receptors consisting of the extracellular domain of the EPO receptor and the transmembrane and/or cytoplasmic domains of the IL-3 receptor β subunit. Chimeras containing the transmembrane domain and cytoplasmic domain from the IL-3 receptor β subunit were mitogenically active following stimulation with EPO. However, this chimeric receptor could not be activated by gp55 although it did associate with gp55. The association of gp55 and the receptor is also dependent upon the amino terminal, MCF-derived glycoprotein as evidenced by the ability of the MCF glycoprotein to associate with the receptor (Li and Baltimore, 1991). Thus the fusion protein combines two potential sites of interaction with the EPO receptor and together provide binding that is capable of activating the receptor. It can be hypothesized that gp55 promotes receptor dimerization in a manner comparable to EPO.

FUNCTIONAL RESPONSES OF HAEMATOPOIETIC GROWTH FACTOR RECEPTORS

Haematopoietic growth factors, through their receptors, can mediate a plethora of responses and it is beyond the scope of this review to survey all the types of responses that have been described. However, an important and common functional response of most cytokines is the ability to support proliferation and to maintain the viability of cells at a variety of stages of differentiation and in various lineages. In addition, various cytokines can initiate functional responses or may contribute to directing differentiation. The extent to which the latter reflect the functional properties or the cellular context in which the receptor is functioning is only beginning to be understood.

The ability of a number of cytokine receptors to support cell cycle progression, resulting in cellular proliferation, has been demonstrated by introduction of the receptors into murine IL-3-dependent cell lines. In particular, introduction of the receptors for IL-6, human IL-3, human GM-CSF, EPO, G-CSF, IL-2, IL-5 and others into IL-3-dependent cells results in acquisition of the ability to proliferate in response to the respective growth factors. This observation suggests that all these receptors are capable of initiating a proliferative response, possibly by utilizing a common signal transducing pathway. As noted below this hypothesis is further supported by the identification of a membrane proximal region in the cytoplasmic domain that is required for mitogenesis.

Whether haematopoietic growth factors are capable of mitogenic function in other lineages of cells has been somewhat more problematic. We have introduced the receptor for EPO into fibroblasts and obtained levels of expression of high affinity receptors that are comparable to those seen in myeloid lineage cells. Although EPO can induce tyrosine phosphorylation in these cells, it is not capable of inducing growth. Similarly, introduction of a constitutively-active and myeloid-transforming mutant of the EPO receptor into fibroblasts did not cause morphological transformation (Longmore and Lodish, 1991). Together the results suggest that some critical components of the signalling pathway are not present in fibroblasts.

The ability of the receptor for EPO to function in a cytotoxic, IL-2-dependent cell line (CTLL-2) has also been examined (Showers et al, 1992; Yamamura et al, 1992) with contradictory results. In one study (Yamamura et al, 1992), introduction of the receptor resulted in cell surface expression and the ability to internalize EPO. However, EPO was unable to induce a mitogenic response. Co-transfection with the IL-3 receptor β chain did not reconstitute the response, although transfection of the IL-3 receptor α and β chains together conferred the ability to respond mitogenically to IL-3. The results were interpreted to indicate that T cells lack a critical signalling subunit for the EPO receptor. In contrast, Showers et al (1992) found that transfection of the receptor for EPO into CTLL-2 cells conferred the ability to proliferate in response to EPO and to induce tyrosine phosphorylation of substrates that are also seen in myeloid cells. The basis for these quite different results is not known. Both groups studied the same cell line although different expression constructs were used. In unpublished studies, we have also introduced the EPO receptor into CTLL-2 cells and found that clones expressing the receptor at levels comparable to those seen in myeloid cells (DA-3 or 32Dcl13) failed to respond mitogenically to EPO.

Similar studies have assessed the function of the GM-CSF receptor in fibroblasts (Areces et al, 1993; Eder et al, 1993; Sasaki et al, 1993; Watanabe et al, 1993) with somewhat different results. In all cases introduction of the α and β subunits of the GM-CSF receptor into fibroblasts reconstituted a high affinity receptor complex. The receptors were found to be capable of initiating some events in signal transduction. In three of the studies (Areces et al, 1993; Sasaki et al, 1993; Watanabe et al, 1993) GM-CSF could support the long-term growth of the cells, while it could not do so in the other study. The possibility exists that some fibroblast lines express functions that can complement the normally deficient signal transmitted through the GM-CSF receptor.

FUNCTIONAL DOMAINS OF THE CYTOPLASMIC PORTIONS OF CYTOKINE RECEPTORS

The ability to introduce cytokine receptors into IL-3-dependent cell lines has provided a valuable system with which to begin to define the functional domains within the cytoplasmic portions of the receptor. Studies with the receptor for EPO have been particularly extensive and are the focus of this discussion, although results from other receptors are brought in as appropriate. The emerging concepts are that there exists a membrane proximal region of the cytoplasmic domain that is required for mitogenesis and that the membrane distal region may be responsible for much of the specificity associated with individual receptors.

Several studies have begun to define the domains of haematopoietic growth factors that are required for mitogenesis. These studies have shown that the carboxyl-half of the cytoplasmic domain is not required for a mitogenic response in IL-6 receptor-associated gp130 (Murakami et al, 1991), granulocyte colony-stimulating factor (G-CSF) receptor (Devos et al, 1991), the IL-4 receptor (Harada et al, 1992) and the IL-2 receptor β chain (Hatakeyama et al, 1989a). The cytoplasmic portion of the EPO receptor consists of 236 amino acids. In the membrane proximal region there is some sequence homology with the IL-2 receptor β chain and more limited similarity to regions initially defined in the IL-6 signal transducing gp130 protein that have been termed the box 1 and box 2 domains (Figure 2) (Murakami et al, 1991). Because of the similarity, this region has been hypothesized to be important for the common ability of the receptors to induce mitogenesis. This concept has been supported by demonstrating that carboxyl truncations do not eliminate the ability to induce growth.

In the EPO receptor (Figure 2) a number of carboxyl truncations have been examined which result in the maintenance of 459, 455, 443, 392, 389, 375, 372, 350, 337, 328, 280 and 262 amino acids relative to the mature processed receptor (D'Andrea et al, 1991; Miura et al, 1991; Quelle and Wojchowski, 1991; Nakamura et al, 1992). The results have been remarkably consistent in demonstrating that receptors of greater than 372 amino acids are mitogenically active while the receptors of 350 amino acids or less are mitogenically inactive. Carboxyl truncations that retain mitogenic activity have been reported to have alterations of other biological effects. Initially it was demonstrated that carboxyl truncations actually increased the mitogenic activity of the receptor in BaF3 cells (D'Andrea et al, 1991) although a comparable effect was not evident in other studies (Miura et al, 1991; Quelle and Wojchowski, 1991). The difference could be due to the use of different recipient cell lines. Carboxyl truncations have also been shown to reverse the ability of the EPO receptor to down-regulate the response of FDC-P1 cells to GM-CSF (Quelle and Wojchowski, 1991). The importance of the carboxyl end of the EPO receptor has been shown dramatically in recent studies (De La Chapelle et al, 1993): a mutation resulting in a carboxyl truncation of 70 amino acids is associated with erythrocytosis in humans.

One study has indicated that the carboxyl region of the receptor may contain a domain that prevents programmed cell death (Nakamura et al, 1992). In particular, the biological properties of a truncated receptor consisting of 280 amino acids were examined. In contrast to what might be predictions from other studies, this receptor functioned to support cell growth and thymidine incorporation at $10 \, \text{units} \, \text{ml}^{-1}$ of EPO. When cells

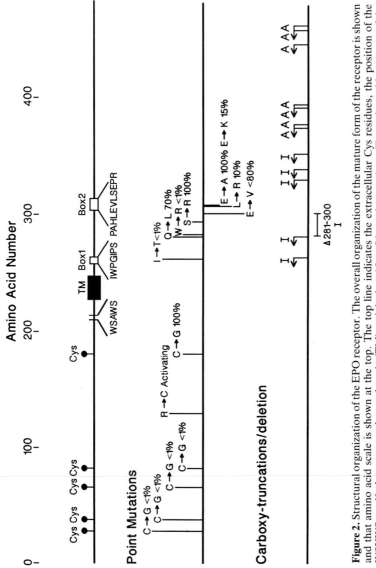

Figure 2. Structural organization of the EPO receptor. The overall organization of the mature form of the receptor is shown and that amino acid scale is shown at the top. The top line indicates the extracellular Cys residues, the position of the WSXWS motif, the transmembrane domain (TM) and the box 1/box 2 homology regions. The amino acid sequence of the box 1/box 2 regions are shown. The second line shows the point mutations that have been studied. The changes are indicated and their effect on mitogenesis is given as a percentage relative to the wild type receptor. The Arg→Cys mutation results in a constitutively active receptor. The third line indicates the carboxyl truncations and the deletion mutate that have been studied. The point of truncation is shown and whether the receptor is active (A) or inactive (I) in mitogenesis.

expressing the truncated receptor were removed from EPO or were cultured in 0.1 unit ml^{-1} of EPO, they showed an increased loss of viability relative to cells expressing the wild type receptor. This was interpreted to suggest that a carboxyl domain of the wild type receptor, in either low EPO concentrations or in the absence of EPO, can suppress programmed cell death.

The effects of various truncations on the ability of the receptor to induce tyrosine phosphorylation have also been examined (Miura et al, 1991). Importantly, there was a complete correlation between the ability of a truncated receptor to induce mitogenesis and to induce tyrosine phosphorylation. In general, there was also no differential effect of carboxyl truncations on the induction of tyrosine phosphorylation of specific cellular substrates resolved by two-dimensional gel electrophoresis. Since point mutations also fail to show a differential effect on tyrosine phosphorylation, it can be hypothesized that there exists a single domain that couples ligand binding and tyrosine phosphorylation.

The effects of deletions and point mutations in the membrane proximal region have been examined to define more precisely the domains that are required for signal transduction (Miura et al, 1991, 1993). Deletion of 20 amino acids (280–301) within the conserved region of the EPO receptor inactivates it for mitogenesis, induction of tyrosine phosphorylation and induction of immediate early genes. This deletion is similar in position and effect to a deletion that has been found to inactivate the IL-2 receptor β chain (Hatakeyama et al, 1989a).

Point mutations have focused on conserved amino acids in the region of the receptor that is required for mitogenesis (Miura et al, 1993). One of the most distinctive mutants is a Trp^{282}→Arg which completely inactivates the receptor for mitogenesis, induction of tyrosine phosphorylation and for the induction of immediate early genes. Trp^{282} is between the box 1 and box 2 sequences and is conserved in a number of haematopoietic growth factor receptors. For this reason, the same mutation was introduced into the IL-2 receptor β chain and the mutated receptor was assayed in 32Dcl3 cells. In contrast to EPO receptor, the mutated IL-2 receptor β chain retained its activity (unpublished data). Therefore conservation of particular amino acids may not necessarily imply a functional role in all the receptors.

Also of interest is the L^{306}EVL sequence that is found in the box 2 region and is conserved in the IL-2 receptor β chain. Mutation of both Leu^{306}→Arg or Glu^{307}→Lys significantly affected receptor function, supportive of the concept that this region of the receptor is essential for function. Mutation of the equivalent residue of Leu^{306} to Pro in the IL-2 receptor β chain inactivates the receptor (Mori et al, 1991). The more conservative mutation of Glu^{307}→Ala had no effect on the receptor.

The concept that haematopoietic growth factor receptors contain at least two functional domains has been supported by studies with both the G-CSF and GM-CSF receptors. In the case of the G-CSF receptor, stimulation of cells with G-CSF induces both mitogenesis and the expression of a series of acute-phase proteins. The membrane proximal domain is required for mitogenesis while the membrane distal region is required for the induction of acute-phase genes (Ziegler et al, 1993). Similarly, there are two functionally definable domains in the common β subunit for the IL-3/GM-CSF/IL-5 receptors (Sakamaki et al, 1992). In this case the membrane proximal domain was required for mitogenesis while the membrane distal region was required for the tyrosine phosphorylation of certain cellular substrates.

Recent studies (Hatakeyama et al, 1992) have indicated that the IL-2 receptor β chain contains two domains that can be distinguished in functional assays. In particular, the activation of c-*fos* by IL-2 requires both a serine-rich domain and a more distal acidic region that is not required for mitogenesis. This distal carboxyl region also mediates association of p56^{lck} and the β chain (Hatakeyama et al, 1991) as discussed below. In contrast, similar carboxyl-truncations of the EPO receptor have no effect on its ability to induce c-*fos* (Miura et al, 1993). Deletional analysis has also been done with the IL-2 receptor γ subunit. The γ chain contains a small cytoplasmic domain of 86 amino acids which has a region resembling an SH2 domain (Takeshita et al, 1992).

SH2 domains were initially defined as a region of 100 amino acids that are conserved among the *src* family member (Sadowski et al, 1986) and have also been found in a number of cytoplasmic signalling proteins including phospholipase C-$_γ$ (PLC$_γ$) (Stahl et al, 1988; Suh et al, 1988), GTPase activating protein (GAP) (Trahey et al, 1988; Vogel et al, 1988) and the 85 kDa regulatory α-subunit of phosphatidylinositol 3-kinase (PI 3-kinase) (Escobedo et al, 1991; Otsu et al, 1991; Skolnik et al, 1991). The SH2 domains of GAP, PI 3-kinase and PLC$_γ$ bind phosphorylated tyrosine residues on activated growth factor receptors and thereby mediate association (Koch et al, 1991). Deletional analysis of the IL-2 receptor γ chain demonstrated that the SH2-like domain was required for c-*myc* induction and mitogenesis while the more distal region of the receptor was required for induction of c-*jun* and c-*fos*. The carboxyl deletions of as little as 62 amino acids have recently been shown to have dramatic consequences in vivo. In particular, X-linked severe combined immunodeficiency is associated with carboxyl-truncation of the γ chain (Noguchi et al, 1993).

Together the data support the general concept that cytokine receptors contain at least two functional domains. The membrane proximal domain is essential for mitogenesis and may be involved in the activation of a common signalling pathway that ultimately induces cell cycle progression and proliferation. Two human conditions have been associated with truncations of cytokine receptor cytoplasmic domains. In the EPO receptor it is associated with excess proliferation (De La Chapelle et al, 1993) while in the IL-2 receptor γ chain it is associated with loss of function (Noguchi et al, 1993). It has been hypothesized that a common kinase may associate with the conserved sequences within the membrane proximal region and be activated by ligand binding. As noted below, considerable evidence supports the hypothesis that this is the Jak2 kinase. The membrane proximal domains can be hypothesized to be required for activating distinct pathways for receptor-specific functions. In the case of the IL-2 receptor, this may also involve kinases of the *src*-gene family as noted below. It is equally possible that the membrane distal regions may contribute in other ways to defining a receptor-specific response.

TYROSINE KINASES IN SIGNAL TRANSDUCTION

Although most haematopoietic growth factors rapidly induce tyrosine phosphorylation, the tyrosine kinases that associate with the receptors have been elusive until very recently. We have used oligonucleotides to conserve regions of tyrosine protein kinases in polymerase chain reactions (PCR) to amplify cDNA fragments from IL-3-dependent cell lines. Thus, we have been able to catalogue the kinases that are present and which might contribute to signal transduction (Yi et al, 1991a). The kinases which are consistently expressed are lyn, Tec, fes, Jak1 and Jak2, the structures of which are shown in Figure 3.

In haematopoietic cells two, differentially spliced forms of the src-related kinase, lyn are expressed (Yi et al, 1991a). This kinase is of particular interest since recent studies have indicated that IL-3 regulates the activity of lyn kinase in myeloid cell lines (O'Connor et al, 1992; Torigoe et al, 1992). However, in our experience, in cell lines expressing the EPO receptor, neither IL-3 nor EPO results in any significant change in the extent of phosphorylation of lyn nor do these growth factors affect in vitro kinase activity in immunoprecipitates. Therefore it is not clear that lyn plays a consistent role in the response to IL-3 nor does lyn play a detectable role in the response to EPO.

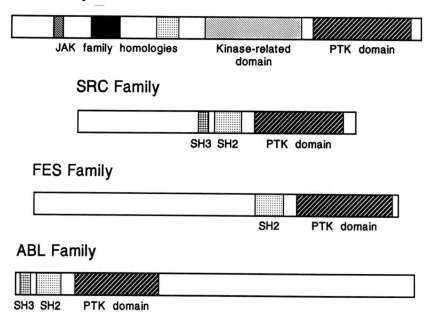

Figure 3. Structure of protein tyrosine kinases expressed in IL-3-dependent cells. The overall organization of the kinase is indicated. The kinase catalytic domains are shown as well as the SH2 and SH3 domains.

Considerable evidence has been obtained to suggest that the *src*-related gene, *lck* plays a role in some of the signalling pathways activated by IL-2. Similar to the receptor for EPO, a restricted region of the cytoplasmic domains of the IL-2 β chain (Hatakeyama et al, 1989a) and the γ chain (Asao et al, 1993) are required for mitogenesis. A second, more membrane proximal domain of each of the subunits is required for c-*fos* induction. Several studies have shown an association of lck with IL-2 receptor β chain (Hatakeyama et al, 1991) or activation of lck kinase activity following IL-2 binding (Horak et al, 1991). Lck associates through its tyrosine kinase catalytic domain with the region of the receptor that is not required for a mitogenic response (Hatakeyama et al, 1991) and this association is critical for IL-2 induced activation of lck (Minami et al, 1993). In haematopoietic cells, which do not express lck, the IL-2 receptor can activate and associate with the related kinases fyn and lyn (Kobayashi et al, 1993). Although the interactions between the IL-2 receptor β chain and the *src*-family kinases are associated with the ability of IL-2 to induce c-*fos*, they are not required for mitogenesis.

One of the major tyrosine kinases present in IL-3-dependent cells is the Tec kinase (Mano et al, 1993). This kinase was initially thought to be limited in its expression to liver and lung cells (Mano et al, 1990). The cDNAs isolated from myeloid cells differed from the initial Tec cDNAs in two important regards. First, myeloid Tec contains longer amino terminus and secondly the initial clones contained a deletion of a portion of the SH3 domain. The Tec kinase is distantly related to the *src* gene family and is most closely related to a *Drosophila* gene termed *Dsrc28C* (Gregory et al, 1987; Vincent III et al, 1989; Wadsworth et al, 1992). Tec contains a carboxyl kinase domain, although it lacks the carboxyl tyrosine residue found in all *src* family members which has been associated with down-regulation of kinase activity. Tec kinase also contains the SH2 and SH3 domains found in src kinases, but differs by having a unique amino terminus that is characterized by having a high number of basic amino acids, particularly lysine residues. Lastly, Tec does not contain a putative myristylation signal.

The potential importance of Tec in myeloid cells is suggested by recent studies that indicate that it is a member of a subfamily of tyrosine kinases that may be involved in lymphoid signalling pathways. In particular, a highly related kinase, termed itk (IL-2 inducible T-cell kinase), has been identified in T-cells and IL-2 has been shown to regulate the levels of itk transcripts (Silicano et al, 1992). Similarly a highly related kinase, termed BPK (B-cell progenitor kinase) or atk (agammaglobulinaemia tyrosine kinase), has been identified in B cells (Tsukada et al, 1993; Vetrie et al, 1993). BPK genetically maps near probes that are tightly linked to X-linked agammaglobulinaemia (XLA) and kinase activity is reduced or absent in XLA pre-B and B cell lines. Moreover, genetically acquired mutations that would be predicted to inactivate the kinase have been detected in atk in patients with XLA (Vetrie et al, 1993). Therefore BPK/atk is likely to play a critical role in B-cell signalling. With regard to myeloid cells, in preliminary experiments we did not detect any effects of IL-3 or EPO stimulation on tyrosine phosphorylation of Tec. However it will be important to assess other aspects such as association with receptors or alterations in kinase activity.

The c-*fes* gene is expressed at relatively low levels in the myeloid cell lines that have been used. With differentiation, the levels of c-fes protein increase significantly which initially suggested that this tyrosine kinase may be involved in some aspect of differentiation. Recent studies have supported this hypothesis by demonstrating that the introduction of an activated form of c-fes into myeloid cells promotes their differentiation (Borellini et al, 1991). Likewise, expression of c-*fes* antisense constructs interferes with differentiation (Ferrari et al, 1990). It should be noted however that v-fes can induce haematopoietic growth factor independence (Meckling-Gill et al, 1992) suggesting that the oncogenic version of the gene can impinge on pathways that are involved in growth regulation. A potentially important role for the fes kinase was recently suggested (Hanazono et al, 1993). In these studies it was demonstrated that in a human growth factor-independent cell line (TF-1), $p92^{c\text{-}fes}$ is tyrosine phosphorylated and its kinase activity is activated following stimulation with IL-3 or GM-CSF. The authors also demonstrated a physical association of fes kinase with the β subunit. We have examined a number of IL-3-dependent cell lines for similar effects on fes kinase activity and have failed to obtain comparable results.

Lastly, PCR with oligonucleotide primers to the conserved domains of protein tyrosine kinases have identified two related, novel kinases that are expressed in myeloid cells (Wilks, 1989; Wilks et al, 1991; Harpur et al, 1992; Pritchard et al, 1992). The Janus kinase (Jak) family (also referred to as just another kinase family) is characterized by containing two protein kinase-related domains in the carboxyl region. The most carboxyl domain contains the consensus sequences of tyrosine protein kinases (Figure 4) and has kinase activity, while the more amino domain contains less sequence homology and has not been shown to be catalytically active. The family does not contain the characteristic SH2 and SH3 domains found in other *src* gene-related protein tyrosine kinases although one region contains some similarity to the core elements of SH2 domains. The Jak kinases are further characterized by an amino terminal region that contains several areas of homology among the family members. The Jak kinase family currently consists of three members, termed Jak1 (Wilks et al, 1991), Jak2 (Harpur et al, 1992; Silvennoinen et al, 1993) and tyk2 (Firmbach-Kraft et al, 1990; Bernards, 1991). Importantly, tyk2 has been recently shown to be involved in signal transduction through the interferon-α receptor (Velazquez et al, 1992) and is speculated to be the kinase that is responsible for the tyrosine phosphorylation of proteins that are integral to the induction of the transcription of genes associated with the response to IFN-α (Fu, 1992; Schindler et al, 1992).

To examine the potential role of Jak1 and Jak2 in myeloid cells we have cloned full length cDNAs for the murine *Jak1* and *Jak2* genes (Silvennoinen et al, 1993). Both encode proteins with a predicted size of 130 kDa and, consistent with this, antipeptide antisera immunoprecipitate proteins of 130 kDa from IL-3/EPO-dependent cell lines. Following stimulation of cells with IL-3 or EPO, Jak2 is rapidly tyrosine phosphorylated as assessed by its ability to be detected with monoclonal antibodies against phosphotyrosine (Silvennoinen et al, 1993; Witthuhn et al, 1993) and its kinase activity is

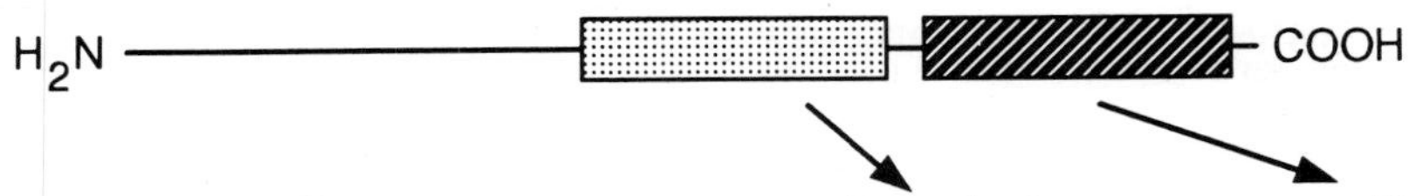

Domain	Consensus	Domain 2	Domain 1
I	273 L G x G x x G x V	L G Q G T F T K I	L G K G N F G S V
II	293 A_I^V K x $_M^{L,V,C}$	L L K V L	A V K K L
VI	373 G x x $_Y^F$ L	A L S Y L	G M E Y L
VII	384 H R D L A A R N	K N I L L A R E	H R D L A A R N
VIII	402 I x D F G x $_{9-10}$ Y (V)	L S D G F (x)$_9$ I L	I G D F G (x)$_{10}$ Y
IX	425 P $_I$ V R W $_K$ M $_T$ A P E	R I P W V P P E	P I F W Y A P E
IX	444 D V W S $_F^Y$ G $_I^V$	D K W S F G T	D V W S F G V

Figure 4. Sequences of the kinase and kinase-like domains of Jak2. The sequence of the conserved subdomains of tyrosine kinases are taken from Hanks et al (1988) and are indicated on the left with the consensus sequences in the second column. The sequences in the kinase domain of Jak2 and the kinase-like domain are shown on the right.

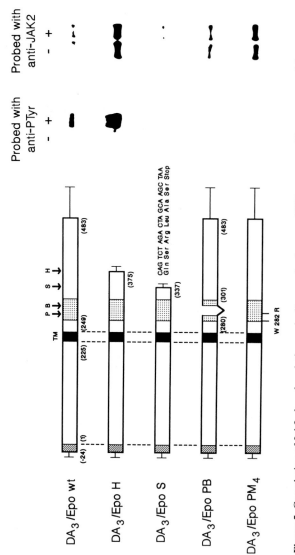

Figure 5. Correlation of Jak2 phosphorylation and mitogenesis of mutant EPO receptors. The structure of the receptor mutants are shown on the left. These mutants were introduced into IL-3-dependent, DA-3 cells and clones expressing the receptors were isolated. The cells were removed from IL-3 overnight and were stimulated with EPO for 10 minutes. The cells were lysed and Jak2 was immunoprecipitated from the cell lysates. The proteins were resolved by SDS-PAGE and blot to membranes. The membranes were subsequently probed with an antiserum against Jak2 (right) or with a monoclonal antibody against phosphotyrosine (left). The data show that, while comparable levels of Jak2 were immunoprecipitated, tyrosine phosphorylation of Jak2 only occurred in cells expressing the mitogenically active wild-type receptor or the carboxyl-truncated H mutant. Tyrosine phosphorylation of Jak2 did not occur in cells expressing mitogenetically-inactive mutants (S, PB, PM4).

dramatically increased following ligand binding. A comparable level of phosphorylation of Jak1 is not seen nor is the kinase activity of Jak1 induced. As illustrated in Figure 5, there is a correlation between the mitogenesis and activation of Jak2 among a series of mutants of the receptor for EPO. Truncations which do not affect mitogenesis are still capable of inducing Jak2 tyrosine phosphorylation while mutations or deletions in the membrane proximal region, which inactivate the receptor for mitogenesis, similarly are unable to induce tyrosine phosphorylation of Jak2. Lastly, Jak2 physically associates with the membrane proximal region of the receptor for EPO (Witthuhn et al, 1993) and is hypothesized to be the protein detected by Yoshimura and Lodish (1992).

In addition to playing a role in IL-3 and EPO signalling, Jak2 is involved in the signalling of a number of the cytokine receptors. In particular, growth hormone had been shown rapidly to induce the tyrosine phosphorylation of a 120 kDa protein that physically associated with the receptor (Wang et al, 1993). Recent studies have shown that this protein is Jak2 (Artgetsinger et al, 1993). Other receptors which induce Jak2 tyrosine phosphorylation and activation of its kinase activity include G-CSF, GM-CSF, IL-6 and prolactin (B. Witthuhn, F. Quelle & J. N. Ihle, unpublished data). Lastly, IFN-γ induces Jak2 tyrosine phosphorylation and activation of its kinase activity. In addition, Jak2 is able to rescue one class of complementation mutants that were selected for their inability to respond to IFN-γ. These mutant cells respond normally to IFN-α. Notably, to date, we have not seen tyrosine phosphorylation or activation of the kinase activity of Jak2 or Jak1 by IL-2, supporting previous studies which indicated that the signalling pathways for EPO and IL-2 were distinct (Yamamura et al, 1992). It can be hypothesized that another Jak family member exists which is essential for the IL-2 signalling events that are specifically required for mitogenesis.

In summary, the Jak family of kinases appear to play a major role in the general signalling of the cytokine receptor superfamily (Figure 6). Thus tyk2 is essential for signalling through the IFN-α/β pathway while Jak2 plays a central role in the signalling pathway activated by a number of cytokines. The available evidence demonstrates that, in those cases examined, Jak2 associates with the membrane proximal domain and thus may be the common kinase that is essential for the mitogenic response of all these receptors.

The model for activation of Jak2 kinase activity following EPO binding is indicated in Figure 6. Based on the available evidence, Jak2 associates with the receptor for EPO in the absence of ligand. Following binding of EPO, there is rapid formation of dimeric and oligomeric structures which may result from the ability of EPO dimers to cause association of receptor molecules. The oligomerization of the receptor–Jak2 complexes may bring Jak2 molecules in proximity resulting in their cross-phosphorylation (auto-phosphorylation) and activation. This model is very similar to the models that have emerged for the activation of receptors containing tyrosine kinase domains (Ullrich and Schlessinger, 1990). In the case of the growth hormone receptor (Artgetsinger et al, 1993), binding of Jak2 occurs only after receptor dimerization, indicating that association of receptor cytoplasmic domains is necessary to create a high affinity binding site for Jak2. Similarly, preliminary studies indicate that neither the α or β subunits of the IL-3 receptor bind Jak2, but the complex formed by IL-3 binding creates a Jak2 binding site. Although the binding site for Jak2 has been localized to the membrane proximal region of the cytoplasmic domain of the receptors, the binding site on Jak2 has not been identified.

The diverse group of cytokine receptors that utilize Jak2 often mediate quite different biological responses. Therefore, the biological specificity must occur at levels other than Jak2 activation and may be related to differences in the substrates available to Jak2. The targets of phosphory-lation by Jak2 could be selected by their ability to associate with individual receptor–Jak2 complexes or phosphorylated derivatives. This possibility is

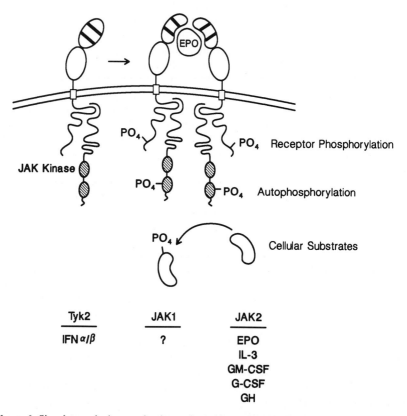

Figure 6. Signal transducing mechanisms of cytokine receptors. The model for signal trans-duction through the EPO receptor is shown. It associates with Jak2. Following ligand binding there is a rapid dimerization of receptors which brings Jak2 kinase molecules in sufficient proximity to cross-phosphorylate (autophosphorylate), resulting in the activation of kinase activity. One of the substrates of protein tyrosine phosphorylation is the EPO receptor. In addition a number of cellular substrates are inducibly tyrosine phosphorylated. As indicated, IFN-α/β signalling requires tyk2 while EPO, IL-3, GM-CSF, G-CSF and growth hormone activate Jak2. Cytokines which activate Jak1 have not yet been identified.

supported by the observation that both GM-CSF and IFN-γ activate Jak2 in macrophages but only GM-CSF induces mitogenesis (Witthuhn et al, unpublished data). Receptor phosphorylation could influence association of potential substrates with the complex; however, in the case of the receptor for EPO the membrane distal region, containing the receptor phosphorylation sites, does not contribute to the mitogenic response. Alternatively, cells of different lineages or stages of differentiation may express distinct constellations of substrates for Jak2. For example, the EPO receptor activates Jak2 in fibroblasts but is unable to initiate a mitogenic response comparable to that seen in haematopoietic cells. For these reasons, it will be important to characterize and compare the substrates of Jak2 phosphorylation in various cell types and in response to various cytokines.

SUBSTRATES OF TYROSINE PHOSPHORYLATION

Following the binding of most of the cytokines, there is the rapid induction of tyrosine phosphorylation and in most cases one of the substrates is the receptor itself (Isfort et al, 1988; Sharon et al, 1989; Sorensen et al, 1989; Murakami et al, 1991; Duronio et al, 1992; Farrar et al, 1992; Sakamaki et al, 1992; Izuhara and Harada, 1993). For example, the EPO receptor is rapidly phosphorylated following EPO binding (Miura et al, 1991; Dusanter-Fourt et al, 1992; Yoshimura and Lodish, 1992). The phosphorylation sites have not been precisely mapped, but by examining the phosphorylation of truncated receptors it is clear that one or more of the three tyrosines in the last 30 amino acids of the receptor are phosphorylated. Since Jak2 associates with the receptor and can phosphorylate the receptor in vitro, it is likely that Jak2 is responsible for receptor phosphorylation. Critical, potential sites of tyrosine phosphorylation, have also been identified in the receptor for IFN-γ (Farrar et al, 1992).

Only recently have the consequences of the phosphorylation of the EPO receptor become apparent. As noted above, truncations of the receptor that remove the phosphorylation sites are still able to induce mitogenesis, thus ruling out these sites in signalling events for cell division. However, a negative regulatory function has been proposed for the membrane distal region based on the increased EPO sensitivity of truncated mutants (D'Andrea et al, 1991). This has been further supported by the association of carboxyl-truncations with erythrocytosis in vivo (De La Chapelle et al, 1993). The basis for these effects is not known but may be related to the ability of a protein tyrosine phosphatase termed haematopoietic cell phosphatase (HCP) to associate with the tyrosine phosphorylated carboxy-terminus of the receptor for erythropoietin.

HCP was identified in approaches to define novel protein tyrosine phosphatases that are expressed in haematopoietic cells (Yi et al, 1991b). Full-length cDNA clones for HCP have been isolated by several groups (Shen et al, 1991; Matthews et al, 1992; Plutzky et al, 1992; Yi et al, 1992). HCP contains a carboxyl-terminal tyrosine phosphatase domain and an amino-terminal region that contains two contiguous SH2 domains. HCP has been shown to bind the tyrosine phosphorylated c-*kit* gene product through the amino terminal SH2 domain (Yi and Ihle, 1993). More recently we have found that HCP also specifically binds the tyrosine-phosphorylated derivatives of the receptor for EPO and the β subunit of the IL-3 receptor. It is hypothesized that following receptor activation, HCP is recruited to the receptor/Jak2 kinase complex and is responsible for down-regulating the response. In the absence of the carboxyl region, the response to EPO is sustained by allowing activated Jak2 to persist.

The role of HCP in down-regulating the response of haematopoietic cells has been amply illustrated by the phenotype of a mutation in mice termed 'motheaten' (Shultz, 1991). Mice with the lethal form of *me* die within a few weeks after birth, primarily from the accumulation of activated macrophages in the lungs. In addition, there are a number of haematopoietic abnormalities including increased sensitivity to EPO (Van Zant and Shultz, 1989). The condition can be cured by bone marrow transplants and can be transmitted via bone marrow. It has recently been shown (Shultz et al, 1993; Tsui et al, 1993) that the *me* mutation results in a functional deletion of the *HCP* gene due to a point mutation that results in aberrant splicing of the *HCP* transcript.

The tyrosine-phosphorylated carboxy-terminus of the receptor for EPO has also been shown to be a binding site for the p85 subunit of phosphatidylinositol 3-kinase through its SH2 domains (Damen et al, 1993). Similar results have recently been obtained for the response to IL-4 (Izuhara and Harada, 1993). Binding of the p85 subunit to tyrosine phosphorylated residues results in an increase in PI 3-kinase activity. The heterodimeric enzyme complex phosphorylates PI, PI 4-phosphate and PI 4,5-bisphosphate at the D-3 position of the inositol ring. Although PI 3-kinase is activated through comparable mechanisms by a number of growth factor receptors, the significance for cell cycle regulation has been obscure. In the EPO receptor, the association and activation of PI 3-kinase is not required for mitogenesis.

A number of cytokines have been shown to phosphorylate additional substrates, the significance of which are not known. In certain mast cell lines Vav has been shown to be inducibly tyrosine phosphorylated (Margolis et al, 1992). The *Vav* gene was initially cloned based on its ability to transform fibroblasts (Katzav et al, 1989a) but is normally expressed primarily in haematopoietic cells (Katzav et al, 1989b), although its normal function has not been determined. Recent studies have shown that Shc may also be a substrate (McGlade et al, 1992). The gene for Shc was cloned with probes from the SH2 domain of c-fes in an attempt to isolate novel SH2-containing genes (Pelicci et al, 1992). When Shc is tyrosine phosphorylated it binds to Grb2 which is involved in the ras signalling pathway (Rozakis-Adcock et al, 1992) and thus has been speculated to mediate the activation of ras by haematopoietic growth factors. Considerable studies remain to establish definitively a role for Shc in haematopoietic signalling.

A variety of cytokines induce activation of ras through pathways that do not involve the tyrosine phosphorylation of ras itself (Satoh et al, 1991, 1992). Ras is a membrane-associated guanylate nucleotide binding protein which cycles between a GTP-bound active state and a GDP-bound inactive state. The two states are controlled through the intrinsic GTPase activity of ras which is influenced by a GTPase-activating enzyme (GAP) or by GDP/GTP nucleotide exchange factors. The downstream consequences of ras activation are not clear. EPO has been shown to phosphorylate p120 GAP which may be involved in EPO-induced ras activation (Torti et al, 1992). Similarly, Gulbins et al (1993) have suggested that Vav may have guanine nucleotide exchange factor activity, which may contribute to ras activation by cytokines that can induce the tyrosine phosphorylation of Vav.

The potential role of the *ras* gene family is of interest because of the frequency of mutations that have been identified in haematopoietic malignancies. Infection of primary cultures of bone marrow cells with H-ras in the presence of IL-3 results in the immortalization of mast cells (Redemann et al, 1988). The lines retain a requirement for IL-3 but proliferate more rapidly than normal mast cells and can be established into cell lines. Similarly introduction of v-ras into IL-3-dependent myeloid cells does not abrogate IL-3 dependence but blocks the ability to terminally differentiate (Mavilio et al, 1989). Interestingly, this phenotype is similar to the one seen with c-*myc* expression constructs (Askew et al, 1991). In other cells lines, ras was found to abrogate IL-3 dependence by a non-autocrine mechanism (Boswell et al, 1990) while in another cell line mutant c-H-*ras* caused increased proliferation without abrogating growth factor requirements (Boswell et al, 1989). These differences are probably due to the variable background of transformation and their ability, or inability, to complement ras in affecting growth factor dependence.

A common cellular substrate of cytokine-induced tyrosine phosphorylation is a 90–95 kDa protein. This is of particular interest because studies have identified a 91 kDa protein that is inducibly tyrosine phosphorylated in response to IFN-γ. Since IFN-γ and many cytokines activate Jak2, a key question is whether the 90–95 kDa protein is the same protein in all cases. The 91 kDa, IFN-γ-inducible protein is a component of the ISGF3α complex (Shuai et al, 1992; Pearse et al, 1993). The ISGF3α complex is composed of the 91 kDa protein and a 113 kDa protein, both of which are inducibly tyrosine phosphorylated in the response to IFN-α. When phosphorylated, the 113 kDa and 91 kDa proteins associate with a 48 kDa DNA-binding component (ISGF3γ), migrate to the nucleus and bind to the interferon response element. In the IFN-γ response only the 91 kDa is inducibly tyrosine phosphorylated and subsequently migrates to the nucleus and binds to an interferon activation sequence.

CYTOKINE-MEDIATED GENE TRANSCRIPTION

Haematopoietic growth factors can induce the transcription of a number of genes, comparable to those initially described in the response of fibroblasts to serum or platelet-derived growth factor (Lau and Nathans, 1985, 1987; Rittling and Baserga, 1987; Sukhatme et al, 1987; Zumstein and Stiles, 1987; Chavrier et al, 1988). Among these the c-*myc* gene is of considerable interest since its deregulated expression has been implicated in the transformation of a variety of haematopoietic lineages (Cory, 1986). In most IL-3-dependent cells, the levels of c-*myc* transcripts are regulated by IL-3 (Conscience et al, 1986; Dean et al, 1987; Harel-Bellan and Farrar, 1987). Removal of IL-3 results in a rapid loss of transcripts, and stimulation of factor-deprived cells results in the re-appearance of transcripts to maximal levels within 30 minutes. A role for tyrosine phosphorylation has been postulated because abrogation of IL-3-dependence by oncogenes containing tyrosine protein kinases results in constitutive transcription of c-*myc*. More strikingly, in cells infected with temperature-sensitive mutants of v-*abl*, c-*myc* transcription is also temperature sensitive. Thus, at the permissive temperature transcription is independent of IL-3 while at the non-permissive temperature transcription requires IL-3 (Cleveland et al, 1989).

The significance of cytokine-regulated expression of c-*myc* transcription is suggested by an increased ability to survive in the absence of IL-3 when c-*myc* is constitutively expressed (Hume et al, 1988; Cory et al, 1987; Dean et al, 1987). The role of c-myc in maintaining viability is not known, but part of its effect may be to control the expression of the ornithine decarboxylase gene (ODC). Initially (Bowlin et al, 1986) it was demonstrated that IL-3 induced rapid increases in ODC and that inhibition of ODC activity inhibited the growth of IL-3-dependent cells. It was subsequently demonstrated that the levels of transcripts for ODC are dependent on IL-3 (Dean et al, 1987). The kinetics of the induction of transcripts were different than the induction of the transcripts for c-*myc* in that ODC transcripts came up later than c-*myc* transcripts. The role of c-myc was more definitively demonstrated by the observation that IL-3-dependent cells, infected with retroviral vectors which constitutively express c-*myc*, constitutively expressed transcripts for ODC (Dean et al, 1987). Therefore it has been proposed that one component of the response to IL-3 involves the induction of transcription of the c-*myc* gene through mechanisms involving tyrosine phosphorylation. C-myc in turn regulates the transcription of the ODC gene and results in the ultimate production of a gene product which is required for proliferation.

In addition, the c-*fos* gene is transiently expressed in response to IL-3 (Conscience et al, 1986; Dean et al, 1987; Harel-Bellan and Farrar, 1987). Curiously c-*fos* expression is also transiently induced by serum stimulating the cells or by simply spinning out the cells and resuspending them. The significance of this expression has not been examined. As noted above, the induction of c-*fos* by IL-2 requires the membrane distal region of the IL-2 receptor β chain which is distinct from the requirement for c-*myc* induction. In all cases examined, there has been a complete correlation between the ability to induce mitogenesis and induction of c-*myc*. This correlation does not exist for c-*fos*, suggesting that its induction may have physiological consequences other than promoting cell cycle progression.

IL-3 has also been shown to regulate the transcription of the c-*pim*-1 gene (Dautry et al, 1988). *Pim*-1 (Preferred Integration site of Moloney MuLV) was initially identified as the gene that is activated by retroviral insertions in thymic lymphomas that are induced by Moloney leukaemia virus (Cuypers et al, 1984). The gene encodes a serine/threonine protein kinase (Selten et al, 1986; Telerman et al, 1988) of 33 kDa that is distantly related to the cdc2 kinases that control cell cycle progression in a variety of species. The *pim*-1 gene is uniquely expressed in haematopoietic cells and may be involved in cell cycle progression in these cells. It also complements with the c-*myc* or N-*myc* gene in the transformation of lymphoid cells. In particular, c-*pim*-1 transgenic mice have a low incidence of leukaemia unless infected with retroviruses to allow for activation of complementing genes. When the tumours that are induced in these mice were examined it was found that the c-*myc* or N-*myc* genes were activated (van Lohuizen et al, 1989). Thus efficient induction of lymphomas requires the constitutive production of both c-*pim*-1 and c-*myc*. Irrespective, the results suggest that the IL-3-dependent transcription of both genes may provide two quite distinct requirements for maintenance of viability and cell cycle progression.

Although the IL-3 regulation of c-*myc* expression has been implicated in growth regulation it is clear that IL-3 also regulates the expression of genes which are more likely to be involved in differentiation. In particular, most IL-3-dependent cell lines express transcripts derived from one or more of the T-cell γ receptor loci (Weinstein et al, 1989). This transcription is from non-rearranged loci and initiates approximately 200 bp 5' from the site of recombination with the V gene segments. Removal of IL-3 results in the rapid loss of transcripts and addition of IL-3 induces the appearance of transcripts with kinetics which are comparable to the induction c-*myc* transcripts. In cells transformed with v-*abl*, expression of transcripts is independent of IL-3 suggesting that tyrosine phosphorylation may be important in signal transduction.

IL-3 has also been shown to regulate the levels of transcripts for the 55 kDa (TAC) gene which encodes the α subunit of the IL-2 receptor (Birchenall-Sparks et al, 1986). The significance of this expression is not known however since the cells do not have high affinity receptors for IL-2 and do not proliferate in response to IL-2. As above, it might be hypothesized that the regulation of this gene may be associated with differentiation rather than growth regulation by IL-3.

From these studies it is clear that cytokine signal transduction will have an important role in the regulation of expression of various genes. It will be important to determine the 'link' between ligand binding, tyrosine phosphorylation and transcriptional activation. The simplest hypothesis might suggest that tyrosine phosphorylation is directly involved in the activation of a transcriptional regulatory protein, however more steps may be involved, such as the tyrosine phosphorylation of a serine protein kinase which then serine phosphorylates a transcriptional regulatory protein. In any event, the advances which have been made in the identification, purification and cloning of transcriptional regulatory proteins will allow direct approaches to studying the role of cytokine signal transduction in gene regulation.

SUMMARY AND CONCLUSIONS

The past few years have seen an explosion in the identification, cloning and characterization of cytokines and their receptors. The pleiotropic effects of many of the growth factors and the considerable redundancy in the actions of growth factors have contributed to a mass of descriptive literature that often seems to defy summary. Only recently have common concepts begun to emerge. First, cytokines mediate their effects through a large family of receptors that have evolved from a common progenitor and retain structural and functional similarities. Within the haematopoietic system, the cytokines are not usually instructive in differentiation, but rather supportive, and may contribute to some differentiation-specific responses. The patterns of expression of cytokine receptors are therefore a product of differentiation and provide for changes in physiological regulation.

The second important concept that is emerging is that the cytokines mediate their mitogenic effects through a common signal-transducing pathway involving tyrosine phosphorylation. Thus, although the cytokine receptor superfamily members do not have intrinsic protein tyrosine kinase activity, by coupling to activation of tyrosine phosphorylation they may affect cell growth by pathways that are common with the large family of growth factor receptors that contain intrinsic protein tyrosine kinase activity. The coupling of cytokine binding to tyrosine phosphorylation and mitogenesis requires a relatively small membrane-proximal domain of the receptors. This region has limited sequence similarity which may be required for the association of individual receptors with an appropriate kinase. Activation of kinase activity results from the dimerization or oligomerization of receptor homodimers or heterodimers. Again this requirement is similar to that seen with the growth factor receptors which have intrinsic protein tyrosine kinase activity.

The protein tyrosine kinases that couple cytokine binding to tyrosine phosphorylation are members of the Jak family of kinases. The ubiquitous expression of these kinases provides a common cellular background on which the cytokine receptors can function and on which unique functionally distinct receptors have evolved. In particular, tyk2 is required for the responses initiated by IFN-α while Jak2 has been implicated in the responses to G-CSF, IL-3, EPO, growth hormone, prolactin and IFN-γ. Very shortly it will be known whether the other cytokines use either tyk2 or Jak2. It will be of particular interest to determine whether some cytokines might use Jak1. Just as common domains of the receptors have been identified that are required for biological activity, it can be anticipated that the Jak family of kinases will contain common domains that are involved in association with the receptors. Moreover, it can be predicted that these regions will be within the unique Jak homology domains found in the amino terminal half of the proteins.

Unlike the common, membrane-proximal domain that is required for association with Jak kinases, the membrane distal regions may contribute to the unique properties of individual receptors. Two mechanisms have been hypothesized for how these domains may contribute to the biological responses. In some cases, the membrane distal domains may contain regions that allow the association of additional protein tyrosine kinases with the receptor complex. Alternatively, the membrane distal region, either alone or following tyrosine phosphorylation, recruits cellular substrates into the kinase complex and activates their function. Again, the similarity with the receptor containing kinase activity is striking and suggests the evolution of common signalling mechanisms in the two systems. Although considerable insight is being gained in the early events in signal transduction, the subsequent events that are responsible for activation of gene expression have been more elusive. In particular, the hallmark for mitogenesis is the induction of transcription of c-*myc* and virtually nothing is known concerning the mechanisms involved in its regulation. However, recent studies on the mechanisms by which IFN-α activates gene transcription, through tyk2, may be an important model for how other Jak kinases couple ligand binding to gene activation. In any case, it can be anticipated that future studies will reveal the precise pathways that are involved in gene regulation. In addition, future studies will be necessary to define more precisely the role of cytokines in differentiation by identifying critical regulatory steps in haematopoiesis.

Acknowledgements

This work was supported in part by the National Cancer Institute Cancer Center Support (CORE) grant P30 CA21765, by grant RO1 DK42932 from the National Institute of Diabetes and Digestive and Kidney Diseases and by the American Lebanese Syrian Associated Charities (ALSAC). We would like to thank Linda Snyder and Cynthia Miller for excellent technical assistance in these studies.

REFERENCES

Arai K, Lee F, Miyajima A et al (1990) Cytokines: Cordinators of immune and inflammatory responses. *Annual Reviews of Biochemistry* **59**: 783–836.
Areces LB, Jucker M, San Miguel JA et al (1993) Ligand-dependent transformation by the receptor for human granulocyte/macrophage colony-stimulating factor and tyrosine phosphorylation of the receptor β subunit. *Proceedings of the National Academy of Sciences, USA* **90**: 3963–3967.
Artgetsinger LS, Campbell GS, Yang X et al (1993) Identification of JAK2 as a growth hormone receptor-associated tyrosine kinase. *Cell* **74**: 237–244.
Asao H, Takeshita T, Ishii N et al (1993) Reconstitution of the functional interleukin 2 receptor complexes on fibroblastoid cells: Involvement of the cytoplasmic domain of the τ chain in two distinct signaling pathways. *Proceedings of the National Academy of Sciences, USA* **90**: 4127–4131.
Askew DS, Ashmun RA, Simmons BC & Cleveland JL (1991) Constitutive c-myc expression in an IL-3-dependent myeloid cell line suppresses cell cycle arrest and accelerates apoptosis. *Oncogene* **6**: 1915–1922.
Bazan JF (1989) A novel family of growth factor receptors: a common binding domain in the growth hormone, prolactin, erythropoietin and IL-6 receptors, and the p75 IL-2 receptor beta-chain. *Biochemical and Biophysical Research Communications* **164**: 788–795.
Bazan JF (1990) Structural design and molecular evolution of a cytokine receptor superfamily. *Proceedings of the National Academy of Sciences, USA* **87**: 6934–6938.
Ben-David Y & Bernstein A (1991) Friend virus-induced erythroleukemia and the multistage nature of cancer. *Cell* **66**: 831–834.
Bernards A (1991) Predicted tyk2 protein contains two tandem protein kinase domains. *Oncogene* **6**: 1185–1187.
Birchenall-Sparks MC, Farrar WL, Rennick D et al (1986) Regulation of expression of the interleukin-2 receptor on hematopoietic cells by interleukin-3. *Science* **233**: 455–458.

Borellini F, He YF, Aquino A et al (1991) Increased DNA binding and transcriptional activity associated with transcription factor Sp1 in K562 cells transfected with the myeloid-specific c-fes tyrosine kinase gene. *Journal of Biological Chemistry* **266**: 15850–15854.

Boswell HS, Harrington MA, Burgess GS et al (1989) A mutant RAS gene acts through protein kinase C to augment interleukin-3 dependent proliferation in a fastidious immortal myeloid cell line. *Leukemia* **3**: 662–668.

Boswell HS, Nahreini TS, Burgess GS et al (1990) A RAS oncogene imparts growth factor independence to myeloid cells that abnormally regulate protein kinase C: A nonautocrine transformation pathway. *Experimental Hematology* **18**: 452–460.

Bowlin TL, McKown BJ & Sunkara PS (1986) Ornithine decarboxylase induction and polyamine biosynthesis are required for the growth of interleukin-2- and interleukin-3-dependent cell lines. *Cellular Immunology* **98**: 341–350.

Chavrier P, Zerial M, Lemaire P et al (1988) A gene encoding a protein with zinc fingers is activated during G0/G1 transition in cultured cells. *EMBO Journal* **7**: 29–35.

Chiba T, Amanuma H & Todokoro K (1992) Tryptophan residue of Trp–Ser–X–Trp–Ser motif in extracellular domains of erythropoietin receptor is essential for signal transduction. *Biochemical and Biophysical Research Communications* **184**: 485–490.

Clark SC & Kamen R (1987) The human hematopoietic colony-stimulating factors. *Science* **236**: 1229–1237.

Cleveland JL, Dean M, Rosenberg N et al (1989) Tyrosine kinase oncogenes abrogate interleukin-3 dependence of murine myeloid cells through signalling pathways involving c-myc: conditional regulation of c-myc transcription by temperature-sensitive v-abl. *Molecular and Cellular Biology* **9**: 5685–5695.

Conscience JF, Verrier B & Martin G (1986) Interleukin-3-dependent expression of the c-myc and c-fos proto-oncogenes in hemopoietic cell lines. *EMBO Journal* **5**: 317–323.

Cory S (1986) Activation of cellular oncogenes in hemopoietic cells by chromosome translocation. *Advances in Cancer Research* **47**: 189–234.

Cory S, Bernard O, Bowtell D et al (1987) Murine c-myc retroviruses alter the growth requirements of myeloid cell lines. *Oncogene Research* **1**: 61–76.

Cuypers HT, Selten G, Quint W et al (1984) Murine leukemia virus-induced T-cell lymphomagenesis: integration in a distinct chromosomal region. *Cell* **37**: 141–150.

D'Andrea AD, Yoshimura A, Youssoufian H et al (1991) The cytoplasmic region of the erythropoietin receptor contains nonoverlapping positive and negative growth-regulatory domains. *Molecular and Cellular Biology* **11**: 1980–1987.

Damen JE, Mui AL-F, Puil L et al (1993) Phosphatidylinositol 3-kinase associates, via its src homology 2 domains, with the activated erythropoietin receptor. *Blood* **81**: 3204–3210.

Dautry F, Weil D, Yu J & Dautry-Varsat A (1988) Regulation of pim and myb mRNA accumulation by interleukin 2 and interleukin 3 in murine hematopoietic cell lines. *Journal of Biological Chemistry* **263**: 17615–71620.

Davis S, Aldrich TH, Valenzuela DM et al (1991) The receptor for ciliary neurotrophic factor. *Science* **253**: 59–63.

Davis S, Aldrich TH, Stahl N et al (1993) LIFRβ and gp130 as heterodimerizing signal transducers of the tripartite CNTF receptor. *Science* **260**: 1805–1808.

De La Chapelle A, Traskelin A-L & Juvonen E (1993) Truncated erythropoietin receptor causes dominantly inherited benign human erythrocytosis. *Proceedings of the National Academy of Sciences, USA* **90**: 4495–4499.

De Vos AM, Ultsch M & Kossiakoff AA (1992) Human growth hormone and extracellular domain of its receptor: crystal structure of the complex. *Science* **255**: 306–312.

Dean J, Cleveland JL, Rapp UR & Ihle JN (1987) Role of myc in the abrogation of IL3 dependence of myeloid FDC-P1 cells. *Oncogene Research* **1**: 279–296.

Devos R, Plaetinck G, Van der Heyden J et al (1991) Molecular basis of a high affinity murine interleukin-5 receptor. *EMBO Journal* **10**: 2133–2137.

Duronio V, Clark-Lewis I, Federsppiel B et al (1992) Tyrosine phosphorylation of receptor beta subunits and common substrates in response to interleukin-3 and granulocyte-macrophage colony-stimulating factor. *Journal of Biological Chemistry* **267**: 21856–21863.

Dusanter-Fourt I, Casadevall N, Lacombe C et al (1992) Erythropoietin induces the tyrosine phosphorylation of its own receptor in human erythropoietin-responsive cells. *Journal of Biological Chemistry* **267**: 10670–10675.

Eder M, Griffin JD & Ernst TJ (1993) The human granulocyte–macrophage colony-stimulating factor receptor is capable of initiating signal transduction in NIH3T3 cells. *EMBO Journal* **12:** 1647–1656.

Escobedo JA, Navankasattusas S, Kavanaugh WM et al (1991) cDNA cloning of a novel 85 kd protein that has SH2 domains and regulates binding of PI3-kinase to the PDGF β-receptor. *Cell* **65:** 75–82.

Farrar MA, Campbell JD & Schreiber RD (1992) Identification of a functionally important sequence in the C terminus of the interferon-τ receptor. *Proceedings of the National Academy of Sciences, USA* **89:** 11706–11710.

Ferrari S, Donelli A, Manfredini R et al (1990) Differential effects of c-myb and c-fes antisense oligodeoxynucleotides on granulocytic differentiation of human myeloid leukemia HL60 cells. *Cell Growth and Differentiation* **1:** 543–548.

Firmbach-Kraft I, Byers M, Shows T et al (1990) Tyk2, prototype of a novel class of non-receptor tyrosine kinase genes. *Oncogene* **5:** 1329–1336.

Fu XY (1992) A transcription factor with SH2 and SH3 domains is directly activated by an interferon alpha-induced cytoplasmic protein tyrosine kinase(s). *Cell* **70:** 323–335.

Gearing DP, King JA, Gough NM & Nicola NA (1989) Expression cloning of a receptor for human granulocyte-macrophage colony-stimulating factor. *EMBO Journal* **8:** 3667–3676.

Gearing DP, Comeau MR, Friend DJ et al (1992) The IL-6 signal transducer, gp130: An oncostatin M receptor and affinity converter for the LIF receptor. *Science* **255:** 1434–1437.

Gorman DM, Itoh N, Kitamura T et al (1990) Cloning and expression of a gene encoding an interleukin 3 receptor-like protein: identification of another member of the cytokine receptor gene family. *Proceedings of the National Academy of Sciences, USA* **87:** 5459–5463.

Gorman DM, Itoh N, Jenkins NA et al (1992) Chromosomal localization and organization of the murine genes encoding the beta subunits (AIC2A and AIC2B) of the interleukin 3, granulocyte/macrophage colony-stimulating factor, and interleukin 5 receptors. *Journal of Biological Chemistry* **267:** 15842–15848.

Gregory RJ, Kammermeyer KL, Vincent III WS & Wadsworth SC (1987) Primary sequence and developmental expression of a novel Drosophila src gene. *Molecular and Cellular Biology* **7:** 2119–2127.

Gulbins E, Coggeshall K, Baier G et al (1993) Tyrosine kinase-stimulated guanine nucleotide exchange activity of VAV in T cell activation. *Science* **260:** 822–825.

Hanazono Y, Chiba S, Sasaki K et al (1993) c-fps/fes protein-tyrosine kinase is implicated in a signaling pathway triggered by granulocyte-macrophage colony-stimulating factor and interleukin-3. *EMBO Journal* **12:** 1641–1646.

Hanks SK, Quinn AM & Hunter T (1988) The protein kinase family: conserved features and deduced phylogeny of the catalytic domains. *Science* **241:** 42–52.

Hara T & Miyajima A (1992) Two distinct functional high affinity receptors for mouse interleukin-3 (IL-3). *EMBO Journal* **11:** 1875–1884.

Harada N, Yang G, Miyajima A & Howard M (1992) Identification of an essential region for growth signal transduction in the cytoplasmic domain of the human interleukin-4 receptor. *Journal of Biological Chemistry* **267:** 22752–22758.

Harel-Bellan A & Farrar WL (1987) Modulation of proto-oncogene expression by colony stimulating factors. *Biochemical and Biophysical Research Communications* **148:** 1001–1008.

Harpur AG, Andres AC, Ziemiecki A et al (1992) JAK2, a third member of the JAK family of protein tyrosine kinases. *Oncogene* **7:** 1347–1353.

Hatakeyama M, Mori H, Doi T & Taniguchi T (1989a) A restricted cytoplasmic region of IL-2 receptor b chain is essential for growth signal transduction but not for ligand binding and internalization. *Cell* **59:** 837–845.

Hatakeyama M, Tsudo M, Minamoto S et al (1989b) Interleukin-2 receptor beta chain gene: generation of three receptor forms by cloned human alpha and beta chain cDNA's. *Science* **244:** 551.

Hatakeyama M, Kono T, Kobayashi N et al (1991) Interaction of the IL-2 receptor with the src-family kinase p56[lck]: Identification of novel intermolecular association. *Science* **252:** 1523–1528.

Hatakeyama M, Kawahara A, Mori H et al (1992) f-cos gene induction by interleukin 2: identification of the critical cytoplasmic regions within the interleukin 2 receptor beta chain. *Proceedings of the National Academy of Sciences, USA* **89:** 2022–2026.

Hayashida K, Kitamura T, Gorman DM et al (1990) Molecular cloning of a second subunit of the receptor for human granulocyte–macrophage colony-stimulating factor (GM-CSF): reconstitution of a high-affinity GM-CSF receptor. *Proceedings of the National Academy of Sciences, USA* **87**: 9655–9659.

Hibi M, Murakami M, Saito M et al (1990) Molecular cloning and expression of an IL-6 signal transducer, gp130. *Cell* **63**: 1149–1157.

Hoatlin ME, Kozak SL, Lilly F et al (1990) Activation of erythropoietin receptors by Friend viral gp55. *Proceedings of the National Academy of Sciences, USA* **87**: 9985–9989.

Horak ID, Gress RE, Lucas PJ et al (1991) T-lymphocyte interleukin 2-dependent tyrosine protein kinase signal transduction involves the activation of p56^{lck}. *Proceedings of the National Academy of Sciences, USA* **88**: 1996–2000.

Hume CR, Nocka KH, Sorrentino V et al (1988) Constitutive c-myc expression enhances the response of murine mast cells to IL-3, but does not eliminate their requirement for growth factors. *Oncogene* **2**: 223–226.

Ihle JN (1990) Interleukin 3: Biochemistry and mechanism of action. In Sporn M & Roberts A (eds) *Peptide Growth Factors and Their Receptors.* New York: Springer Verlag.

Ihle JN (1992) Interleukin-3 and hematopoiesis. In Kishimoto T (ed.) *Interleukins: Molecular biology and immunology*, pp 65–106. Basel: Karger.

Ip NY, Nye SH, Stahl N et al (1992) CNTF and LIF act on neuronal cells via shared signalling pathways that involve the IL-6 signal transducing component gp130. *Cell* **69**: 1121–1132.

Isfort RJ, Stevens D, May WS & Ihle JN (1988) IL-3 binding to a 140 kd phosphotyrosine containing cell surface protein. *Proceedings of the National Academy of Sciences, USA* **85**: 7982–7986.

Itoh N, Yonehara S, Schreurs J et al (1990) Cloning of an interleukin-3 receptor gene: a member of a distinct receptor gene family. *Science* **247**: 324–327.

Izuhara K & Harada N (1993) Interleukin-4 (IL-4) induces protein tyrosine phosphorylation of the IL-4 receptor and association of phosphatidylinositol 3-kinase to the IL-4 receptor in a mouse T cell line, HT2. *Journal of Biological Chemistry* **268**: 13097–13102.

Katzav S, Martin-Zanca D & Barbacid M (1989a) vav, a novel human oncogene derived from a locus ubiquitously expressed in hematopoietic cells. *EMBO Journal* **8**: 2283–2290.

Katzav S, Martin-Zanca D, Barbacid M et al (1989b) The trk oncogene abrogates growth factor requirements and transforms hematopoietic cells. *Oncogene* **4**: 1129–1135.

Kitamura T, Sato N, Arai K & Miyajima A (1991) Expression cloning of the human IL-3 receptor cDNA reveals a shared beta subunit for the human IL-3 and GM-CSF receptors. *Cell* **66**: 1165–1174.

Kobayashi N, Kono T, Hatakeyama M et al (1993) Functional coupling of the src-family protein tyrosine kinases p59^{fyn} and p53/56^{lyn} with the interleukin 2 receptor: Implications for redundancy and pleiotropism in cytokine signal transduction. *Proceedings of the National Academy of Sciences, USA* **90**: 4201–4205.

Koch CA, Anderson D, Moran MF et al (1991) SH2 and SH3 domains: elements that control interactions of cytoplasmic signaling proteins. *Science* **252**: 668–674.

Lau LF & Nathans D (1985) Identification of a set of genes expressed during the G0/G1 transition of cultured mouse cells. *EMBO Journal* **4**: 3145–3151.

Lau LF & Nathans D (1987) Expression of a set of growth-related immediate early genes in Balb/c3T3 cells: Coordinate regulation with c-fos and c-myc. *Proceedings of the National Academy of Sciences, USA* **84**: 1182–1186.

Leonard WJ, Depper JM, Crabtree GR et al (1984) Molecular cloning and expression of cDNAs for the human interleukin-2 receptor. *Nature* **311**: 626–631.

Li J-P & Baltimore D (1991) Mechanism of leukemogenesis induced by the MCF murine leukemia viruses. *Journal of Virology* **65**: 2408–2414.

Li JP, D'Andrea AD, Lodish HF & Baltimore D (1990) Activation of cell growth by binding of Friend spleen focus-forming virus gp55 glycoprotein to the erythropoietin receptor. *Nature* **343**: 762–764.

Longmore GD & Lodish HF (1991) An activating mutation in the murine erythropoietin receptor induces erythroleukemia in mice: a cytokine receptor superfamily oncogene. *Cell* **67**: 1089–1102.

McGlade J, Cheng A, Pelicci G et al (1992) Shc proteins are phosphorylated and regulated by the v-src and v-fps protein-tyrosine kinases. *Proceedings of the National Academy of Sciences, USA* **89**: 8869–8873.

Mano H, Ishikawa F, Nishida J et al (1990) A novel protein-tyrosine kinase, tec, is preferentially expressed in liver. *Oncogene* **5:** 1781–1786.

Mano H, Mano K, Tang B et al (1993) Expression of a novel form of tec kinase in hematopoietic cells and mapping of the gene to chromosome 5 near kit. *Oncogene* **8:** 417–424.

Matthews RJ, Bowne DB, Flores E & Thomas ML (1992) Characterization of hematopoietic intracellular protein tyrosine phosphatases: description of a phosphatase containing an SH2 domain and another enriched in proline-, glutamic acid-, serine-, and threonine-rich sequences. *Molecular and Cellular Biology* **12:** 2396–2405.

Mavilio F, Kreider BL, Valtieri M et al (1989) Alteration of growth and differentiation factors response by Kirsten and Harvey sarcoma viruses in the IL-3-dependent murine hematopoietic cell line 32D C13(G). *Oncogene* **4:** 301–308.

Meckling-Gill KA, Yee SP, Schrader JW & Pawson T (1992) A retrovirus encoding the v-fps protein-tyrosine kinase induces factor-independent growth and tumorigenicity in FDC-P1 cells. *Biochimica et Biophysica Acta* **1137:** 65–72.

Metcalf D (1989) The molecular control of cell division, differentiation commitment and maturation in haemopoietic cells. *Nature* **339:** 27–30.

Minami Y, Kono T, Yamada K et al (1993) Association of p56^{lck} with IL-2 receptor β chain is critical for the IL-2-induced activation of p56^{lck}. *EMBO Journal* **12:** 759–768.

Miura O & Ihle JN (1993) Dimer- and oligomerization of erythropoietin receptor by disulfide bond formation and significance of WSXWS motif on intracellular transport. *Archives of Biochemistry and Biophysics* **306(1):** 200–208.

Miura O, D'Andrea A, Kabat D & Ihle JN (1991) Induction of tyrosine phosphorylation by the erythropoietin receptor correlates with mitogenesis. *Molecular and Cellular Biology* **11:** 4895–4902.

Miura O, Cleveland JL & Ihle JN (1993) Inactivation of erythropoietin receptor function by point mutations in a region having homology with other cytokine receptors. *Molecular and Cellular Biology* **13:** 1788–1795.

Miyajima A, Kitamura T, Harada N et al (1992) Cytokine receptors and signal transduction. *Annual Reviews of Immunology* **10:** 295–331.

Mori H, Barsoumian EL, Hatakeyama M & Taniguchi T (1991) Signal transduction by interleukin 2 receptor beta chain: importance of the structural integrity as revealed by site-directed mutagenesis and generation of chimeric receptors. *International Immunology* **3:** 149–156.

Murakami M, Narazaki M, Hibi M et al (1991) Critical cytoplasmic region of the interleukin 6 signal transducer gp130 is conserved in the cytokine receptor family. *Proceedings of the National Academy of Sciences, USA* **88:** 11349–11353.

Murakami M, Hibi M, Nakagawa N et al (1993) IL-6-induced homodimerization of gp130 and associated activation of a tyrosine kinase. *Science* **260:** 1808–1810.

Nakamura Y, Komatsu N & Nakauchi H (1992) A truncated erythropoietin receptor that fails to prevent programmed cell death of erythroid cells. *Science* **257:** 1138–1141.

Nicola NA (1989) Hematopoietic cell growth factors and their receptors. *Annual Reviews of Biochemistry* **58:** 45–77.

Noguchi M, Yi H, Rosenblatt HM et al (1993) Interleukin-2 receptor γ chain mutation results in X-linked sever combined immunodeficiency in humans. *Cell* **73:** 147–157.

O'Connor R, Torigoe T, Reed JC & Santoli D (1992) Phenotypic changes induced by interleukin-2 (IL-2) and IL-3 in an immature T-lymphocytic leukemia are associated with regulated expression of IL-2 receptor beta chain and of protein tyrosine kinases LCK and LYN. *Blood* **80:** 1017–1025.

Otsu M, Hiles I, Gout I et al (1991) Characterisation of two 85 kd proteins that associate with receptor tyrosine kinases, middle T/pp60^{c-src} complexes, and PI 3-kinase. *Cell* **65:** 91–104.

Park LS, Martin U, Sorensen R et al (1992) Cloning of the low-affinity murine granulocyte-macrophage colony-stimulating factor receptor and reconstitution of a high-affinity receptor complex. *Proceedings of the National Academy of Sciences, USA* **89:** 4295–4299.

Pearse RN, Feinman R, Shuai K et al (1993) Interferon γ-induced transcription of the high-affinity Fc receptor for IgG requires assembly of a complex that includes the 91-kDa subunit of transcription factor ISGF3. *Proceedings of the National Academy of Sciences, USA* **90:** 4314–4318.

Pelicci G, Lanfrancone L, Grignani F et al (1992) A novel transforming protein (SHC) with an SH2 domain is implicated in mitogenic signal transduction. *Cell* **70:** 93–104.

Plutzky J, Neel BG & Rosenberg RD (1992) Isolation of a src homology 2-containing tyrosine phosphatase. *Proceedings of the National Academy of Sciences, USA* **89**: 1123–1127.

Polotskaya A, Zhao Y, Lilly ML & Kraft AS (1993) A critical role for the cytoplasmic domain of the granulocyte-macrophage colony-stimulating factor α receptor in mediating cell growth. *Cell Growth and Differentiation* **4(6)**: 523–531.

Pritchard MA, Baker E, Callen DF et al (1992) Two members of the JAK family of protein tyrosine kinases map to chromosomes 1p31.3 and 9p24. *Mammalian Genome* **3**: 36–38.

Quelle DE & Wojchowski DM (1991) Localized cytosolic domains of the erythropoietin receptor regulate growth signaling and down-modulate responsiveness to granulocyte-macrophage colony-stimulating factor. *Proceedings of the National Academy of Sciences, USA* **88**: 4801–4805.

Redemann N, Gaul U & Jackle H (1988) Disruption of a putative Cys-zinc interaction eliminates the biological activity of the Kruppel finger protein. *Nature* **332**: 90–92.

Rittling SR & Baserga R (1987) Regulatory mechanisms in the expression of cell cycle dependent genes. *Anticancer Research* **7**: 541–552.

Rozakis-Adcock M, McGlade J, Mbamalu G et al (1992) Association of the Shc and Grb/Sem5 SH2-containing proteins is implicated in activation of the Ras pathway by tyrosine kinases. *Nature* **360**: 689–692.

Sadowski I, Stone JC & Pawson T (1986) A non-catalytic domain conserved among cytoplasmic tyrosine kinases modifies the kinase function and transforming activity of Fujinami sarcoma virus p130$^{gag-fps}$. *Molecular and Cellular Biology* **6**: 4396–4408.

Sakamaki K, Miyajima I, Kitamura T & Miyajima A (1992) Critical cytoplasmic domains of the common β subunit of the human GM-CSF, IL-3 and IL-5 receptors for growth signal transduction and tyrosine phosphorylation. *EMBO Journal* **11**: 3541–3549.

Sasaki K, Chiba S, Hanazono Y et al (1993) Coordinate expression of the α and β chains of human granulocyte-macrophage colony-stimulating factor receptor confers ligand-induced morphological transformation in mouse fibroblasts. *Journal of Biological Chemistry* **268**: 13697–13702.

Satoh T, Nakafuku M, Miyajima A & Kaziro Y (1991) Involvement of ras p21 protein in signal-transduction pathways from interleukin 2, interleukin 3, and granulocyte/macrophage colony-stimulating factor, but not from interleukin 4. *Proceedings of the National Academy of Sciences, USA* **88**: 3314–3318.

Satoh T, Minami Y, Kono T et al (1992) Interleukin 2-induced activation of ras requires two domains of interleukin 2 receptor β subunit, the essential region for growth stimulation and lck-binding domain. *Journal of Biological Chemistry* **267**: 25423–25427.

Schindler C, Shuai K, Prezioso VR & Darnell JE Jr (1992) Interferon-dependent tyrosine phosphorylation of a latent cytoplasmic transcription factor. *Science* **257**: 809–813.

Selten G, Cuypers HT, Boelens W et al (1986) The primary structure of the putative oncogene pim-1 shows extensive homology with protein kinases. *Cell* **46**: 603–611.

Sharon M, Gnarra JR & Leonard WJ (1989) The beta-chain of the IL-2 receptor (p70) is tyrosine-phosphorylated on YT and HUT-102B2 cells. *Journal of Immunology* **143**: 2530–2533.

Shen SH, Bastien L, Posner BI & Chrëtien P (1991) A protein-tyrosine phosphatase with sequence similarity to the SH2 domain of the protein-tyrosine kinases. *Nature* **352**: 736–739 [Erratum in *Nature* (1991) **353**: 868].

Showers MO, Moreau J-F, Linnekin D et al (1992) Activation of the erythropoietin receptor by the Friend spleen focus-forming virus gp55 glycoprotein induces constitutive protein tyrosine phosphorylation. *Blood* **12**: 3070–3078.

Shuai K, Schindler C, Prezioso VR & Darnell JE Jr (1992) Activation of transcription by IFN-τ: tyrosine phosphorylation of a 91-kD DNA binding protein. *Science* **259**: 1808–1812.

Shultz LD (1991) Hematopoiesis and models of immunodeficiency. *Seminars in Immunology* **3**: 397–408.

Shultz LD, Schweitzer PA, Rajan TV et al (1993) Mutations at the murine motheaten locus are within the hematopoietic cell protein tyrosine phosphatase (Hcph) gene. *Cell* **73**: 1445–1454.

Silicano JD, Morrow TA & Desiderio SV (1992) itk, a T-cell-specific tyrosine kinase gene inducible by interleukin 2. *Proceedings of the National Academy of Sciences, USA* **89**: 11194–11198.

Silvennoinen O, Witthuhn B, Quelle FW et al (1993) Structure of the JAK2 protein tyrosine kinase and its role in IL-3 signal transduction. *Proceedings of the National Academy of Sciences, USA* **90:** 8429–8433.

Skolnik EY, Margolis B, Mohammadi M et al (1991) Cloning of PI3 kinase-associated p85 utilizing a novel method for expression/cloning of target proteins for receptor tyrosine kinases. *Cell* **65:** 83–90.

Sorensen P, Mui ALF & Krystal G (1989) Interleukin-3 stimulates the tyrosine phosphorylation of the 140-kilodalton interleukin-3 receptor. *Journal of Biological Chemistry* **264:** 19253–19258.

Srinivas RV, Kilpatrick DR, Tucker S et al (1991) The hydrophobic membrane-spanning sequences of the gp55 glycoprotein are required for the pathogenicity of Friend spleen focus-forming virus. *Journal of Virology* **65:** 5272–5280.

Stahl ML, Ferenz CR, Kelleher KL et al (1988) Sequence similarity of phospholipase C with the non-catalytic region of src. *Nature* **332:** 269–272.

Suh P-G, Ryu SH, Moon KH et al (1988) Inositol phospholipid-specific phospholipase C: complete cDNA and protein sequences and homology to tyrosine kinase-related oncogene products. *Proceedings of the National Academy of Sciences, USA* **85:** 5419–5423.

Sukhatme VP, Kartha S, Toback FG et al (1987) A novel early growth response gene rapidly induced by fibroblast, epithelial and lymphocyte mitogens. *Oncogene Research* **1:** 343–355.

Taga T, Hibi M, Hirata Y et al (1989) Interleukin-6 triggers the association of its receptor with a possible signal transducer, gp130. *Cell* **58:** 573–581.

Takaki S, Tominaga A, Hitoshi Y et al (1990) Molecular cloning and expression of the murine interleukin-5 receptor. *EMBO Journal* **9:** 4367–4374.

Takeshita T, Asao H, Ohtani K et al (1992) Cloning of the τ chain of the human IL-2 receptor. *Science* **257:** 379–382.

Tavernier J, Devos R, Cornelis S et al (1991) A human high affinity interleukin-5 receptor (IL5R) is composed of an IL5-specific alpha chain and a beta chain shared with the receptor for GM-CSF. *Cell* **66:** 1175–1184.

Telerman A, Amson R, Zakut-Houri R & Givol D (1988) Identification of the human pim-1 gene product as a 33-kilodalton cytoplasmic protein with tyrosine kinase activity. *Molecular and Cellular Biology* **8:** 1498–1503.

Torigoe T, O'Connor R, Santoli D & Reed JC (1992) Interleukin-3 regulates the activity of the LYN protein-tyrosine kinase in myeloid-committed leukemic cell lines. *Blood* **80:** 617–624.

Torti M, Marti KB, Altschuler D et al (1992) Erythropoietin induces p21^{ras} activation and p120GAP tyrosine phosphorylation in human erythroleukemia cells. *Journal of Biological Chemistry* **267:** 8293–8298.

Trahey M, Wong G, Halenbeck R et al (1988) Molecular cloning of two types of GAP complementary DNA from placenta. *Science* **242:** 1697–1700.

Tsui HW, Siminovitch KA, de Souza L & Tsui FWL (1993) Motheaten and viable motheaten mice have mutations in the haematopoietic cell phosphatase gene. *Nature Genetics* **4:** 124–129.

Tsukada S, Saffran DC, Rawlings DJ et al (1993) Deficient expression of a B-cell cytoplasmic tyrosine kinase in human X-linked agammaglobulinemia. *Cell* **72:** 279–290.

Ullrich A & Schlessinger J (1990) Signal transduction by receptors with tyrosine kinase activity. *Cell* **61:** 203–212.

van Lohuizen M, Verbeek S, Krimpenfort P et al (1989) Predisposition to lymphomagenesis in pim-1 transgenic mice: cooperation with c-myc and N-myc in murine leukemia virus-induced tumors. *Cell* **56:** 673–682.

Van Zant G & Shultz L (1989) Hematopoietic abnormalities of the immunodeficient mouse mutant, viable motheaten (*mev*). *Experimental Hematology* **17:** 81–87.

Velazquez L, Fellous M, Stark GR & Pellegrini S (1992) A protein tyrosine kinase in the interferon alpha/beta signaling pathway. *Cell* **70:** 313–322.

Vetrie D, Vorechovsky I, Sideras P et al (1993) The gene involved in X-linked agamma-globulinaemia is a member of the src family of protein-tyrosine kinases. *Nature* **361:** 226–233.

Vincent III WS, Gregory RJ & Wadsworth SC (1989) Embryonic expression of a Drosophila src gene: alternate forms of the protein are expressed in segmental stripes and in the nervous system. *Genes & Development* **3:** 334–347.

Vogel US, Dixon RAF, Schaber MD et al (1988) Cloning of bovine GAP and its interaction with oncogenic ras. *Nature* **335**: 90–93.

Wadsworth SC, Muckenthaler FA & Vincent III WS (1992) Differential expression of alternate forms of a Drosophila src protein during embryonic and larval tissue differentiation. *Developmental Biology* **138**: 296–312.

Wang X, Moller C, Norstedt B & Carter-Su C (1993) Growth hormone-promoted tyrosyl phosphorylation of a 121-kDa growth hormone receptor-associated protein. *Journal of Biological Chemistry* **268**: 3573–3579.

Watanabe S, Mui AL-F, Muto A et al (1993) Reconstituted human granulocyte-macrophage colony-stimulating facctor receptor transduces growth-promoting signals in mouse NIH 3T3 cells: comparison with signalling in BA/F3 pro-B cells. *Molecular and Cellular Biology* **13**: 1440–1448.

Weinstein Y, Morishita K, Cleveland JL & Ihle JN (1989) Interleukin 3 (IL-3) Induces transcription from non-rearranged gamma T cell Loci in IL-3-dependent cell lines. *Journal of Experimental Medicine* **169**: 2059–2071.

Wilks AF (1989) Two putative protein-tyrosine kinases identified by application of the polymerase chain reaction. *Proceedings of the National Academy of Sciences, USA* **86**: 1603–1607.

Wilks AF, Harpur AG, Kurban RR et al (1991) Two novel protein-tyrosine kinases, each with a second phosphotransferase-related catalytic domain, define a new class of protein kinase. *Molecular and Cellular Biology* **11**: 2057–2065.

Witthuhn B, Quelle FW, Silvennoinen O et al (1993) JAK2 associates with the erythropoietin receptor and is tyrosine phosphorylated and activated following EPO stimulation. *Cell* **74**: 227–236.

Yamamura Y, Kageyama Y, Matuzaki T et al (1992) Distinct downstream signaling mechanism between erythropoietin receptor and interleukin-2 receptor. *EMBO Journal* **11**: 4909–4915.

Yamasaki K, Taga T, Hirata Y et al (1988) Cloning and expression of the human interleukin-6 (BSF-2/IFN beta 2) receptor. *Science* **241**: 825–828.

Yi T & Ihle JN (1993) Association of hematopoietic cell phosphatase with c-kit after stimulation with c-kit ligand. *Molecular and Cellular Biology* **13**: 3350–3358.

Yi T, Bolen JB & Ihle JN (1991a) Hematopoietic cells express two forms of lyn kinase differing by 21 amino acids in the amino terminus. *Molecular and Cellular Biology* **11**: 2391–2398.

Yi T, Cleveland JL & Ihle JN (1991b) Identification of novel protein tyrosine phosphatases of hematopoietic cells by PCR amplification. *Blood* **78**: 2222–2228.

Yi T, Cleveland JL & Ihle JN (1992) A protein tyrosine phosphatase containing SH2 domains: Characterization, preferential expression in hematopoietic cells and localization to human chromosome 12p12–13. *Molecular and Cellular Biology* **12**: 836–846.

Yoshimura A & Lodish HF (1992) In vitro phosphorylation of the erythropoietin receptor and an associated protein, pp130. *Molecular and Cellular Biology* **12**: 706–715.

Yoshimura A, D'Andrea AD & Lodish HF (1990a) Friend spleen focus-forming virus glycoprotein gp55 interacts with the erythropoietin receptor in the endoplasmic reticulum and affects receptor metabolism. *Proceedings of the National Academy of Sciences, USA* **87**: 4139–4143.

Yoshimura A, Longmore G & Lodish HF (1990b) Point mutation in the exoplasmic domain of the erythropoietin receptor resulting in hormone-independent activation and tumorigenicity. *Nature* **348**: 647–649.

Yoshimura A, Zimmers T, Neumann D et al (1992) Mutations in the Trp–Ser–X–Trp–Ser motif of the erythropoietin receptor abolish processing, ligand binding, and activation of the receptor. *Journal of Biological Chemistry* **267**: 11619–11625.

Ziegler SF, Bird TA, Morella KK et al (1993) Distinct regions of the human granulocyte-colony-stimulating factor receptor cytoplasmic domain are required for proliferation and gene induction. *Molecular and Cellular Biology* **13**: 2384–2390.

Zon LI, Moreau JF, Koo JW et al (1992) The erythropoietin receptor transmembrane region is necessary for activation by the Friend spleen focus-forming virus gp55 glycoprotein. *Molecular and Cellular Biology* **12**: 2949–2957.

Zumstein P & Stiles CD (1987) Molecular cloning of gene sequences that are regulated by insulin-like growth factor I. *Journal of Biological Chemistry* **262**: 11252–11260.

3

Cytokines acting early in human
haematopoiesis

DONNA E. HOGGE
HEATHER J. SUTHERLAND
JOHANNE D. CASHMAN
PETER M. LANSDORP
R. KEITH HUMPHRIES
CONNIE J. EAVES

The functional and phenotypic characterization of primitive human haematopoietic progenitors has, until recently, relied primarily on the use of in vitro assays. However, by definition, in such systems the classical 'stem cell' phenotype, i.e. a cell with multilineage bone marrow repopulating ability, can never be conclusively identified. Nevertheless, the culture of various populations of human haematopoietic cells has allowed the identification and partial purification of rare constituents with many of the properties expected of stem cells (Sutherland et al, 1989a,b; Udomsakdi et al, 1991). By analogy with murine studies, where detailed and quantitative in vivo and in vitro experiments are possible, it appears likely that multipotent human progenitors with marrow repopulating ability can be maintained for many weeks in culture and under appropriate conditions may proliferate (Fraser et al, 1990). Thus, for a number of years, we have used the long-term culture system not only to characterize very primitive types of human haematopoietic cells but also to define the molecular mechanisms that control their behaviour (Eaves et al, 1991a). This review summarizes the progress made from our investigations in this area.

HUMAN LONG-TERM CULTURES

When unseparated human bone marrow cells are placed in suspension culture at a high cell density ($>10^6$ cells ml^{-1}), an adherent layer of mesenchymal 'stromal' cells forms with which primitive haematopoietic cells become associated (Coulombel et al, 1983). These stromal cells support the continued generation of haematopoietic progenitors and their differentiation into some types of mature progeny in the absence of any exogenous growth factors (Eaves et al, 1986; Hogge et al, 1991). The clonogenic cells detected in such long-term cultures (LTC) after 5 weeks are derived from more primitive precursor cells termed LTC-initiating cells (LTC-IC). In contrast to LTC-IC, directly clonogenic cells fail to sustain their numbers beyond 3 to 4 weeks under the same culture conditions (Sutherland et al, 1989a).

LTC-IC are highly enriched in populations of human marrow cells which are CD34+, and HLADR−, CD71±, CD45RA−, Thy-1^{low} or Rh123^{dull} and exhibit low forward and side light scatter on flow cytometric analysis (Sutherland et al, 1989a; Lansdorp et al, 1990; Udomsakdi et al, 1991; Craig et al, 1993). When assayed at limiting dilution, a single LTC-IC may generate up to 30 (with a mean of 4) clonogenic cells after 5 weeks in culture regardless of the purity of the starting cell population. Moreover, in up to 20% of cases these progeny include clonogenic cells from more than one lineage (Sutherland et al, 1990). Thus, LTC-IC are cells with a primitive phenotype, at least some of which are multipotent and have considerable proliferative capacity. LTC-IC can also be physically separated from the majority of clonogenic cells in bone marrow by their greater resistance to killing by 4-hydroperoxycyclophosphamide, a property expected of quiescent progenitors (Winston and Colenda, 1987; Udomsakdi et al, 1992a). Autologous marrow cells maintained in human LTC have been used successfully as haematopoietic support for high-dose myelosuppressive therapy (Chang et al, 1986; Barnett et al, 1989). Thus, characterization of human LTC-IC to date suggests that they and marrow repopulating stem cells may belong to overlapping, if not identical, populations.

REGULATION OF THE PROLIFERATIVE STATUS OF PRIMITIVE PROGENITOR CELLS IN LTC

In standard LTC, LTC-IC numbers remain unchanged for the first 10 days and then gradually decline to 25% and 10% of input values by 5 and 8 weeks, respectively (Figure 1) (Eaves et al, 1991b; Udomsakdi et al, 1992b). The maintenance of these cells, like the support of their differentiating progeny requires the presence of an adherent mesenchymal feeder layer. This may be generated from stromal cells (or their precursors) present in unseparated marrow, or provided by pre-established fibroblast feeders from a variety of sources (Sutherland et al, 1991). The feeder layers generate signals recognized by haematopoietic progenitors, some of which stimulate their proliferation and some of which may act as inhibitors. This was first demonstrated by analysis of the cell cycle status of the primitive clonogenic cells that are in contact with stromal cells as components of the adherent layer of LTC of normal marrow. By ^{3}H-thymidine suicide analysis, these cells have been shown to remain quiescent until stimulated to enter active cell cycle following the addition of fresh medium to established cultures. Thus, 2–3 days following a half medium change, primitive erythroid and granulocyte–macrophage progenitors in LTC adherent layers are cycling but, by the time of the next weekly medium change, they have returned to a quiescent state. In contrast, proliferation of the same types of progenitors found in the

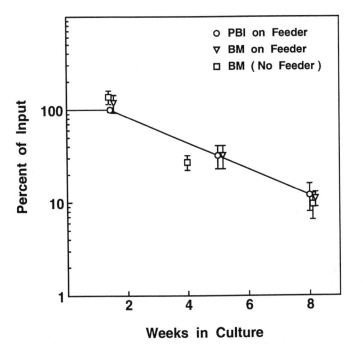

Figure 1. Kinetics of LTC-IC maintenance when normal peripheral blood, or marrow cells are seeded onto irradiated normal marrow feeders as compared to LTC initiated with normal unseparated marrow without feeders (Udomsakdi et al, 1992b). Values shown are mean ± SEM after normalization of data in individual experiments by setting LTC-IC values in the primary innoculum in each experiment to 100%. $n = 5$ for LTC-IC in normal blood (open circles) and $n = 2$ for LTC-IC in normal marrow (open triangles). Open squares show data for LTC-IC in normal unseparated marrow cultured in the absence of pre-established feeders (Eaves et al, 1991b).

non-adherent fraction of the LTC, where their contact with stromal cells is presumably much less, occurs continuously (Cashman et al, 1985). The predominantly non-cycling state of primitive progenitors in the adherent layer of LTC is reminiscent of their normally quiescent state in the bone marrow. This suggests that stromal cells in the marrow microenvironment may perform a similar regulatory function in vivo.

A series of experiments was performed to investigate the role of various components of the culture medium in regulating haematopoietic progenitor cycling, and then to analyse the effects of specific molecular species. The first experiments demonstrated that the stimulatory effect of a half-medium change on progenitor cycling could be mimicked by horse serum but not by other components of the fresh LTC medium. However, stimulation of progenitor cell cycling could also be achieved following the addition of IL-1β, TGF-α, IL-2 or PDGF. None of these factors were able to stimulate haematopoietic colony-forming cells directly in methylcellulose assays, although all were known to stimulate mesenchymal cells to release various cytokines (Sieff et al, 1988; Eaves et al, 1991c). Co-addition of TGF-β, a direct-acting negative regulator of primitive haematopoietic cells, was found to block the stimulatory effect of IL-1 or fresh medium on progenitor cycling (Cashman et al, 1990). These results suggested a model of regulation in which varying production of positive and negative regulatory factors by mesenchymal stromal cells controls the proliferative status of adjacent haematopoietic cells.

To test such a model, Northern analysis was performed on RNA derived from LTC adherent layers after addition of factors thought to activate progenitor cycling by indirect mechanisms (Eaves et al, 1991c). Increased levels of messenger RNA for IL-1β, IL-6, G-CSF and, in some cases, GM-CSF were seen in the stimulated stromal cells with corresponding increases in the bioactivity of these same growth factors found to be in the overlying medium. In contrast, TGF-β mRNA and bioactivity were found to be constitutively produced by LTC adherent layers and these were relatively unaffected by the addition of mesenchymal cell activators. Interestingly, the levels of TGF-β detected in LTC media were similar to the amounts of exogenous TGF-β $(5\,\text{ng}\,\text{ml}^{-1})$ that inhibited adherent layer progenitor cycling. To assess the functional significance of endogenous TGF-β, neutralizing anti-TGF-β antibody was added to cultures in which primitive progenitors in the adherent layers were already actively cycling. Their return to a quiescent state was consistently inhibited. Similar addition of anti-TGF-β antibody to cultures in which these progenitors had again become quiescent allowed progenitor entry into S phase in some, but not all, experiments (Eaves et al, 1991c). Thus, the ability of stromal cells to down-regulate the proliferative status of primitive haematopoietic cells appears to involve endogenously produced TGF-β.

More recently, similar experiments have been undertaken with MIP-1α, another negative regulator of haematopoiesis (Graham and Pragnell, 1992). MIP-1α is also produced in LTC adherent layers (Otsuka et al, 1991a) and addition of MIP-1α has been shown to have the same ability as TGF-β to block the stimulatory effect of a half-medium change or the addition of IL-1β (Eaves et al, 1992). Moreover, addition of MIP-1β (which is able to neutralize the activity of MIP-1α) (Broxmeyer et al, 1991) to activated cultures can also prolong primitive progenitor cycling (Cashman and Eaves, unpublished data). Taken together, these data underscore the likely importance of the relative (rather than the absolute) levels of positive and negative regulators to which primitive haematopoietic cells are exposed in determining their proliferative state.

EFFECTS OF POSITIVE REGULATORS OF HAEMATOPOIESIS IN LTC

A variety of cytokines which stimulate the proliferation and differentiation of haematopoietic cells in short-term assays are produced, at least transiently, in standard LTC (Eaves et al, 1991c). However, analyses of adherent layer RNAs for cytokine message or LTC medium for bioactive factor does not allow identification of specific regulators that may play a direct and determining role in any particular response. As a first approach to this latter question, a series of experiments were designed specifically to alter the concentration of one or more growth factors of interest. This was done either by simply adding the factor to the LTC medium or by establishing LTC on adherent layer feeders that had been genetically engineered by retroviral infection to constitutively produce one or more factor (Hogge et al, 1991; Otsuka et al, 1991b,c; Sutherland et al, 1991). Addition of soluble factors to the medium allows a high concentration to be achieved throughout the LTC which then declines over the next few days. This makes repeated additions of factor necessary if effects are to be studied over a period of several weeks. Constitutive production of growth factor by cells within the adherent layer results in very high concentrations of factor in that location relative to elsewhere in the culture. However, with this strategy it is possible to achieve overall cytokine levels that remain relatively steady over time. This second situation may also be relatively 'physiological' since many growth factors are thought to mediate their effects in vivo in a similarly spatially-restricted fashion. Since a number of cytokines have been shown to exist in both a cell surface-bound and free (soluble) form, there is also the possibility that some factors may have different mechanisms of action on target cells when presented in a cellular context (Rettenmier et al, 1987; Flanagan et al, 1991). Thus, it was of interest to compare and contrast the effects of both exogenously and endogenously presented growth factors in the LTC system.

Initially our efforts focused on two factors known to be produced in LTC and to stimulate the growth of haematopoietic cells in short-term methylcellulose assays, i.e., GM-CSF and G-CSF (Hogge et al, 1991). Neither of these stimulated progenitor cycling when added individually to LTC, even in a very high single dose (Table 1). Similar results were obtained with feeder layers generated by fibroblasts constitutively producing GM-CSF. In contrast, engineered feeders releasing relatively small amounts of G-CSF into the culture medium maintained primitive progenitors in the adherent layer in a continuously dividing state with the same effect resulting from three consecutive daily additions of G-CSF. Interestingly this could not be achieved with two daily additions of exogenous G-CSF suggesting that continuous exposure for a minimal period of 72 hours is critical for progenitor activation. On the other hand, when G-CSF and GM-CSF were combined and added together as a single dose, even low doses of both were effective in stimulating primitive progenitor proliferation. This synergistic action on progenitor cycling in LTC may be similar to the synergism between these two factors observed on haematopoietic cells assayed in other systems (McNiece et al, 1989).

Interleukin-3 (IL-3) is a well-characterized multilineage haematopoietin normally produced by activated T cells (Kannourakis and Johnson, 1990). In LTC of human marrow, it is not produced at levels sufficient to detect by bioactivity assays (Eaves et al, 1991c). Nevertheless, the possibility that IL-3 production by the T cells present in the marrow microenvironment plays a physiological role in regulating haematopoiesis in vivo cannot be discounted. Moreover, known IL-3 effects suggest that its addition to LTC should

Table 1. Effect of increasing the concentrations of specific growth factor on the proliferative status of primitive clonogenic cells in the adherent layer of LTC.

Growth factor	Concentration (ng/ml)	Mode of increased presentation*	Primitive progenitor† cycling status
GM-CSF	4	Human feeders	Quiescent
GM-CSF	80	Single addition	Quiescent
G-CSF	20	Human feeders	Cycling
G-CSF	150	One or two daily additions	Quiescent
G-CSF	150	Three daily additions	Cycling
GM-CSF+	2	Human feeders	Cycling
G-CSF	10		
GM-CSF+	10	Single addition	Cycling
G-CSF	5		
IL-3	7	Human feeders	Cycling
IL-3	100	Single addition	Quiescent
IL-3	10	Three daily additions	Cycling
IL-6	20	Murine fibroblasts (M2-10B4 cells)	Cycling
IL-6	100	Single addition	Quiescent
IL-6	20	Three daily additions	Cycling
IL-3+	25	M2-10B4	Cycling
IL-6	10		

* By genetically engineered fibroblasts of the origin stated or by addition of soluble factor to the culture medium as indicated.
† Determined 2–3 days after a mock medium change with addition of a specific factor or 7 days after a previous half-medium change (for cultures containing genetically engineered feeders) at which time progenitors in control LTC with no growth factor manipulations are quiescent.

enhance haematopoiesis in these cultures. Experiments to test this showed that the continuous presence of IL-3 in LTC, whether provided by IL-3-producing feeder cells, or by daily addition of factor for at least 3 days, *does* activate and sustain primitive progenitor cell cycling (Otsuka et al, 1991b). Similar results have been obtained with IL-6 (Table 1) (Otsuka et al, 1991c). Thus, direct-acting haematopoietins produced by stromal cells in LTC can be implicated in activating the proliferation of early haematopoietic progenitors in this system (Eaves et al, 1991c).

Further experiments were performed to see if the addition of these same factors would lead to an expansion of any of the various populations of haematopoietic cells maintained in LTC. In these studies one or more growth factors was provided continuously for 5 weeks through the use of genetically engineered human growth-factor producing murine fibroblast (M2-10B4) feeders. The influence of these feeders on the output of mature non-adherent cells, clonogenic progenitors and LTC-IC was assessed. As shown in Table 2, provision of IL-3, IL-6, G-CSF and GM-CSF (alone or in combination) was able to modify the number of cells accumulated in one or more of these compartments after 5 weeks of culture except in the case of LTC containing only feeders producing $6 \, mg \, ml^{-1}$ of human IL-3. IL-6 alone was also relatively unsuccessful in stimulating marrow cells in LTC, causing only a modest (twofold) increase in clonogenic cells. Maintenance of higher levels of IL-3 ($50 \, ng \, ml^{-1}$) or provision of G-CSF, GM-CSF or any combination of two or three of the four growth factors increased mature cell

Table 2. Changes in cell content of 5-week-old LTC containing human growth factor-producing murine fibroblast feeders.

Feeder	Growth factor	Concentration (ng/ml)	NAC*	CFU*	LTC-IC*
A. M2-10B4	IL-3	50	↑ (6)†	↑ (3)†	<->
	IL-3	6	<->	<->	<->
	IL-6	20	<->	↑ (2)†	<->
	G-CSF	20	↑ (2)†	↑ (2)†	<->
	GM-CSF	1	↑ (21)†	<->	↓ (2)
	IL-3 + IL-6	25 + 10	↑ (5)†	↑ (3)†	↑ (2)†
	IL-3 + G-CSF	3 + 10	↑ (4)†	↑ (3)†	↑ (2)†
	IL-3 + GM-CSF	3 + 0.5	↑ (14)†	<->	<->
	G-CSF + GM-CSF	10 + 0.5	↑ (25)†	<->	↓ (3)
	IL-3 + G-CSF + GM-CSF	3 + 10 + 0.5	↑ (14)†	<->	<->
B. Human marrow fibroblast			↑ (3)†	<->	<->
C. Plastic			↓ (11)†	↓ (33)†	↓ (2)

* <->, no change; ↑, increase; ↓, decrease; (fold change) as compared to unmodified M2-10B4 feeders.
† $p \leq 0.05$ as compared to M2-10B4 feeders.

output; the most dramatic increase was obtained whenever GM-CSF was present in increased amounts (Otsuka et al, 1991c; Sutherland et al, 1991). In contrast, increased GM-CSF levels did not change the progenitor content of 5-week-old LTC and effects on LTC-IC, if any, were negative. Increased levels of IL-3 in combination with G-CSF or IL-6 were the only conditions that significantly enhanced LTC-IC maintenance although even these effects were not marked ($\leq$2-fold) (Otsuka et al, 1991c; Sutherland et al, 1991). Not surprisingly, the same conditions were also effective in supporting the output of clonogenic cells from LTC-IC. However, as with LTC-IC maintenance, the increases observed were modest (threefold). When LTC-IC were assayed at limiting dilution with these various growth factor-producing feeders, the mean number of clonogenic cells produced per LTC-IC remained unchanged (Sutherland et al, 1991).

The relative effectiveness of exogenous factor additions versus factor-producing feeder cells in stimulating primitive progenitors was directly compared in the case of IL-3 (Table 3) (Otsuka et al, 1991b). To change the dose of IL-3 provided by feeders, IL-3-producing cells were mixed in various proportions with non-IL-3-producing cells of the same kind. Even when the number of IL-3-producing feeder cells was decreased to the point where no bioactive IL-3 could be detected in the medium, continuous cycling of primitive progenitors could be maintained. Addition of exogenous factor, which resulted in much higher levels of IL-3 in the medium, was, however, unable to achieve the same effect, even when IL-3 was present throughout the entire 5-week duration of the culture. The greater effectiveness of the IL-3-producing cells as compared to repeated factor additions is most likely due to the relatively high local concentrations of IL-3 near progenitors in the adherent layer obtainable by endogenous production. However, increased

Table 3. Comparison of the effect of maintaining various concentrations of IL-3 (using IL-3-producing feeders or exogenous IL-3) on the proliferative status of primitive adherent layer progenitors in 3–5-week-old LTC.

Method of IL-3 presentation	Dose of IL-3 added	IL-3 detected in LTC medium (ng ml^{-1})†	Progenitor cycling†
Exogenous addition	$10\,\text{ng ml}^{-1}$ once per week	<0.1	Quiescent
	$10\,\text{ng ml}^{-1}$ twice per week	1–2	Quiescent
	$10\,\text{ng ml}^{-1}$ daily × 5 week	10–15	Cycling
% IL-3-producing feeders*	0	<0.1	Quiescent
	10	<0.1	Cycling
	30	1	Cycling
	100	7	Cycling

* Of human marrow origin.
† Measured 7 days after the regular half-medium change.

potency of IL-3 presented in association with cell surface or extracellular matrix components could be envisaged. There is some evidence that both IL-3 and GM-CSF can bind to extracellular matrix produced by marrow stroma (or fibroblasts) suggesting that even small amounts of such factors produced in the marrow may be retained where they can interact with responsive haematopoietic target cells (Gordon et al, 1987; Roberts et al, 1988). Although fibroblasts have not been found to produce IL-3, small numbers of activated T cells may be present in the normal marrow microenvironment where they could play a regulatory role by presenting IL-3 to haematopoietic cells.

One of the more intriguing observations emerging from experiments with genetically engineered murine bone marrow fibroblasts has been that these cells in their unmanipulated state can support all levels of human haematopoiesis. In particular, they are able to support the maintenance of LTC-IC and their ability to generate clonogenic cells to a degree that is comparable to that achieved with human marrow fibroblasts. Since these cells could not be found to produce known species cross-reactive factors such as IL-6 and G-CSF, even after stimulation with agents such as IL-1, it appears likely that their supportive activity is due to other, as yet uncharacterized, activities. Subsequently, a number of groups have described the expression, in mesenchymal cells, of a factor whose deficiency in homozygous Steel (Sl/Sl) mutant mice gives rise to congenital anaemia (Copeland et al, 1990; Huang et al, 1990). Cloning of the gene for the Steel factor and studies of its activity on a variety of specific haematopoietic cell subpopulations raised the question of whether endogenously produced Steel factor might be responsible for some of the ability of fibroblasts to support haematopoiesis in LTC (Flanagan et al, 1991). Steel factor can be expressed as a membrane-bound protein that subsequently undergoes proteolytic cleavage to release an active derivative from the cell surface (Flanagan et al, 1991). An alternatively-spliced mRNA which lacks the extracellular proteolytic cleavage site gives rise to an obligate membrane-bound form of the molecule, which might contribute to local mechanisms of regulation of haematopoiesis in the marrow microenvironment. The receptor for Steel factor, c-kit, is expressed on all primitive murine and human haematopoietic progenitors examined to date (Ashman et al, 1991; Okada et al, 1991, 1992; Papayannopoulou et al, 1991). Murine Steel factor has significant cross-activity on human haematopoietic cells and is expressed by murine marrow stromal cells (Brandt et al, 1992).

To examine specifically the role of Steel factor in regulating human haematopoiesis in the LTC system, strategies both to deplete and increase the level of Steel factor present were pursued. Populations of human marrow cells highly enriched for LTC-IC and depleted of normal marrow stromal elements were cultured, together with fibroblast feeders from Sl/Sl or normal littermate (+/+) mouse embryos, to examine the effect of removing Steel factor from the cultures. The same types of haematopoietic cells were also cultured in suspension with single or multiple defined recombinant growth factors (including Steel factor) to examine the effects of Steel factor in the absence of any other fibroblast-derived cytokine (Sutherland et al, 1993). Addition of Steel factor to suspension cultures of these purified progenitors was equivalent to maintaining these cells on competent fibroblasts when LTC-IC numbers were evaluated after 5 weeks, but was no more effective in this regard than a combination of IL-3 and G-CSF or all three factors together. In contrast, directly clonogenic cells showed greater amplification in cultures containing the combination of Steel factor, IL-3 and G-CSF by comparison to cultures to which only Steel factor or G-CSF plus IL-3 was added. Of particular interest is the equivalence of homozygous Steel deleted (Sl/Sl) feeders to both +/+ and human marrow feeders in maintaining LTC-IC numbers and clonogenic cell output. In these experiments all feeders (or growth factor additions) tested were superior to conditions of no growth factor supplementation including those in which no source of Steel factor was present. Thus, Steel factor appears not to be necessary for the proliferation of early haematopoietic progenitors, including LTC-IC, although this factor can, under certain circumstances, contribute to the process by which these cells are activated. The ability of Sl/Sl feeders also to enhance progenitor maintenance implies that species cross-reactive factor(s) other than Steel, possibly as yet uncharacterized, must be produced by these cells.

MODEL OF HUMAN HAEMATOPOIETIC CELL REGULATION IN LTC

A hierarchy of haematopoietic cells is present in LTC initiated with human cells, ranging from LTC-IC, the most primitive cells known, through their clonogenic progeny to mature cells of the granulocyte and macrophage lineages. Regulation of the production and maintenance of all these cell types appears to be a function of the mesenchymal stromal cells present in this system and the growth factors they produce. Additional cytokines, such as IL-3, which are normally not detectable in LTC, will also stimulate haematopoietic cells in this system and may interact with other, endogenously

58

Table 4. The ability of various growth factors and feeders to support human progenitors in 5-week-old LTC.

		Clonogenic cells†		LTC-IC†	
Factor added*	Feeder present	Start	Week 5	Start	Week 5
None	None	4.0	0.22	1.0	0.04
Steel factor	None	3.0	1.0	1.1	0.16
G-CSF + IL-3	None	3.0	5.9	1.1	0.18
Steel + G-CSF + IL-3	None	3.0	20.7	1.1	0.16
None	Sl/Sl	8.5	3.2	1.0	0.14
None	+/+	8.5	4.4	1.0	0.14
None	Human marrow	4.2	4.0	1.0	0.11

* Recombinant human Steel factor (Amgen Corp., Thousand Oaks, Ca.) was added to LTC three times per week at a concentration of $100\,\mathrm{ng\,ml^{-1}}$. Transfected COS cell supernatants containing G-CSF or IL-3 were added three times per week at concentrations of $20\,\mathrm{ng\,ml^{-1}}$.
† CD34+, HLA-DR± human marrow cells with low to intermediate forward light scatter and low 90° light scatter were isolated using a FACScan Plus cell sorter. Results shown are expressed per 100 cells initially cultured.

produced factors. Supplementation of LTC with one or more growth stimulatory molecules can enhance haematopoietic activity in the cultures even when the growth factor in question can be detected at significant levels prior to its addition (Tables 1–4; Figure 2). This demonstrates that progenitor responses are influenced by the concentration, as well as the type of factors to which they are exposed. The ultimate responses seen may be the end result of a variety of additive or synergistic interactions between different cytokines.

Finally, individual factors show different activities on haematopoietic cell targets at different stages of development. For example, GM-CSF appears to act almost exclusively on the terminal stages of granulopoiesis (Hogge et al, 1991; Sutherland et al, 1991) whereas IL-3 has little activity of this type but instead, as a single factor, can enhance the generation of clonogenic cells from LTC-IC. In combination with G-CSF or IL-6, IL-3 also enhances the maintenance of LTC-IC themselves (Otsuka et al, 1991b,c; Sutherland et al, 1991). Steel factor on its own has little ability to support the generation of clonogenic cells from LTC-IC or the generation of mature non-adherent cells from clonogenic cells. However, Steel factor alone can support LTC-IC self-maintenance, and, in combination with G-CSF and IL-3, induces a marked expansion in their output of clonogenic cells and their mature granulocyte and macrophage progeny (Sutherland et al, 1993).

It has proven possible to achieve a twentyfold or greater expansion of non-adherent cell numbers in LTC with a variety of growth factor(s). Clonogenic cells can be similarly increased with combinations including Steel factor (Table 4; Sutherland et al, 1993). Unfortunately, thus far conditions to support a significant, net expansion of LTC-IC numbers have not been identified. Thus, although LTC-IC maintenance can be enhanced slightly by supplementing cultures with growth factors, their gradual decline over a 5–8-week period in LTC cannot yet be reversed (Figure 1). On the other hand, these cells seem relatively tolerant of a wide variety of culture conditions, perhaps reflecting an initial quiescent state.

Negative regulators of haematopoiesis are also endogenously produced in LTC by both stromal cells and macrophages (Eaves et al, 1991c; Otsuka et al, 1991a). The level of at least one of these factors, TGF-β, appears to change very little with various manipulations of the culture. Nevertheless, up-regulation of specific stimulatory factors or down-regulation of TGF-β are equally effective in releasing primitive haematopoietic cells from their quiescent state in LTC adherent layers (Eaves et al, 1991c). Conversely, addition of sufficient TGF-β or MIP-1α to LTC media can counteract positive stimulus which would otherwise induce progenitor cycling (Cashman et al, 1990; Eaves et al, 1992). The proliferative status of primitive haematopoietic cells in the adherent layer of LTC is thus

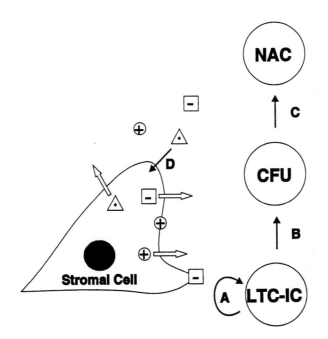

Figure 2. Proposed model of human haematopoiesis in LTC. Haematopoietic cells, including LTC-IC, clonogenic cells (CFU) and mature non-adherent cells (NAC) of the granulocyte–macrophage lineage, interact with stromal cells (such as fibroblasts, endothelial cells or macrophages) and the regulatory factors they produce. In addition to being secreted by stromal cells (white arrows) such factors may be bound to the cell surface, presented as part of the extracellular matrix, or introduced exogenously as soluble regulators. Factors act at various levels in the haemopoietic hierarchy (or on stromal cells themselves) to generate stimulatory or inhibitory signals. ⊕, positive regulator of haematopoietic cells; (⊟), negative regulator of haematopoietic cells; (△), regulator which has no effect on haematopoietic cells but may stimulate stromal cells to produce haematopoietic regulators. Solid arrows, cellular responses that may be influenced by regulators; A, LTC-IC maintenance/self-renewal; B, LTC-IC differentiation to clonogenic cells; C, CFU proliferation and differentiation to mature NAC; D, stimulation of stromal cells to produce growth factors. The net effect observed on any of these processes depends on the nature of the factor(s) present, their relative and absolute concentration and their interaction with a specific target cell.

determined by the net result of additive, synergistic and antagonistic interactions among multiple molecular species and the target cell. Rather small perturbations in the level of any one regulator may cause significant effects by altering this subtle balance. The apparent redundancy of the effects of several of these factors when their activities are studied in short-term methylcellulose assay (e.g. G-CSF, GM-CSF) can be further dissected in LTC to reveal discrete differences in the responses of different haematopoietic cells.

Such a complex regulatory system, embodying multiple factors that can interact with several different types of targets at different levels in the developmental hierarchy, offers enormous opportunities for flexibility. At first glance, this may appear to be at odds with the observed consistency in the number of mature blood cells in the adult circulation. However, given the amplification potential of haematopoietic differentiation processes, tight control of terminal cells may be entirely compatible with independent regulation of early compartments. Moreover, as complex as the regulation of haematopoiesis already appears to be, current evidence suggests that additional, uncharacterized regulators participate in the maintenance of primitive human progenitor cells (Sutherland et al, 1993).

A number of haematopoietic growth factors, including M-CSF and Steel factor are known to exist in both soluble and membrane-bound forms (Rettenmier et al, 1987; Flanagan et al, 1991). Some data suggest that the bound form of Steel may function more effectively as a stimulator of haematopoiesis than the secreted molecule (Toksoz et al, 1992). Even secreted molecules, such as IL-3, can provide a local stimulus to primitive progenitors when neither bioactive factor nor haematopoietic effects can be detected more distantly. Resolution of the most likely mechanisms responsible for such 'local' effects has not yet been possible. Such mechanisms include increased local factor availability dictated by the laws of diffusion or binding to available molecules in the extracellular matrix or on the cell surface, as well as mechanisms of enhanced bioactivity due to the presence locally of other, as yet uncharacterized, co-stimulatory molecules.

SUMMARY

In long-term cultures (LTC) of human haematopoietic cells, primitive progenitors termed LTC-initiating cells can be maintained for several months and will differentiate to produce clonogenic cells and mature granulocytes and macrophages when provided with a supportive feeder layer of adherent mesenchymal cells. Primitive haematopoietic cells become associated with this feeder layer and their proliferative status and differentiation are regulated by their interaction with these feeder cells and the growth factors they produce. Both positive and negative regulators are generated in LTC and the balance between these diverse factors is readily manipulated by both direct and indirect mechanisms which appear to operate in a localized fashion. These features parallel those believed to characterize the mechanisms that regulate haematopoiesis in the bone marrow microenvironment in vivo and suggest that further analysis of the LTC system will be useful in delineating the full mystery of this process.

Acknowledgements

These investigations were supported by grants from the National Cancer Institute of Canada (NCIC) and the Medical Research Council of Canada. CJE is a Terry Fox Cancer Research Scientist of the NCIC.

REFERENCES

Ashman LK, Cambareri AC, To LB et al (1991) Expression of the YB5.B8 antigen (c-kit proto-oncogene product) in normal human bone marrow. *Blood* **78:** 30–37.
Barnett MJ, Eaves CJ, Phillips GL et al (1989) Successful autografting in chronic myeloid leukaemia after maintenance of marrow in culture. *Bone Marrow Transplantation* **4:** 345–351.
Brandt J, Briddell RA, Srour EF et al (1992) Role of c-kit ligand in the expansion of human hematopoietic progenitor cells. *Blood* **79:** 634–641.
Broxmeyer HE, Sherry B, Cooper S et al (1991) Macrophage inflammatory protein (MIP)-1. *Journal of Immunology* **147:** 2586–2594.
Cashman J, Eaves AC & Eaves CJ (1985) Regulated proliferation of primitive hematopoietic progenitor cells in long-term human marrow cultures. *Blood* **66:** 1002–1005.
Cashman JD, Eaves AC, Raines EW et al (1990) Mechanisms that regulate the cell cycle status of very primitive hematopoietic cells in long-term human marrow cultures. I. Stimulatory role of a variety of mesenchymal cell activators and inhibitory role of TGF-β. *Blood* **75:** 96–101.
Chang J, Coutinho L, Morgenstern G et al (1986) Reconstitution of haemopoietic system with autologous marrow taken during relapse of acute myeloblastic leukaemia and grown in long-term culture. *Lancet* **i:** 294–295.
Copeland NG, Gilbert DJ, Cho BC et al (1990) Mast cell growth factor maps near the steel locus on mouse chromosome 10 and is deleted in a number of steel alleles. *Cell* **63:** 175–183.
Coulombel L, Eaves AC & Eaves CJ (1983) Enzymatic treatment of long-term human marrow cultures reveals the preferential location of primitive hemopoietic progenitors in the adherent layer. *Blood* **62:** 291–297.
Craig W, Kay R, Cutler RL & Lansdorp PM (1993) Expression of Thy-1 on human hemato-poietic progenitor cells. *Journal of Experimental Medicine*, in press.
Eaves AC, Cashman JD, Gaboury LA et al (1986) Unregulated proliferation of primitive chronic myeloid leukemia progenitors in the presence of normal marrow adherent cells. *Proceedings of the National Academy of Sciences, USA* **83:** 5306–5310.
Eaves CJ, Cashman JD & Eaves AC (1991a) Methodology of long-term culture of human hematopoietic cells. *Journal of Tissue Culture Methods* **13:** 55–62.
Eaves CJ, Cashman JD, Sutherland HJ et al (1991b) Molecular analysis of primitive hemato-poietic cell proliferation control mechanisms. *Annals of the New York Academy of Sciences* **628:** 298–306.
Eaves CJ, Cashman JD, Kay RJ et al (1991c) Mechanisms that regulate the cell cycle status of very primitive hematopoietic cells in long-term human marrow cultures. II. Analysis of positive and negative regulators produced by stromal cells within the adherent layer. *Blood* **78:** 110–117.
Eaves CJ, Cashman JD, Wolpe SD & Eaves AC (1992) Primitive chronic myeloid leukemia (CML) cells are unresponsive to MIP-1α, an inhibitor of primitive normal hematopoietic cells (Abstract). *Blood* **80 (supplement 1):** 155a.
Flanagan JG, Chan DC & Leder P (1991) Transmembrane form of the kit ligand growth factor is determined by alternative splicing and is missing in the SI^d mutant. *Cell* **64:** 1025–1035.
Fraser CC, Eaves CJ, Szilvassy SJ & Humphries RK (1990) Expansion in vitro of retrovirally marked totipotent hematopoietic stem cells. *Blood* **76:** 1071–1076.

Gordon MY, Riley GP, Watt SM & Greaves MF (1987) Compartmentalization of a haemato-poietic growth factor (GM-CSF) by glycosaminoglycans in the bone marrow micro-environment. *Nature* **326:** 403–405.

Graham GJ & Pragnell IB (1992) SCI/MIP-1α: A potent stem cell inhibitor with potential roles in development. *Developmental Biology* **151:** 377–381.

Hogge DE, Cashman JD, Humphries RK & Eaves CJ (1991) Differential and synergistic effects of human granulocyte-macrophage colony-stimulating factor and human granulo-cyte colony-stimulating factor on hematopoiesis in human long-term marrow cultures. *Blood* **77:** 493–499.

Huang E, Nocka K, Beier DR et al (1990) The hematopoietic growth factor KL is encoded by the Sl locus and is the ligand of the c-kit receptor, the gene product of the W locus. *Cell* **63:** 225–233.

Kannourakis G & Johnson GR (1990) Proliferative properties of unfractionated, purified, and single cell human progenitor populations stimulated by recombinant human interleukin-3. *Blood* **75:** 370–377.

Lansdorp PM, Sutherland HJ & Eaves CJ (1990) Selective expression of CD45 isoforms on functional subpopulations of CD34+ hemopoietic cells from human bone marrow. *Journal of Experimental Medicine* **172:** 363–366.

McNiece I, Andrews R, Stewart M et al (1989) Action of interleukin-3, G-CSF, and GM-CSF on highly enriched human hematopoietic progenitor cells: Synergistic interaction of GM-CSF plus G-CSF. *Blood* **74:** 110–114.

Okada S, Nakauchi H, Nagayoshi K et al (1991) Enrichment and characterization of murine hematopoietic stem cells that express c-kit molecule. *Blood* **78:** 1706–1712.

Okada S, Nakauchi H, Nagayoshi K et al (1992) In vivo and in vitro stem cell function of c-kit- and Sca-1-positive murine hematopoietic cells. *Blood* **80:** 3044–3050.

Otsuka T, Eaves CJ, Humphries RK et al (1991a) Lack of evidence for abnormal autocrine or paracrine mechanisms underlying the uncontrolled proliferation of primitive chronic myeloid leukemia progenitor cells. *Leukemia* **5:** 861–868.

Otsuka T, Thacker JD, Eaves CJ & Hogge DE (1991b) Differential effects of microenviron-mentally presented interleukin 3 versus soluble growth factor on primitive human hematopoietic cells. *Journal of Clinical Investigation* **88:** 417–422.

Otsuka T, Thacker JD & Hogge DE (1991c) The effects of interleukin 6 and interleukin 3 on early hematopoietic events in long-term cultures of human marrow. *Experimental Hematology* **19:** 1042–1048.

Papayannopoulou T, Brice M, Broudy VC & Zsebo KM (1991) Isolation of c-kit receptor-expressing cells from bone marrow, peripheral blood, and fetal liver: Functional properties and composite antigenic profile. *Blood* **78:** 1403–1412.

Rettenmier CW, Roussel MF, Ashmun RA et al (1987) Synthesis of membrane-bound colony-stimulating factor 1 (CSF-1) and downmodulation of CSF-1 receptors in NIH 3T3 cells transformed by cotransfection of the human CSF-1 and c-fms (CSF-1 receptor) genes. *Molecular and Cellular Biology* **7:** 2378–2387.

Roberts R, Gallagher J, Spooncer E et al (1988) Heparan sulphate bound growth factors: A mechanism for stromal cell mediated haemopoiesis. *Nature* **332:** 376–378.

Sieff CA, Niemeyer CM, Mentzer SJ & Faller D (1988) Interleukin-1, tumour necrosis factor, and the production of colony-stimulating factors by cultured mesenchymal cells. *Blood* **72:** 1316–1323.

Sutherland HJ, Eaves CJ, Eaves AC et al (1989a) Characterization and partial purification of human marrow cells capable of initiating long-term hematopoiesis in vitro. *Blood* **74:** 1563–1570.

Sutherland HJ, Eaves CJ, Eaves AC & Lansdorp PM (1989b) Differential expression of antigens on cells that initiate haemopoiesis in long-term human marrow culture. In Knapp W et al (eds) *Leucocyte Typing IV. White Cell Differentiation Antigens*, pp 910–912. Oxford: Oxford University Press.

Sutherland HJ, Lansdorp PM, Henkelman DH et al (1990) Functional characterization of individual human hematopoietic stem cells cultured at limiting dilution on supportive marrow stromal layers. *Proceedings of the National Academy of Sciences, USA* **87:** 3584–3588.

Sutherland HJ, Eaves CJ, Lansdorp PM et al (1991) Differential regulation of primitive human hematopoietic cells in long-term cultures maintained on genetically engineered murine stromal cells. *Blood* **78:** 666–672.

Sutherland HJ, Hogge DE, Cook D & Eaves CJ (1993) Alternative mechanisms with and without steel factor support primitive human hematopoiesis. *Blood* **81:** 1465–1470.

Toksoz D, Zsebo KM, Smith KA et al (1992) Support of human hematopoiesis in long-term bone marrow cultures by murine stromal cells selectively expressing the membrane-bound and secreted forms of the human homolog of the steel gene product, stem cell factor. *Proceedings of the National Academy of Sciences, USA* **89:** 7350–7354.

Udomsakdi C, Eaves CJ, Sutherland HJ & Lansdorp PM (1991) Separation of functionally distinct subpopulations of primitive human hematopoietic cells using rhodamine-123. *Experiental Hematology* **19:** 338–342.

Udomsakdi C, Lansdorp PM, Hogge DE et al (1992a) Characterization of primitive hemato-poietic cells in normal human peripheral blood. *Blood* **80:** 2513–2521.

Udomsakdi C, Eaves CJ, Swolin B et al (1992b) Rapid decline of chronic myeloid leukemic cells in long-term culture due to a defect at the leukemic stem cell level. *Proceedings of the National Academy of Sciences, USA* **89:** 6192–6196.

Winton EF & Colenda KW (1987) Use of long-term human marrow cultures to demonstrate progenitor cell precursors in marrow treated with 4-hydroperoxycyclophosphamide. *Experimental Hematology* **15:** 710–714.

4

Cytokines acting on committed haematopoietic progenitors

ZHONG CHAO HAN
JACQUES PHILIPPE CAEN

The old concepts of haematopoiesis and its regulation were simple and convenient. The stem cell is able to self-renew and under appropriate conditions to proliferate and differentiate into different committed progenitors which subsequently give rise to mature and functional haematopoietic cells in the presence of lineage-specific growth factors (Till and McCulloch, 1961; Dexter et al, 1971). Many advances have occurred since, stimulated by the development of new methodologies for assaying progenitors and by the identification and biotechnical production of a variety of haematopoietic growth factors. It is now clear that haematopoiesis is a complex multistage cellular and biological process, and that the haematopoietic tissue of adult mammals can broadly be divided into several types of cell population: pluripotent stem cells, multipotent progenitors, committed progenitors and maturing/mature cells (Moore, 1991; Wright and Lord,

Table 1. Developmental process of human haematopoietic cells and in vitro assays available to the various stages.

Cell compartment	In vitro assay	Original report
Stem cells	Blast-CFC	Brandt et al (1988)
	HPP-CFC	McNiece et al (1989)
Multipotent progenitors	CFU-Mix	Fauser and Messner (1978)
Committed progenitors		
Granulocyte/macrophage	CFU-GM, CFU-G	
	CFU-M	Pike and Robinson (1970)
Erythroid/megakaryocyte	Immunostaining	Han et al (1991c)
Erythroid lineage	BFU-E, CFU-E	Teppermann et al (1974)
Megakaryocytes	CFU-Meg	Vainchenker et al (1979)
	BFU-Meg	Hoffman et al (1987)
Eosinophils	CFU-Eo	Chervenick and Boggs (1971)
Basophils	CFU-Baso	Denburg et al (1985)
Maturing/mature cells	Morphology, function	
	Cell quantitation	

Abbreviations: EC, endothelial cell; G, granulocyte; M, monocyte–macrophage; E, erythroblast; F, fibroblast; Eo, eosinophil; Meg, megakaryocyte; Stem, stem cell; Strom, stromal cell; Mast, mast cell; T, T lymphocyte; B, B lymphocyte.

Baillière's Clinical Haematology—
Vol. 7, No. 1, March 1994
ISBN 0–7020–1819–8

65

1992). Table 1 illustrates this process and indicates the assays capable of enumerating the cells.

It is also known that almost no cytokine is specific to a certain lineage of cells as originally expected, but are pleiotropic and have multiple biological functions on various tissues and cells. This chapter is limited to the cytokines having obvious effects on the committed progenitors, including colony-

Table 2. Cytokines acting on committed haematopoietic progenitors.

Cytokine	Major cell source	Responding progenitors
GM-CSF	EC, F, M, T, B	G, M, Eo, Meg, E
G-CSF	EC, F	G, M
M-CSF	Most tissues	M, G
Epo	Kidney, Liver	E, Meg
Meg-CSF	?	Meg
IL-1	M, EC, F	T, Stem, Meg
IL-2	T	T, B
IL-3	T, Mast	G, M, E, Meg, Eo, Stem, Mast
IL-5	T, Mast	Eo, B
IL-6	B, M, Meg, Eo, F, Strom	Stem, G, M, Meg
IL-9	T	T, E, Meg, Mast
IL-11	Strom, F	M, Meg, B
SCF	Strom, EC, M	Stem, Meg, G, E, Mast
LIF	T, M, Strom	Meg
bFGF	EC, Meg, M	Meg, G, Strom
TGF-β1	Meg, platelets, M, T, F, EC	G, M, E, Meg, Stem
PF-4	Meg, platelets	Meg, G, E, M
AcSDKP	Fetal calf marrow	Stem, G, M, E
MIP-1α	M, T, F	Stem, E, G, M

Abbreviations: EC, endothelial cell; G, granulocyte; M, monocyte–macrophage; E, erythroblast; F, fibroblast; Eo, eosinophil; Meg, megakaryocyte; Stem, stem cell; Strom, stromal cell; Mast, mast cell; T, T lymphocyte; B, B lymphocyte.

Table 3. Haematopoietic progenitors to particular cytokines.

Responding progenitor	Cytokines active
Strom	bFGF
Stem	IL-1, IL-3, IL-6, SCF, TGF-β, AcSDKP, MIP-1α
G	GM-CSF, G-CSF, M-CSF, IL-3, IL-6, SCF, bFGF, TGF-β1, PF-4, AcSDKP, MIP-1α
M	GM-CSF, G-CSF, M-CSF, IL-3, IL-6, IL-11, TGF-β1, PF-4, AcSDKP, MIP-1α
Eo	IL-3, IL-5, GM-CSF
E	GM-CSF, EPO, IL-3, IL-9, SCF, TGF-β1, PF-4, AcSDKP, MIP-1α
Meg	Meg-CSF, GM-CSF, EPO, IL-1, IL-6, IL-9, IL-11, SCF, bFGF, TGF-β1, PF-4
Mast	IL-3, IL-9, SCF
T	IL-1, IL-2, IL-9
B	IL-1, IL-2, IL-5, IL-11

Abbreviations: EC, endothelial cell; G, granulocyte; M, monocyte–macrophage; E, erythroblast; F, fibroblast; Eo, eosinophil; Meg, megakaryocyte; Stem, stem cell; Strom, stromal cell; Mast, mast cell; T, T lymphocyte; B, B lymphocyte.

stimulating factors for: granulocyte-macrophage (GM-CSF), granulocyte (G-CSF), macrophage (M-CSF) or megakaryocyte (Meg-CSF); interleukins-1 (IL-1), IL-3, IL-5, IL-6, IL-9, IL-11; erythropoietin (EPO), stem cell factor (SCF), basic fibroblast growth factor (bFGF), leukaemia inhibitory factor (LIF), transforming growth factor-β1 (TGF-β1), platelet factor-4 (PF-4) and related peptides, tetrapeptide acetyl-N-Ser–Asp–Lys–Pro (AcSDAP), macrophage inflammatory protein-1 (MIP-1) and interferon-α (IFN-α) (Tables 2 and 3).

POSITIVE REGULATORS OF COMMITTED HAEMATOPOIETIC PROGENITORS

GM-CSF

GM-CSF is produced by a variety of normal and neoplastic cells (Wong et al, 1985) and is growth factor-active on a number of cell types of haemato-poietic and non-haematopoietic origins (Dedhar et al, 1988). It stimulates the proliferation of granulocyte, macrophage, eosinophil and basophil progenitors and also exerts a variety of direct or indirect effects on mature cells including neutrophils, eosinophils, monocytes and macrophage at concentrations below that required to promote proliferation of progenitor cells (Coffey, 1989; Rapoport et al, 1992). In addition, GM-CSF supports growth of megakaryocyte colonies in vitro (Hoffman, 1989; Han et al, 1992a). In vivo, however, animal experiments have shown that GM-CSF enhances the numbers of megakaryocytes but not of platelets. An effective stimulation of megakaryocytopoiesis in vivo, bringing about an increase in the levels of blood platelets, may require interaction of GM-CSF with other cytokines (Ishibashi et al, 1990; Vannucchi et al, 1990). In addition, GM-CSF acts in synergy with IL-3 and EPO to increase multipotential and erythroid colony formation, and with M-CSF to induce optimal growth of macrophages (Sieff et al, 1985; Donahue et al, 1988).

G-CSF

Mouse G-CSF was first purified by Nicola et al (1983) from medium conditioned by lung tissue obtained from mice injected with bacterial endo-toxin; human G-CSF was purified later (Welte et al, 1985) and molecularly cloned soon after this success (Nagata et al, 1986). The mouse and human G-CSF amino acid sequences exhibit more than 70% homology so that they are highly species cross-reactive. G-CSF acts primarily to stimulate prolifer-ation, differentiation and activation of committed progenitor cells of the neutrophil–granulocyte lineage into functionally mature neutrophils. These cells are also further stimulated by G-CSF to show increased activity at sites of infection and inflammation (Asano, 1991). In combination with IL-3, G-CSF can enhance the proliferation of multipotent haematopoietic pro-genitors (Ikebuchi et al, 1989) and megakaryocyte progenitors (McNiece et al, 1988).

M-CSF

M-CSF is a relatively specific monocyte–macrophage growth factor and is produced by a variety of cell types. M-CSF purified from either mouse L-cell supernatants or human urine exhibits similar properties with respect to the formation of monocyte–macrophage colonies in culture. Like other CSFs M-CSF has effects on the functions of mature cells, and is also able to enhance the antibody-mediated antitumour cytotoxicity of monocytes (Bajorin et al, 1991). M-CSF has circulating concentrations in healthy individuals of 2–$7\,\mathrm{ng\,ml}^{-1}$ (Bartocci et al, 1987). Patients with myeloproliferative disease have increased serum levels ranging from 7 to $28\,\mathrm{ng\,ml}^{-1}$ (Guilbert et al, 1987). Studies in vivo in a number of animal species show that the administration of M-CSF induces peripheral monocytosis, neutrophilia and lymphocytopenia (Ulich et al, 1990).

IL-1

IL-1 is able to promote granulopoiesis and thrombopoiesis either by stimulating the release of other haematopoietic growth factors such as GM-CSF, G-CSF, M-CSF and IL-6 or by synergizing with IL-3 (Golde, 1990; Moore, 1991). In vivo, in mice, IL-1 stimulates the growth of monocytic progenitors and accelerates haematopoietic recovery from myelosuppression induced by anticancer drugs (Ido et al, 1992). IL-1 also induces thrombopoiesis in mice (Kimura H et al, 1990) and in humans (Tewari et al, 1990) in vivo.

IL-3

IL-3 is produced by T-lymphocytes, mast cells and possibly skin keratinocytes. Studies in vitro and in vivo in both animals and man have shown that the biological actions of IL-3 are characterized by two distinctive features: the ability to stimulate the growth and differentiation of multiple blood cell lineages including granulocytes, macrophages, megakaryocytes, erythrocytes, eosinophils and mast cells, and to promote cell growth in the stem cell compartment. However, IL-3 alone is unable to support full development of a single lineage. A particularly interesting aspect of IL-3 biology is its apparent synergism with GM-CSF, G-CSF, EPO, IL-11 and IL-6 in augmenting respectively the formation of granulocyte/macrophage, neutrophil, erythroid and megakaryocyte colonies (Emerson et al, 1988; Spivak, 1989; Donahue et al, 1988; Asano, 1991; Geissler et al, 1992; Yonemura et al, 1992). In addition, IL-3 promotes the proliferation of mast cells and eosinophils, and also potentiates the activities of eosinophils, basophils and monocytes (Lu et al, 1990; Niskanen, 1991; Denburg, 1992; Sanderson, 1992).

   Among the well characterized factors, IL-3 is the most potent in stimulating in vitro growth of megakaryocyte progenitors (Hoffman, 1989; Han et al, 1992a). There are similarities in the functional activities of IL-3 and

GM-CSF. GM-CSF is not as potent as IL-3 in promoting megakaryocyte growth but can act additively with IL-3 or IL-6 (Emerson et al, 1988; Han et al, 1992a). The additive effect of IL-3 and GM-CSF has been further demonstrated by studies using a GM-CSF/IL-3 fusion protein. In both the serum-free cultures of megakaryocyte progenitors and the long-term bone marrow cultures, Bruno et al (1992) have observed that this fusion protein is able to stimulate megakaryocytopoiesis at a level equivalent to that of the GM-CSF/IL-3 combination and was superior to either IL-3 and GM-CSF alone.

IL-5

IL-5 is a peptide hormone produced from activated T lymphocytes and mast cells, and exhibits activity on eosinophils, B cells and thymocytes. Both mouse IL-5 and human IL-5 have an approximate M_r of 12 kDa and a sequence homology of 77% at the DNA level and 70% at the protein level. Recombinant IL-5 produced in mammalian cells is a disulphide-linked dimer. Dimerization of the IL-5 molecule is essential for its biological activity. Monomeric mouse IL-5 is inactive on both IL-5 dependent B-cell lines and murine eosinophils. The C-terminal region of IL-5 seems important for interaction with its receptors and for producing subsequent transmembrane signals, because substituting only eight residues in this region of human IL-5 for those of murine IL-5, can result in an increase in the activity of the human variety (McKenzie et al, 1991; Sanderson 1992; Tominaga et al, 1992). Binding studies of IL-5 to human eosinophils showed cross-competition with IL-3 and GM-CSF, suggesting some common components for each of these cytokines (Lopez et al, 1991).

In vitro, IL-5 is able to induce eosinophil proliferation and maturation (Yamaguchi et al, 1988; Lu et al, 1990). In vivo, administration of anti-IL-5 antibody to mice infected with several parasites completely blocked the development of eosinophilia, suggesting an essential role of IL-5 in the control of eosinophil production (Sanderson, 1992). In IL-5 transgenic mice, eosinophils in peripheral blood were seventyfold higher than control mice, and infiltration of eosinophils into various tissues was also significant (Tominaga et al, 1992).

IL-6

IL-6, a glycoprotein produced by various types of lymphoid and non-lymphoid cells and tumour cells and with multiple activities, is able to support the proliferation and differentiation of granulocyte–macrophage progenitor cells (Kishimoto, 1989; Han et al, 1992a). In the presence of IL-3, G-CSF, GM-CSF or M-CSF, IL-6 significantly enhances the growth of granulocyte and macrophage progenitors (Rennick et al, 1989). In addition, IL-6 alone or in combination with IL-3 can accelerate haematopoietic recovery after myeloid depression (Patchen et al, 1991; Geissler et al, 1992).

IL-6 also has apparent effect on megakaryocytopoiesis. In serum-free cultures in vitro, IL-6 does not affect megakaryocyte colony formation but enhances their diameter, the ploidy, the acetylcholinesterase activity and the protein synthesis of megakaryocytes (Ishibashi et al, 1989; Ishida et al, 1991). In the presence of normal plasma IL-6 is able to stimulate, although moderately, megakaryocyte proliferation (Lotem et al, 1989; Han et al, 1992a). This stimulating effect of IL-6 becomes obvious in the presence of optimal and suboptimal concentrations of IL-3 (Carrington et al, 1992; Han et al, 1992a). In rodents and primates in vivo, administration of IL-6 results in a significant increase in the number of platelets and megakaryocytes (Hill et al, 1991; Stahl et al, 1991). The effects of IL-6 on the proliferation of megakaryocyte and other progenitors are thought to be caused by recruitment of quiescent progenitors into the G_1 phase in which they are more sensitive to the effects of other growth factors (Kishimoto, 1989).

SCF

SCF (Stem Cell Factor) alone has limited effect on myeloid colony formation. However, it does stimulate directly the development of colony-forming unit–granulocyte macrophage (CFU-GM) and promotes the effects of other factors (Heyworth et al, 1992). It enhances myeloid and erythroid colony growth when combined with GM-CSF, G-CSF, IL-3 or EPO (McNiece et al, 1991). It acts in synergy with IL-3 and GM-CSF to stimulate megakaryocytopoiesis (Avraham et al, 1992; Hunt et al, 1992; Tanaka et al, 1992). It also induces an increase in CFU-GM and erythroid burst forming unit (BFU-) E from purified CD34 bone marrow cells in combination with IL-3, GM-CSF or G-CSF (Bernstein et al, 1991). In non-human primates in vivo, SCF caused an increase in the peripheral blood of the number of erythrocytes, neutrophils, monocytes, eosinophils, basophils and lymphocytes. In marrow, it caused an increase in marrow cellularity and in the absolute number of CFU-GM and BFU-E (Andrew et al, 1991).

EPO

EPO is produced primarily in the kidneys, and to a small extent in liver, in response to hypoxic conditions resulting from reduced atmospheric oxygen, phlebotomy or any number of anaemic states. EPO is responsible for maintenance of erythrocyte mass and control of erythropoiesis. It acts on erythroid precursors in the bone marrow, spleen, and fetal liver, and stimulates colony formation of the BFU-E and erythroid colony forming unit CFU-E. EPO may further act on erythroblasts to induce proliferation, increase circulating reticulocyte levels and reduce the marrow transit time of erythroid cells with early denucleation of erythroblasts (Spivak JL, 1989; Pedrazzini, 1992).

The effect of EPO on megakaryocytopoiesis had been inconclusive (Hoffman, 1989; Han et al, 1991b). EPO is able to accelerate the DNA and protein synthesis of purified megakaryocytes (Ishida et al, 1991), to enhance megakaryocyte colony formation in vitro (Sakaguchi et al, 1987), and to promote thrombopoiesis in vivo in several studies using animals (McDonald et al, 1989; Shikama et al, 1992). Although megakaryocytes also express specific high-affinity binding sites for EPO (Fraser et al, 1989), it is now clear that the role of EPO in stimulating megakaryocytopoiesis is limited and requires the presence of other factors. Critical analysis of the data on EPO stimulation of megakaryocytopoiesis shows that most data were obtained from serum- or plasma-containing culture experiments. Recently, Tsukada et al (1992) have reported that serum contains a growth factor(s) that is distinct from IL-1, IL-3, IL-4, IL-6, G-CSF and GM-CSF and that synergizes with EPO to stimulate the proliferation and differentiation of megakaryocyte progenitors.

IL-9

Human and mouse IL-9 both support erythroid colony formation (Donahue et al, 1990). This effect seems to be direct since IL-9 stimulates BFU-E and CFU-E colony formation by highly enriched CD34+++ DR+CD33− progenitors in serum-free conditions (Lu et al, 1992).

IL-11

IL-11, in addition to its ability to stimulate B-cell proliferation, also supports the growth of macrophage progenitors (Paul et al, 1990). Like IL-6, IL-11 promotes megakaryocyte maturation and acts synergistically with IL-3 to shorten the G_0 period of early progenitors in both murine and human systems (Teramura et al, 1992). Also, IL-11 increases the tritiated thymidine suicide rate of fetal colony-forming unit–mixed lineages (CFU-MIX), CFU-GM and BFU-E (Schibler et al, 1992), and promotes megakaryocytopoiesis alone or in combination with IL-3, (Burnstein et al, 1992; Teramura et al, 1992; Yonemura et al, 1992).

LIF

LIF increased the number of megakaryocytes and platelets when injected into mice in vivo (Metcalf et al, 1991). In vitro, LIF alone had no effects on the survival or proliferation of murine megakaryocytes or their progenitors, but promoted the maturation of megakaryocytes by augmenting the acetyl-cholinesterase activity and the percentage of 32N megakaryocytes (Burnstein et al, 1992). In addition, LIF acts synergistically with IL-3 to enhance the formation of megakaryocyte colonies. Receptors for LIF have been demonstrated on immature and mature megakaryocytes (Metcalf, 1991; Burnstein et al, 1992).

Meg-CSF and thrombopoietin (TPO)

There are data to suggest that there may be two relatively lineage-specific growth factors that regulate megakaryocyte proliferation and maturation, respectively (Williams, 1982; Hoffman, 1989). A Meg-CSF has been detected in the serum, plasma and urinary extracts obtained from patients with aplastic anaemia or undergoing bone marrow transplantation after chemotherapy (Fauser et al, 1988; Hoffman, 1989). This serum or urinary factor seems to be different from the known cytokines capable of stimulating megakaryocyte colony formation such as IL-3, GM-CSF, IL-1, IL-6 and EPO, since its activity cannot be neutralized by specific antibodies against these cytokines (Mazur et al, 1990; Tsukada et al, 1992). Several laboratories have tried to isolate and characterize this factor using traditional protein purification methods. A homogeneous, biologically active factor capable of stimulating the formation of pure and mixed megakaryocyte colonies has recently been purified from the urine of bone marrow transplant patients (Turner et al, 1991). However, the activity of this factor was reported to be limited (Turner et al, 1991) and further studies on its biological features in vitro and in vivo are required.

A TPO has been found in urine, serum and plasma from thrombo-cytopenic animals and patients; medium from human embryonic kidney (HEK) cell cultures is another potent source. TPO augments megakaryo-cyte maturation by increasing megakaryocyte size, endomitosis and ploidy (Williams et al, 1982; McDonald, 1989). Recent data, however, suggested that the TPO activity in HEK cell conditioned medium, that stimulates megakaryocyte maturation in vitro, is predominantly due to the presence of IL-6 and EPO (Withy et al, 1992).

FGF

Basic and acidic FGF have been shown to be involved in haematopoiesis since they stimulate granulopoiesis in long-term marrow culture (Wilson et al, 1991) and the growth of megakaryocyte progenitor cells (Han et al, 1992a) as well as human erythroleukaemia cells (Bikfalvi et al, 1992). bFGF has an additive effect when combined with IL-3 and GM-CSF, on the proliferation of early haematopoietic progenitor cells, BFU-E or colony-forming unit–megakaryocyte (CFU-MK) (Gabblanelli et al, 1990). The effect of FGF on megakaryocytopoiesis seems to be mediated by IL-6 because its action can be abrogated by a monoclonal antimouse IL-6 antibody. On the other hand, the mRNA specific for FGF receptors has been found in several megakaryocytic cell lines, normal megakaryocytes and platelets (Armstrong et al, 1992; Bikfalvi et al, 1992; Katoh et al, 1992). Normal megakaryocytes, platelets and one megakaryocytic cell line, the Meg-01, express bFGF mRNA (Han and Caen, unpublished observation), suggesting autocrine regulation of megakaryocyte growth by bFGF.

NEGATIVE REGULATORS OF COMMITTED HAEMATOPOIETIC PROGENITORS

It has become increasingly clear that normal haematopoiesis is controlled by the dynamic balance of both positive and negative regulators. Positive regulators stimulate the proliferation and differentiation of their responding progenitors and ultimately result in cell death through an organized process, apoptosis. Negative regulators maintain haematopoietic tissue at constant size by inhibiting cells from undergoing mitosis and therefore prevent both the loss of haematopoietic stem cells and progenitors through apoptosis and the disorders which result from increasing numbers of differentiated or mature cells. Over the past years, a number of negative haematopoietic regulators have been characterized on the basis of their inhibitory effects on progenitors at different stages.

TGF-β1

TGF-β1 is viewed as a growth-stimulating factor for mesenchymal cells and as a growth inhibitor for normal haematopoietic progenitor cells and leukaemic cells (Moses and Yang, 1990). Interestingly, the inhibitory effect of TGF-β1 on haematopoietic progenitors is concentration- and factor-dependent. It acts on normal granulopoiesis at micromolar concentrations but on megakaryocytopoiesis at picomolar levels, mainly by blocking the activity of IL-3 (Ishibashi et al, 1987; Keller et al, 1988; Han et al, 1992a; Kuter et al, 1992).

The in vivo effect of TGF-β1 on haematopoiesis has also been studied in mice. Goey et al (1989) showed that TGF-β1, when injected locoregionally to the bone marrow, inhibited the proliferation of early haematopoietic progenitors. Carlino et al (1990) reported that after subcutaneous daily injection of TGF-β1 for 14 days, there was a decrease in mature erythroid cell and platelet counts, and an increase in the number of white blood cells and granulopoiesis in the spleen and the bone marrow. Furthermore, Bursuker et al (1992) showed that injection of either natural or recombinant TGF-β1 into mice caused an increase in the number of progenitors in the bone marrow that gave rise to granulocytes and macrophages in response to M-CSF and GM-CSF.

These in vivo observations are paralleled by several recent in vitro studies that TGF-β1 enhanced granulocyte and macrophage proliferation in the presence of GM-CSF and M-CSF (Keller et al, 1991; Celada and Maki, 1992; Fan et al, 1992), and indicate that by expanding the early precursor cell population TGF-β1 may effectively act on haematopoiesis either as an inhibitor or promotor.

PF-4 and related peptides

PF-4 and two related peptides, thromboglobulin-β (TG-β) and connective tissue activating peptide III (CTAP-III), which share amino acid sequence homology, are platelet-specific proteins. These platelet proteins are capable of inhibiting the proliferation and maturation of megakaryocyte progenitor cells in vitro (Han et al, 1990a,b, 1991b). PF-4 and TGF-β also inhibit the growth of human erythroleukaemia cell lines (Han et al, 1990b, 1992b) and of megakaryocyte and erythroid progenitors from patients with essential thrombocythaemia. An in vivo inhibitory effect of PF-4 on murine mega-karyocytopoiesis and granulopoiesis has been recently demonstrated. The intraperitoneal injection of PF-4 for 4 days induced a dose-dependent decrease in the number of megakaryocytes and their progenitors, continuing for 1 week after injection. Platelet levels were significantly decreased at days 3–4. There was also a decrease in the number of CFU-GM at days 1–2. However, white blood cells and haemoglobin were unaffected (Han et al, 1991a). It is expected that these findings will lead to PF-4 being used in the management of myeloproliferative disorders.

Tetrapeptide AcSDKP

The AcSDKP was originally described as an inhibitor of murine pluripotent stem cells (Frindel and Guigon, 1977; Lenfant et al, 1989), and subsequently found to inhibit the growth of human CFU-GM and BFU-E, and decrease percentage in DNA synthesis. It was unable to inhibit the growth of leukaemia cells (Bonnet et al, 1992a). In human long-term bone marrow culture, AcSDKP had inhibitory but reversible effects on non-adherent progenitors and did not induce long-term modifications of the microenviron-ment (Bonnet et al, 1992b). All these data suggest a potential clinical application of the tetrapeptide in protecting normal haematopoietic pro-genitors during chemotherapy of cancers and leukaemias.

MIP-1α

MIP-1α is a potent inhibitor of the proliferation of stem cells (Broxmeyer et al, 1990; Dunlop et al, 1992). When injected into mice, MIP-1α rapidly inhibits DNA synthesis in proliferating CFU-S (Wright and Pragell, 1992) and decreases absolute numbers of myeloid progenitors in the marrow and spleen (Maze et al, 1992). These effects of MIP-1α are dose- and time-dependent and reversible, suggesting the possibility that it too may be a useful adjunct to cytotoxic chemotherapy.

IFN-α

Recombinant IFN-α has been reported to inhibit MK colony formation in vitro (Han et al, 1987). Clinical studies in essential thrombocythaemia have confirmed the inhibitory effect of IFN-α on the proliferation of megakaryo-cyte progenitors and on thrombopoiesis (Wadenvik et al, 1991).

GLYCOSAMINOGLYCANS AS MODULATORS OF HAEMATOPOIESIS

Glycosaminoglycans (GAGs) exhibit a variety of different biological activities and have recently stepped closer to the centre stage of cell biology (Ruoslahti and Yamaguchi, 1991). The contribution of GAGs to haemato-poiesis has been suggested by the following observations:

1. Haematopoietically active mouse bone marrow cultures synthesize several types of GAGs including heparan sulfate, hyaluronic acid and chondroitin sulfate. Heparan sulfate is enriched in the adherent cells whereas hyaluronic acid and chondroitin are distributed mainly to the culture medium (Spooncer et al, 1983). Haematopoietic cells such as megakaryocytes at different stages of differentiation synthesize different size of GAGs (Schick et al, 1988).
2. Heparan sulfate derived from bone marrow adherent cells is able to modulate haematopoiesis by retaining and compartmentalizing GM-CSF and IL-3 (Gordon et al, 1987; Roberts et al, 1988).
3. Binding of primitive haematopoietic progenitors to marrow stromal cells involves heparan sulfate (Siczkowski et al, 1992).
4. Heparin and heparan sulfate neutralize the PF4-induced inhibition of the in vitro growth of HEL cells, a megakaryocytic leukaemia cell line (Han et al, 1992b), and abrogate the inhibitory effect of PF-4 on megakaryocyte and platelet production in vitro and in vivo in mice (unpublished data).
5. Heparin and heparan sulfate enhance the biological activity of acidic and basic FGF and prevent them from inactivation (Gospodarowicz and Cheng, 1986).

CLINICAL STUDIES

The biological properties of the cytokines described above have indicated their potential clinical applications, alone or in combination with other factors, in disease states in which a single or multiple lineages are affected (Tables 4 and 5). This chapter only discusses G-CSF, GM-CSF, M-CSF,

Table 4. Potential clinical application of positive regulators alone or in combination in various disease states.

1. Therapy of congenital cytopenias
   Fanconi anaemia (EPO, IL-9, IL-3, SCF)
   Diamond–Blackfan anaemia (IL-3, EPO, SCF, IL-9)
   Cyclic neutropenia (GM-CSF, G-CSF, IL-3)
   Kostmann myelocathexis (GM-CSF, G-CSF, IL-3)
   Osteopetrosis (GM-CSF, M-CSF, G-CSF)
   Thrombocytopenia
       Amegakaryocytic (Meg-CSF, SCF, IL-1, IL-3, IL-6)
       Dysmaturation (Meg-CSF, IL-6, IL-11, LIF, Modulators)
2. Amelioration of cytopenia due to chemotherapy (the use of cytokines alone or in combination depends on the involvement of cell lineages)
3. Recovery from conventional or high-dose radiation or chemotherapy (combination of IL-3, GM-CSF, G-CSF, EPO and IL-6 . . .)
4. Bone marrow transplantation (GM-CSF, G-CSF, IL-3 . . .)
5. Prevention or salvage therapy for infections (G-CSF, GM-CSF, M-CSF . . .)
6. Aplastic anaemia (SCF, IL-3, GM-CSF, EPO, Meg-CSF)
7. Myelodysplastic syndromes (GM-CSF, G-CSF, IL-3, EPO)
8. Idiopathic purpura thrombocytopenia (IL-6, IL-11, LIF, Modulators)
9. Anaemias due to renal failure or inflammation (EPO, IL-9)
10. AIDS
11. Peripheral blood progenitor mobilization

Table 5. Potential clinical application of negative regulators.

1. Protection of stem cells or committed progenitors during chemotherapy for cancers (MIP-1α, AcSDKP)
2. Treatment of myeloproliferative disorders (IFN-α, PF-4 and related peptides)

SCF and IL-3. Other factors being clinically studied will be described in other chapters.

G-CSF

G-CSF was initially used therapeutically in patients with chemotherapy-induced neutropenia. The initial non-randomized trials established an effective dose, route and duration of G-CSF administration (Bronchud et al, 1987; Davis and Morstyn, 1991). Several randomized trials, involving approximately 400 patients with small cell lung cancer or non-Hodgkin's lymphoma, have further demonstrated that G-CSF significantly decreases neutropenia and infectious complications (Crawford et al, 1991; Green, 1992; Pettengell et al, 1992). G-CSF is now being investigated in a wider group of diseases. A number of phase I/II trials of G-CSF have been conducted in severe chronic neutropenia including congenital neutropenia, cyclic neutropenia and chronic idiopathic neutropenia. The initial trials were successful in showing that the administration of G-CSF caused a rapid and sustainable increase in neutrophil counts in most patients (Hammond et al, 1989; Migliaccio et al, 1990; Welte et al, 1990; Asano, 1991). A phase III, randomized clinical trial has subsequently been conducted in 75 patients. A complete response to G-CSF treatment was seen in 69 patients. G-CSF decreased the incidence and duration of infections, antibiotic use and hospitalization by up to 80% (Bonilla et al, 1990). Now, more than 200 patients with severe chronic neutropenia have received long-term G-CSF treatment. G-CSF appears an effective and well-tolerated long-term therapy for severe chronic neutropenia.

In other haematopoietic disease states such as myelodysplastic syndromes (MDS) (Kobayashi et al, 1989; Negrin et al, 1990), drug-induced agranulo-cytosis (Muroi et al, 1989), and relapsed or refractory acute leukaemia undergoing intensive chemotherapy (Ohno et al, 1990), G-CSF enhances the production of functional neutrophils and decreases infectious compli-cations. There is insufficient evidence to make any conclusion concerning the potential use of G-CSF in aplastic anaemia, AIDS and hairy cell leukaemia, although some encouraging preliminary findings have been reported (Glaspy et al, 1988; Kimura et al, 1990; Kojima et al, 1991).

G-CSF has also been used after high-dose chemotherapy with autologous bone marrow transplantation (ABMT). G-CSF shortened the period of neutropenia and reduced antibiotic usage and duration of hospital stay (Asano, 1991; Gabrilove, 1992; Sheridan, 1992). In patients with inter-mediate or high grade non-Hodgkin lymphoma treated with chemotherapy plus G-CSF, the number of haematopoietic progenitors in the circulation increased to a mean of 226-fold for CFU-Mix, 278-fold for CFU-GM and

29-fold for BFU-E. By contrast, the mean increase was modest (seven- to twelve-fold) for patients treated with chemotherapy alone (Demuynick et al, 1992). These results indicate that G-CSF is very effective at generating or mobilizing progenitors into peripheral blood.

When the peripheral blood progenitors collected from patients after 5–7 days treatment with G-CSF were infused together with autologous bone marrow cells following high-dose chemotherapy, neutrophil and particularly platelet recovery was accelerated (Sheridan et al, 1992; Chao et al, 1992). G-CSF appeared to be the most effective cytokine for 'stem-cell' mobilisation.

GM-CSF

GM-CSF has been used in various clinical settings including cancer chemotherapy, bone marrow transplantation, severe chronic neutropenia, MDS, aplastic anaemia and other haematopoietic disorders and infectious diseases. Initial phase I/II trials using GM-CSF in the setting of myeloablative therapy and ABMT have demonstrated that GM-CSF reduces the duration of leukopenia (Antman et al, 1988; Nemunaitis et al, 1988; Devereux et al, 1989; Scarffe, 1991). The increase in leukocytes observed is mainly attributed to an increase in neutrophils, with some increases in eosinophils and monocytes. Some studies have reported accelerated platelet recovery (Nemunaitis et al, 1988; Ho et al, 1990). Several randomized trials have provided convincing evidence of significantly faster recoveries in neutrophil counts from over 600 patients treated with GM-CSF (Powles et al, 1990; Scarffe, 1991; Khwaja et al, 1992). Other clinical benefits such as a reduction of antibiotic usage, of platelet transfusion and of other hospital resources have been suggested in some studies. For example, Gulati and Bennett (1992) reported that GM-CSF administration was associated with acceleration of myeloid and platelet recovery and was cost-effective in the treatment of patients who received intensive chemotherapy. Similar results were also obtained by Nemunaitis et al (1991). However, the data from a British national lymphoma trial showed that GM-CSF administration accelerates neutrophil, but not platelet, recovery following chemotherapy and ABMT, and that there was no firm evidence of concomitant reductions in infection rates, antibiotic use of hospital stay (Khwaja et al, 1992). The clinical value of GM-CSF in this context used at various doses and schedules, requires further investigation.

The use of GM-CSF in the treatment of severe chronic neutropenia has also been reported. It increased white blood cell counts in most patients, although in others the increase in white blood cell count was predominantly due to increases in eosinophil numbers (Ganser et al, 1989; Welte et al, 1990). GM-CSF may also have a role in the treatment of cyclic neutropenia (Pedrazzoli et al, 1990). In drug-induced agranulocytosis, Nand et al (1991) reported the effectiveness of GM-CSF for their patients but Delannoy (1992) found no benefit in his five patients.

In severe aplastic anaemia, administration of GM-CSF does not induce a significant increase in absolute blood cell counts. However, an increase in neutrophils, eosinophils and monocytes was observed in aplastic anaemia of mild to moderate severity after GM-CSF administration (Nissen et al, 1988; Vadhan-Raj et al, 1988; Scarffe, 1991). These results suggest that sufficient target cells are needed for an adequate response.

In initial phase I/II trials in MDS, GM-CSF was shown to increase leukocyte counts (Estey et al, 1991; Scarffe, 1991). Subsequent randomized trials further demonstrated that GM-CSF administration increased the number of neutrophils, monocytes, eosinophils and lymphocytes, and reduced major infections in most patients treated with GM-CSF (Gerhartz et al, 1990; Schuster et al, 1990). Concerns remain however, that the drug may increase the risk or rate of blast transformation.

GM-CSF has been used in acute myeloid leukaemia (AML) in an attempt to stimulate normal haematopoiesis allowing a reduction in the duration of chemotherapy-induced aplasia, to stimulate leukaemic proliferation allowing a recruitment of leukaemic cells into cell cycle and then rendering them susceptible to S phase-specific cytotoxic drugs, and also to promote differentiation and programmed cell death of leukaemic cells. Although several studies have shown more rapid neutrophil recovery and remission rates (Bettelheim et al, 1991; Scarffe, 1991), some authors reported no benefit with respect to remission rates, infection rates, or neutrophil or platelet recovery. In a recent large clinical trial with this therapy, Estey and his colleagues (1992) gave GM-CSF to 56 patients with AML before and during, or only during ara-C and daunorubicin chemotherapy, and compared the outcome to 176 patients with newly diagnosed AML given the same dose and schedule of ara-C without GM-CSF. They found that therapy of newly diagnosed AML with chemotherapy plus GM-CSF decreased remission rates and survival time compared to chemotherapy alone. Their observation is consistent with an in vitro finding of Koistinen et al (1991) that GM-CSF protected the blast cells from ara-C. These results suggest that the concept of recruitment of blast cells into cycle, at least using GM-CSF for this purpose, should be carefully reviewed.

The ability of GM-CSF to stimulate progenitor proliferation and to enhance the function of neutrophil, monocyte and eosinophil lineages have suggested its use in AIDS. Several investigations have shown that GM-CSF is effective for leukopenia in AIDS (Groopman et al, 1987; Niskanen, 1991; Scarffe, 1991). Neutrophil function may also be improved by GM-CSF (Baldwin et al, 1988).

Several studies have demonstrated that GM-CSF potentiated peripheral blood progenitor cell support of high-dose chemotherapy in cancer (Haas, 1991; Scarffe, 1991). The collected PBPCs are capable of restoring haematopoiesis, especially granulocyte and platelet recoveries, after high-dose chemotherapy, and lead to early haematopoietic recovery, and reduced transfusion requirements and duration of hospital stay.

M-CSF

Clinical trials of M-CSF have been performed in an attempt to ameliorate leukopenia. Komiyama et al (1988) showed that administration of purified human M-CSF increased neutrophil counts in patients with childhood neutropenias. A phase I trial defining the tolerance and haematological effects of M-CSF in patients with metastatic melanoma showed an increase in the number and function of circulating monocytes (Bajorin et al, 1991). In a non-randomized, controlled study (32 patients with urinary tract malignancies) and a randomized controlled study (98 patients with gynaeco-logical malignancies), M-CSF administration reduced the period of post-chemotherapy leukopenia (Motoyshi and Takaku, 1990; Niskanen, 1991).

M-CSF has been successfully used to treat leukopenia after transplan-tation (Masaoka et al, 1988). Recombinant M-CSF was administered to 45 patients after allogeneic or autologous bone marrow transplant (ABMT). Recovery of leukocytes and granulocytes was significantly accelerated. However, in another trial of purified human M-CSF in 20 patients under-going ABMT for malignant lymphoma, the results showed that purified human M-CSF did not improve haematopoietic recovery, except in patients who received relatively large numbers of nucleated marrow cells in whom there was accelerated recovery of platelets (Khwaja et al, 1992). Masaoka et al (1990) have reported a randomized double blind trial of M-CSF following bone marrow transplantation for leukaemia. The recovery of granulocytes was enhanced by M-CSF. Further prospective randomized studies of both purified and recombinant M-CSF in patients receiving ABMT are required to justify the in vivo effect of M-CSF. The effects of M-CSF are also being evaluated in patients with advanced or resistant fungal disease, in whom monocytes may play an important part in control of infection.

IL-3

IL-3 is currently being evaluated in clinical trials worldwide. Recombinant human IL-3, alone or in combination with other growth factors has been used in patients experiencing primary haematopoietic failure and to prevent or treat thrombocytopenia and neutropenia in patients undergoing chemo-therapy with or without ABMT. Several phase I/II studies have demon-strated that IL-3 accelerates recovery of neutrophils, platelets, monocytes and red blood cells after chemotherapy and that the haematological response is dose-dependent (Hoelzer et al, 1991; Kurzrock et al, 1991; Tepler et al, 1991; Biesma et al, 1992). The platelet recovery induced by IL-3 is of particular interest because thrombocytopenia is not significantly affected by G-CSF, GM-CSF, M-CSF or EPO individually. The use of IL-3, alone or in combination with other factors, has the potential to augment megakaryocytopoiesis and may shorten the period for haematopoietic recovery following chemotherapy. In aplastic anaemia and MDS, several studies have shown that IL-3 induced variable improvements in all cell lineages in most patients (Ganser et al, 1990a,b; Gillio et al, 1991a). IL-3 may also have a role in the treatment of Diamond–Blackfan anaemia. In three preliminary reports, some patients had a durable response to IL-3 followed by an improvement of anaemia (Gillio et al, 1991b; Campos et al, 1991; Olivierie et al, 1991).

SCF

Stem cell factor has recently entered study, as a single agent in patients following chemotherapy. Preliminary data suggest that by itself SCF appears to have limited efficacy and significant toxicity—mainly due to mast cell stimulation—at higher doses. However, Tong et al (1993) have shown an increase in primitive progenitor cells in patients receiving SCF, so that combination of this agent with later acting haemopoietins may be highly effective.

Cytokine combinations

In vitro and preclinical in vivo studies described above have shown that some haematopoietic growth factors, like EPO, G-CSF and M-CSF, have relatively restricted biological activities. Other factors such as SCF, IL-3, GM-CSF and IL-6 have a broad range of action and combination of some factors results in a synergistic activity. In addition, it appears that the cytokines acting on early progenitors, like IL-3, increase the number of progenitors capable of responding to cytokines having restricted activity on more committed cells. Based on extensive pre-clinical data, there have been several trials using combination cytokines in human and non-human primates (Table 6). Many have demonstrated a synergistic or additive stimulation of haematopoiesis by the use of two or more cytokines. These or future cytokine combination studies will almost certainly show more dramatic effects on haematopoiesis than any single cytokine alone.

Table 6. In vivo effects of combination of cytokines on haematopoiesis in primates and in humans.

Combinations	Haematopoietic actions	References
Other primates		
IL-3 + GM-CSF	Synergistic effects on multilineages	Donahue et al (1988)
		Mayer et al (1989)
		Krumwieh et al (1990)
		Geissler et al (1990)
IL-3 + G-CSF	Granulopoiesis	Krumwieh et al (1990)
IL-3 + IL-6	Thrombopoiesis	Geissler et al (1992)
IL-1 + IL-3 + GM-CSF	Granulopoiesis	Monroy et al (1988)
Humans		
IL-3 + GM-CSF	Synergistic on granulopoiesis	Brugger et al (1992)
		Kanz et al (1991)
		Hoelzer et al (1991)
		Ganser et al (1992)
G-CSF + EPO	Improvement of neutropenia and anaemia in AIDS	Miles et al (1991)

CONCLUSION

Basic and clinical studies on haematopoietic regulators have rapidly progressed. There is no doubt that these regulators are effective in correcting haematopoietic disorders of various aetiologies. Whether these regulators decrease morbidity and mortality, and the requirements for hospital resources, will require further investigation. In particular, improvements in protocol design including the use of factor combinations will be necessary.

REFERENCES

Andrew RG, Knitter GH, Bartelmez SH et al (1991) Recombinant human stem cell factor, a c-kit ligand, stimulates hematopoiesis in primates. *Blood* **78:** 1975–1980.

Antman KS, Griffin JD, Elias A et al (1988) Effect of recombinant human granulocyte–macrophage colony-stimulating factor on chemotherapy-induced myelosuppression. *New England Journal of Medicine* **319:** 593–598.

Armstrong E, Vainikka S, Partanen J et al (1992) Expression of fibroblast growth factor receptors in human leukemia cells. *Cancer Research* **52:** 2004–2007.

Asano S (1991) Human granulocyte colony-stimulating factor: Its basic aspect and clinical applications. *American Journal of Pediatric Hematology/Oncology* **13:** 400–413.

Avraham H, Vannier E, Cowley S et al (1992) Effect of stem cell factor, c-kit Ligand on human megakaryocytic cells. *Blood* **79:** 365–371.

Bajorin DF, Cheung NKV & Houghton AN (1991) Macrophage colony-stimulating factor: biological effects and potential applications for cancer therapy. *Seminars in Hematology* **28:** 42–48.

Baldwin GC, Gasson JC, Quan SG et al (1988) Granulocyte-macrophage colony-stimulating factor enhances neutrophil function in acquired immunodeficiency syndrome patients. *Proceedings of the National Academy of Sciences, USA* **85:** 2763–2766.

Bartocci A, Mastrogiannis DS, Migliorati G et al (1987) Macrophages specifically regulate the concentration of their own growth factor in the circulation. *Proceedings of the National Academy of Sciences, USA* **84:** 6179–6183.

Bernstein ID, Andrews RG & Szebo KM (1991) Recombinant human stem cell factor enhances the formation of colonies by CD34+ and CD34+ line-cells cultured with interleukin-3, granulocyte colony-stimulating factor, or granulocyte-macrophage colony-stimulating factor. *Blood* **77:** 2316–2321.

Bettelheim P, Valent P, Andreeff M et al (1991) Recombinant human granulocyte-macrophage colony-stimulating factor in combination with standard induction chemotherapy in de novo myeloid leukemia. *Blood* **77:** 700–711.

Biesma B, Willemse HB, Mulder NH et al (1992) Effects of interleukin-3 after chemotherapy for advanced ovarian cancer. *Blood* **80:** 1141–1148.

Bikfalvi A, Han ZC & Furhmann G (1992) Interactions of fibroblast growth factors with murine megakaryocytopoiesis and human megakaryocytic cell lines. *Blood* **80:** 1905–1913.

Bonilla MA, Gillio AP, Ruggiero M et al (1989) Effects of recombinant human granulocyte colony-stimulating factor on neutropenia in patients with congenital agranulocytosis. *New England Journal of Medicine* **320:** 1574–1580.

Bonilla MA and Severe Chronic Neutropenia Study Group (1990) Clinical efficacy of recombinant human granulocyte colony stimulating factor (r-metHuG-CSF) in patients with severe chronic neutropenia. *Blood* **76:** 133a (abstract. supplement 1).

Bonnet D, Césaire R, Lemoine F et al (1992a) The tetrapeptide AcSDKP, an inhibitor of the cell cycle status for normal human bone marrow progenitors, has no effect on leukemic cells. *Experimental Hematology* **20:** 251–255.

Bonnet D, Lemoine FM, Khoury E et al (1992b) Reversible inhibitory effects and absence of toxicity of the tetrapeptide acetyl-*N*-ser–asp–lys–pro (AxSDKP) in human long-term bone marrow culture. *Experimental Hematology* **20:** 1165–1169.

Brandt JE, Baird N, Lu L et al (1988) Characterization of a human hematopoietic progenitor cell capable of forming blast cell containing colonies in vitro. *Journal of Clinical Investigation* **82:** 1017–1021.

Bronchud MH, Scarffe JH, Thatcher N et al (1987) Phase I/II study of recombinant human granulocyte colony-stimulating factor in patients receiving intensive chemotherapy for small cell lung cancer. *British Journal of Cancer* **56:** 809–813.

Broxmeyer HE, Sherry B, Cooper S et al (1990) Macrophage inflammatory protein (MIP)-1β abrogates the capacity of MIP-1α to suppress myeloid progenitor cell growth. *Journal of Immunology* **147**: 2586–2594.

Brugger W, Bross K, Frisch J et al (1992) Mobilization of peripheral blood progenitor cells by sequential administration of interleukin-3 and granulocyte-macrophage colony-stimulating factor following polychemotherapy with etoposide, ifosfamide, and cisplatin. *Blood* **79**: 1193–1200.

Bruno E, Briddell RA, Cooper RJ & Hoffman R (1988) Effect of recombinant interleukin-11 on human megakaryocyte progenitor cells. *Experimental Hematology* **19**: 378–381.

Bruno E, Briddell RA, Cooper RJ et al (1992) Recombinant GM-CSF/IL3 fusion protein. Its effects on in vitro human megakaryocytopoiesis. *Experimental Hematology* **20**: 494–499.

Burnstein SA, Mei RL, Henthorn J et al (1992) Leukemia inhibitory factor and interleukin-11 promote maturation of murine and human megakaryocytes in vitro. *Journal of Cell Physiology* **153**: 305–312.

Bursuker I, Neddermann KM, Petty BA et al (1992) In vivo regulation of hemopoiesis by transforming growth factor beta 1: stimulation of GM-CSF- and M-CSF-dependent murine bone marrow precursors. *Experimental Hematology* **20**: 431–435.

Campos L, Bastion Y, Felman P et al (1991) Stem cell stimulation with interleukin-3 (IL3) treatment in patients with Diamond–Blackfan anemia (DBA). *Blood* **78 (supplement 1)**: 94a.

Carlino JA, Higley HR, Avis PD & Ellingsworth LE (1990) Hematologic and hematopoietic changes induced by systemic administration of TGF-β1. *Annals of the New York Academy of Sciences* **593**: 326–333.

Carrington PA, Hill RJ, Levin J & Verotta D (1992) Effects of interleukin 3 and interleukin 6 on platelet recovery in mice treated with 5-fluorouracil. *Experimental Hematology* **20**: 462–469.

Celada A & Maki RA (1992) Transforming growth factor-β enhances the M-CSF and GM-CSF-stimulated proliferation of macrophages. *Journal of Immunology* **148**: 1102–1105.

Chao NJ, Long GD, Negrin RS et al (1992) G-CSF and peripheral blood progenitor cells. *Lancet* **339**: 1410.

Chervenick PA & Boggs DR (1971) In vitro growth of granulocytic and mononuclear cell colonies from blood of normal individuals. *Blood* **66**: 1002–1005.

Coffey RG (1989) Mechanisms of GM-CSF stimulation of neutrophils. *Immunology Research* **8**: 236–248.

Crawford J, Ozer H, Stoller R et al (1991) Reduction by granulocyte colony-stimulating factor of fever and neutropenia induced by chemotherapy in patients with small-cell lung cancer. *New England Journal of Medicine* **315**: 164–170.

Davis I & Morstyn G (1991) The role of granulocyte colony-stimulating factor in cancer chemotherapy. *Seminars in Hematology* **28**: 25–33.

Dedhar S, Gaboury L, Galloway P & Eaves C (1988) Human granulocyte-macrophage colony-stimulating factor is a growth factor active on a variety of cell types of non-hemopoietic origin. *Proceedings of the National Academy of Sciences, USA* **85**: 9253–9257.

Delannoy (1992) GM-CSF therapy for drug-induce agranulocytosis. *Journal of Internal Medicine* **231**: 269–271.

Demuynick H, Pettengell R, de Campos E et al (1992) The capacity of peripheral blood stem cells mobilised with chemotherapy plus G-CSF to repopulate irradiated marrow stroma in vitro is similar to that of bone marrow. *European Journal of Cancer* **28**: 381–386.

Denburg JA (1992) Basophil and mast cell lineages in vitro and in vivo. *Blood* **79**: 846–860.

Denburg JA, Messner H, Lim B et al (1985) Clonal origin of human basophil/mast cells from circulating multipotent hemopoietic progenitors. *Experimental Hematology* **13**: 188–194.

Devereux S, Linch DC, Gribben JG et al (1989) GM-CSF accelerates neutrophil recovery after autologous bone marrow transplantation for Hodgkin's disease. *Bone Marrow Transplantation* **4**: 49–54.

Dexter TM, Allen TD & Lajitha LG (1971) Conditions controlling the proliferation of haemopoietic stem cells in vitro. *Journal of Cell Physiology* **91**: 335–339.

Donahue RE, Seehra J, Metzger M et al (1988) Human IL-3 and GM-CSF act synergistically in stimulating hematopoiesis in primates. *Science* **241**: 1820–1823.

Donahue RE, Yang Y-C & Clark SC (1990) Human P40 T-cell factor (interleukin-9) supports erythroid colony formation. *Blood* **75**: 2271–2275.

Dunlop DJ, Wright EG, Lorimore S et al (1992) Demonstration of stem cell inhibition and myeloprotective effects of SCI/rhMIP-1α in vivo. *Blood* **79**: 2221–2225.

Emerson SG, Yang Y-C, Clark SC et al (1988) Human recombinant granulocyte-macrophage colony stimulating factor and interleukin 3 have overlapping but distinct hematopoietic activities. *Journal of Clinical Investigation* **83**: 1282–1287.

Estey EH, Kurzrock R, Talpaz et al (1991) Effects of low doses of recombinant human granulocyte-macrophage colony-stimulating factor (GM-CSF) in patients with myelodysplastic syndromes. *British Journal of Haematology* **77**: 291–295.

Estey E, Thall PF, Kantarjian H et al (1992) Treatment of newly diagnosed adult myelogenous leukemia with granulocyte-macrophage colony-stimulating factor (GM-CSF) before and during continuous-infusion high-dose ara-C + daunorubicin: comparison to patients treated without GM-CSF. *Blood* **79**: 2246–2255.

Fan K, Ruan Q, Sensenbrenner L & Chen B (1992) Transforming growth factor-β1 bifunctionally regulates murine macrophage proliferation. *Blood* **79**: 1679–1685.

Fauser AA & Messner HA (1978) Granuloerythropoietic colonies in human marrow, peripheral blood and cord blood. *Blood* **52**: 1243–1248.

Fauser AA, Kanz L, Spurill GM & Löhr GW (1988) Megakaryocytic colony-stimulating activity in patients receiving a marrow transplant during hematopoietic reconstitution. *Transplantation* **46**: 543–547.

Fraser JK, Tan AS, Lin FK et al (1989) Expression of specific high-affinity binding sites for erythropoietin on rat and mouse megakaryocytes. *Experimental Hematology* **17**: 10–16.

Frindel E & Guigon M (1977) Inhibition of CFU entry into cycle by a bone marrow extract. *Experimental Hematology* **5**: 74–79.

Gabblanelli M, Sargiacomo M, Pelosi E et al (1990) 'Pure' human hematopoietic progenitors: permissive action of basic fibroblast growth factor. *Science* **28**: 1561–1564.

Gabrilove J (1992) The development of granulocyte colony-stimulating factor in its various clinical applications. *Blood* **80**: 1382–1385.

Ganser A, Ottmann OG, Erdmann H et al (1989) The effect of recombinant human granulocyte-macrophage colony-stimulating factor on neutropenia and related morbidity in chronic severe neutropenia. *Annals of Internal Medicine* **iii**: 887–892.

Ganser A, Lindermann A, Seipelt G et al (1990a) Effects of recombinant human interleukin-3 in aplastic anemia. *Blood* **76**: 1287–1292.

Ganser A, Speipelt G, Lindemann A et al (1990b) Effects of recombinant human interleukin-3 in patients with myelodysplastic syndromes. *Blood* **76**: 455–462.

Ganser A, Lindemann A, Ottmann OG et al (1992) Sequential in vivo treatment with two recombinant human hematopoietic growth factors (interleukin-3 and granulocyte-macrophage colony-stimulating factor) as a new therapeutic modality to stimulate hematopoiesis: results of a phase I study. *Blood* **79**: 2583–2591.

Geissler K, Valent P, Mayer P et al (1990) Recombinant human interleukin-3 expands the pool of circulating hematopoietic progenitor cells—synergism with recombinant human granulocyte-macrophage colony-stimulating factor. *Blood* **75**: 2305–2310.

Geissler K, Valent P, Batteheim P et al (1992) In vivo synergism of recombinant human interleukin-3 and recombinant human interleukin-6 on thrombopoiesis in primates. *Blood* **79**: 1155–1160.

Gerhartz HH, Marcus R, Delmer A et al (1990) Randomized phase II study with GM-CSF and low-dose ARAC in patients with 'high risk' myelodysplastic syndromes (MDS) *Blood* **76 (supplement 1):** 337a (abstract).

Gillio AP, Castro-Malaspina H, Gasparetto C et al (1991a) Human recombinant interleukin-3 treatment in patients with myelodysplastic syndrome and aplastic anemia. *Blood* **78 (supplement 1):** 95a.

Gillio AP, Gasparetto C, Faulkner L et al (1991b) Successful treatment of Diamond–Blackfan-anemia with recombinant human IL-3. *Blood* **78 (supplement 1):** 153a.

Glaspy JA, Baldwin GC, Robertson PA et al (1988) Therapy for neutropenia in hairy cell leukemia with recombinant human granulocyte colony-stimulating factor. *Annals of Internal Medicine* **109**: 789–795.

Goey H, Keller JR, Back T et al (1989) Inhibition of early murine hemopoietic progenitor cell proliferation after in vivo locoregional administration of transforming growth factor β1. *Journal of Immunology* **143**: 877–880.

Golde DW (1990) Overview of myeloid growth factors. *Seminars in Hematology* **27(3)**: 1–7.

Gordon MY, Riley GP, Watt SM & Greaves MF (1987) Compartmentalization of a haemato-poietic growth factor by glycosaminoglycans in the bone marrow microenvironment. *Nature* **326:** 403–405.

Gospodarowicz D & Cheng J (1986) Heparin protects basic and acidic FGF from inactivation. *Journal of Cell Physiology* **1:** 475–484.

Green JA (1992) Recombinant G-CSF reduced neutropenia in patients on chemotherapy—A review of randomised European and USA studies. *Clinician* **10:** 33–40.

Groopman JE, Mitsuyasu RT, Deleo MJ et al (1987) Effect of recombinant human granulocyte-macrophage colony-stimulating factor on myelopoiesis in acquired immuno-deficiency syndrome. *New England Journal of Medicine* **317:** 593–598.

Guilbert HS, Praloran V, Stanley ER (1987) Increased serum concentrations of colony-stimulating factor-1 in myeloproliferative disease. *Blood* **70:** 135–140.

Gulati SC & Bennett CL (1992) Granulocyte-macrophage colony-stimulating factor (GM-CSF) as adjunct therapy in relapsed Hodgkin disease. *Annals of Internal Medicine* **116:** 177–182.

Haas M (1991) Utilization of recombinant human GM-CSF to enhance peripheral progenitor cells yield for autologous transplantation. *Bone Marrow Transplantation* **7:** 13–17.

Hammond WP, Price TH, Souza LM & Dale DC (1989) Treatment of cyclic neutropenia with granulocyte colony-stimulating factor. *New England Journal of Medicine* **320:** 1306–1311.

Han ZC, Briere J, Abgrall JF et al (1987) Effects of recombinant human interferon alpha on human megakaryocyte and fibroblast colony formation. *Journal of Biological Regulators and Homeostatic Agents* **1:** 195–200.

Han ZC, Sensebe L, Abgrall JF & Brière J (1990a) Platelet factor 4 inhibits human mega-karyocytopoiesis in vitro. *Blood* **75:** 1234–1239.

Han ZC, Bellucci S, Tenza D & Caen JP (1990b) Negative regulation of human megakaryo-cytopoiesis by human platelet factor 4 and beta-thromboglobulin: comparative analysis in bone marrow cultures from normal individuals and patients with essential thrombo-cythaemia and immune thrombocytopenic purpura. *British Journal of Haematology* **74:** 395–401.

Han ZC, Bellucci S, Bodevin E et al (1991a) In vivo inhibition of megakaryocyte and platelet production by Platelet factor 4 in mice. *Compte Rendu Academi des Sciences, Paris* **313:** 553–558.

Han ZC, Bellucci S & Caen JP (1991b) Megakaryocytopoiesis: characterization and regulation in normal and pathologic states. *International Journal of Hematology* **54:** 3–14.

Han ZC, Bellucci S, Pidard D & Caen JP (1991c) Coexpression in the same cell in marrow culture of antigens from erythroid and megakaryocytic lineage. In Kaplan-Gouet N, Schlegel Ch & McGregor J (eds) *Platelet Immunology: Functional and Clinical Aspects*, vol. 206, pp 17–18. Colloque INSERM: John Libbey Eurotext.

Han ZC, Bellucci S, Wan HY & Caen JP (1992a) New insights into the regulation of megakaryocytopoiesis by haematopoietic and fibroblast growth factors and transforming growth factor β1. *British Journal of Haematology* **81:** 1–5.

Han ZC, Maurer AM, Bellucci S et al (1992b) Inhibitory effect of platelet factor 4 (PF4) on the growth of human erythroleukemia cells: proposed mechanism of action of PF4. *Journal of Laboratory & Clinical Medicine* **120:** 645–660.

Heyworth CM, Whetton AD, Nicholls S et al (1992) Stem cell factor directly stimulates the development of enriched granulocyte–macrophage colony-stimulating cells and promotes the effects of other colony-stimulating factors. *Blood* **80:** 2230–2236.

Hill RJ, Warren K, Stenberg P et al (1991) Stimulation of megakaryocytopoiesis in mice by human recombinant interleukin-6. *Blood* **77:** 42–48.

Ho AD, Del Valle F, Englehard M et al (1990) Mitoxantrone-highdose Ara-C and recombinant GM-CSF in the treatment of refractory non-Hodgkin's lymphoma. A pilot study. *Cancer* **66:** 423–430.

Hoelzer D, Seipelt G & Ganser A (1991) Interleukin 3 alone and in combination with GM-CSF in the treatment of patients with neoplastic disease. *Seminars in Hematology* **28:** 17–24.

Hoffman R (1989) Regulation of megakaryocytopoiesis. *Blood* **74:** 1196–1212.

Hoffman R, Stravena J, Yang HH et al (1987) New insights into the regulation of human megakaryocytopoiesis. *Blood Cells* **13:** 75–86.

Hunt P, Zsebo KM, Hokom MM et al (1992) Evidence that stem cell factor is involved in the rebound thrombocytosis that follows 5-fluorouracil treatment. *Blood* **80:** 904–911.

Ido M, Harada M, Furuichi H et al (1992) Interleukin-1-induced sequential myelorestoration: dynamic relation between granulopoiesis and progenitor cell recovery in myelosuppressed mice. *Experimental Hematology* **20:** 161–166.

Ikebuchi K, Clark SC, Ihle JN et al (1989) Granulocyte colony stimulating factor enhances interleukin 3-dependent proliferation of multipotent hematopoietic progenitors. *Proceedings of the National Academy of Sciences, USA* **85:** 3445–3449.

Ishibashi T, Miller S & Burstein SA (1987) Type B transforming growth factor is a potent inhibitor of murine megakaryocytopoiesis in vitro. *Blood* **69:** 1737–1741.

Ishibashi T, Kimura H, Shikama Y et al (1989) Interleukin-6 is a potent thrombopoietic factor in vitro in mice. *Blood* **74:** 1241–1244.

Ishibashi T, Kimura H, Shikama Y et al (1990) Effect of recombinant granulocyte–macrophage colony-stimulating factor on murine thrombocytopoiesis in vitro and in vivo. *Blood* **75:** 1433–1438.

Ishida Y, Yano S, Yoshida T et al (1991) Biological effects of recombinant erythropoietin, granulocyte-macrophage colony-stimulating factor, interleukin 3, and interleukin 6 on purified rat megakaryocytes. *Experimental Hematology* **19:** 608–612.

Kanz L, Brugger W, Bross K et al (1991) Combination of cytokines: current status and future prospects. *British Journal of Haematology* **79 (supplement 1):** 96–104.

Katoh O, Hattori Y, Sato T et al (1992) Expression of the heparin-binding growth factor receptor genes in human megakaryocytic leukemia cells. *Biochemical and Biophysical Research Communications* **183:** 83–92.

Keller JR, Mantel C, Sing GK et al (1988) Transforming growth factor β1 selectively regulates early murine hematopoietic progenitors and inhibits the growth of IL3-dependent myeloid leukemia cell lines. *Journal of Experimental Medicine* **168:** 737–750.

Keller JR, Jacobsen SEW, Sill KT et al (1991) Stimulation of granulopoiesis by transforming growth factor β: Synergy with granulocyte/macrophage-colony-stimulating factor. *Proceedings of the National Academy of Sciences, USA* **88:** 7190–7194.

Khwaja A, Linch DC, Goldstone AH et al (1992) Recombinant human granulocyte–macrophage colony-stimulating factor after autologous bone marrow transplantation for malignant lymphoma: a British National Lymphoma Investigation double-blind, placebo-controlled trial. *British Journal of Haematology* **82:** 317–323.

Kimura H, Ishibashi T, Shikama Y et al (1990) Interleukin-1β (IL-1β) induces thrombocytosis in mice: possible implication of IL6. *Blood* **76:** 2493–2500.

Kimura S, Matsuda J, Ikematsu S et al (1990) Efficacy of recombinant human granulocyte colony-stimulating factor on neutropenia in patients with AIDS. *AIDS* **4:** 1251–1255.

Kishimoto T (1989) The biology of interleukin-6. *Blood* **74:** 1–10.

Kobayashi Y, Okabe T, Ozawa K et al (1989) Treatment of myelodysplastic syndromes with recombinant human granulocyte colony-stimulating factor: a preliminary report. *American Journal of Medicine* **86:** 178–182.

Koistinen P, Wang C, Curtis JE & McCulloch EA (1991) Granulocyte–macrophage colony-stimulating factor and interleukin-3 protect blast cells from ara-C toxicity. *Leukemia* **5:** 789–795.

Kojima S, Fukuda M, Miyajima Y et al (1991) Treatment of aplastic anemia in children with recombinant human granulocyte colony-stimulating factor. *Blood* **77:** 937–941.

Komiyama A, Ishiguro A, Kubo T et al (1988) Increases in neutrophil counts by purified human urinary colony-stimulating factor in chronic neutropenia of childhood. *Blood* **71:** 41–45.

Krumwieh D, Weinmann E & Seiler FR (1990) Different effects of interleukin-3 (IL3) on the hematopoiesis of subhuman primates due to various combination with granulocyte–macrophage colony-stimulating factor (GM-CSF) and granulocyte colony-stimulating factor (G-CSF). *International Journal of Cell Cloning* **8:** 229–248.

Kurzrock R, Talper M, Estrov Z et al (1991) Phase I study of recombinant human interleukin-3 in patients with bone marrow failure. *Journal of Clinical Oncology* **9:** 1241–1250.

Kuter DJ, Gminski DM & Rosenberg RD (1992) Transforming growth factor β inhibits megakaryocyte growth and endomitosis. *Blood* **79:** 619–626.

Lenfant M, Wdzieczak-Bakala J, Guittet E et al (1989) Inhibitor of hematopoietic pluripotent stem cell proliferation: purification and determination of its structure. *Proceedings of the National Academy of Sciences, USA* **6:** 779–782.

Lopez AF, Vadas MA, Woodcock JM et al (1991) Interleukin-5, interleukin-3, and granulocyte–macrophage colony-stimulating factor cross-compete for binding to cell

86 Z. C. HAN AND J. P. CAEN

surface receptors on human eosinophils. *Journal of Biological Chemistry* **266:** 24741–24747.

Lotem J, Shabo Y & Sachs (1989) Regulation of megakaryocyte development by interleukin-6. *Blood* **74:** 1545–1551.

Lu L, Lin ZH, Shen RN et al (1990) Influence of interleukin 3, 5, and 6 on the growth of eosinophil progenitors in highly enriched human bone marrow in the absence of serum. *Experimental Hematology* **18:** 1180–1185.

Lu L, Leemhuis, Srour E & Yang YC (1992) Human interleukin (IL)-9 specifically stimulates proliferation of CD34+++DR+CD33– erythroid progenitors in normal human bone marrow in the absence of serum. *Experimental Hematology* **20:** 418–424.

McDonald TP (1989) The regulation of megakaryocyte and platelet production. *International Journal of Cell Cloning* **7:** 139–155.

McKenzie ANJ, Ely B & Sanderson CJ (1991) Mutated interleukin-5 monomers are inactive. *Molecular Immunology* **25:** 155–158.

McNiece IK, McGrath HE & Quesenberry PJ (1988) Granulocyte colony-stimulating factor augments in vitro megakaryocyte colony formation by interleukin-3. *Experimental Hematology* **16:** 807–810.

McNiece IK, Stewart FM, Deacon DM et al (1989) Detection of a human colony forming cell with a high proliferative potential. *Blood* **74:** 609–612.

McNiece IK, Langley KE & Zsebo KM (1991) Recombinant human stem cell factor synergizes with GM-CSF, G-CSF, IL3 and Epo to stimulate human progenitor cells of the myeloid and erythroid lineages. *Experimental Hematology* **19:** 226–230.

Masaoka T, Motoyoshi K, Takaku F et al (1988) Administration of human urinary colony-stimulating factor after bone marrow transplantation. *Bone Marrow Transplantation* **3:** 121–127.

Masaoka T, Shibata H, Ohno R et al (1990) Double-blind test of human urinary macrophage colony-stimulating factor for allogeneic and syngeneic bone marrow transplantation: effectiveness of treatment and 2-year follow-up for relapse of leukemia. *British Journal of Haematology* **76:** 501–505.

Mayer P, Valent P, Schmidt G et al (1989) The in vivo effects of recombinant interleukin-3: demonstration of basophil differentiation factor, histamine-producing activity, and priming of GM-CSF-responsive progenitors in nonhuman primates. *Blood* **74:** 613–621.

Maze R, Sherry B, Know BS et al (1992) Myelosuppressive effects in vivo of purified recombinant murine macrophage inflammatory protein-1α. *Journal of Immunology* **149:** 1004–1009.

Mazur EM, Cohen JL, Newton J et al (1990) Human serum megakaryocyte colony-stimulating activity appears to be distinct from interleukin-3, granulocyte-macrophage colony-stimulating factor, and lymphocyte-conditioned medium. *Blood* **76:** 290–297.

Metcalf D, Hilton D & Nicola NA (1991) Leukemia inhibitory factor can potentiate murine megakaryocyte production in vitro. *Blood* **77:** 2150–2153.

Migliaccio AR, Migliaccio G, Dale DC & Hammond WP (1990) Hematopoietic progenitors in cyclic neutropenia: effect of granulocyte colony-stimulating factor in vivo. *Blood* **75:** 1951–1959.

Miles SA, Mitsuyasu RT, Moreno J et al (1991) Combined therapy with recombinant granulocyte colony-stimulating factor and erythropoietin decreases hematologic toxicity from Zidovudine. *Blood* **77:** 2109–2117.

Monroy RL, Skelly RR, MacVittie TJ et al (1988) Cytokine regulation of hematopoiesis in vivo using a primate model. *Experimental Hematology* **16:** 480–486.

Moore MAS (1991) Clinical implications of positive and negative hematopoietic stem cell regulators. *Blood* **78:** 1–19.

Moses HL & Yang EY (1990) TGF-β stimulation and inhibition of cell proliferation: new mechanistic insights. *Cell* **62:** 245–247.

Motoyshi K & Takaku F (1990) Human monocytic colony-stimulating factor (hM-CSF), phase I/II clinical studies. In Mertelsmann R & Hermann F (eds) *Hematopoietic Growth Factors in Clinical Applications*, pp 161–175. New York: Marcel Dekker.

Muroi K, Ito M, Sasaki R et al (1989) Treatment of drug-induced agranulocytosis with granulocyte colony-stimulating factor. *Lancet* **ii:** 55.

Nagata S, Tsuchiya M, Asano S et al (1986) Molecular cloning and expression of cDNA for human granulocyte colony-stimulating factor. *Nature* **319:** 415–418.

Nand S, Bayer R, Prinz RA et al (1991) Granulocyte macrophage colony stimulating factor for the treatment of drug induced agranulocytosis. *American Journal of Hematology* **37:** 267–269.

Negrin RS, Haeuber DH, Nagler A et al (1990) Maintenance treatment of patients with myelodysplastic syndromes using recombinant human granulocyte colony-stimulating factor. *Blood* **76:** 36–43.

Nemunaitis J, Singer JW, Buckner CD et al (1988) Use of recombinant human granulocyte-macrophage colony-stimulating factor in autologous marrow transplantation for lymphoid malignancies. *Blood* **72:** 834–836.

Nemunaitis J, Rabinowe SN, Singer JW et al (1991) Recombinant granulocyte–macrophage colony-stimulating factor after autologous bone marrow transplantation for lymphoid cancer. *New England Journal of Medicine* **324:** 1773–1778.

Nicola NA, Metcalf D, Matsumoto M & Johnson GR (1983) Purification of a factor inducing differentiation in murine myelomonocytic leukemia cells: identification as granulocyte colony-stimulating factor (G-CSF). *Journal of Biological Chemistry* **258:** 9017–9023.

Niskanen E (1991) Hematopoietic growth factors in clinical hematology. *Annals of Medicine* **23:** 615–624.

Nissen C, Tichelli A, Gratwohl A et al (1988) Failure of recombinant human granulocyte-macrophage colony-stimulating factor therapy in aplastic anemia patients with very severe neutropenia. *Blood* **72:** 2045–2047.

Ohno R, Tomonaga M, Kobayashi T et al (1990) Effect of granulocyte colony-stimulating factor after intensive induction therapy in relapsed or refractory acute leukemia. *New England Journal of Medicine* **323:** 871–877.

Olivierie NF, Berriman AM, Davis S et al (1991) Response to the hematopoietic growth factor IL-3 in patients with Diamond–Blackfan anemia. *Blood* **78 (supplement 1):** 153a.

Patchen ML, MacVittie TJ, Williams JL et al (1991) Administration of interleukin-6 stimulates multilineage hematopoiesis and accelerates recovery from radiation-induced hemato-poietic depression. *Blood* **77:** 472–480.

Paul S, Bennett F, Calvetti J et al (1990) Molecular cloning of cDNA encoding interleukin-11, a stromal cell-derived lymphopoietic and hematopoietic cytokine. *Proceedings of the National Academy of Sciences, USA* **87:** 7512–7516.

Pedrazzini A (1992) Current and potential applications for erythropoietin. *Acta Haematologica* **87 (supplement 1):** 2–3.

Pedrazzoli P, Locatelli F, Zecca M et al (1990) Cyclic neutropenia treated with GM-CSF (abstract). *Blood* **76 (supplement 1):** 160a.

Pettengell R, Gurney H, Radford JA et al (1992) Granulocyte colony-stimulating factor to prevent dose-limiting neutropenia in non-Hodgkin's lymphoma: a randomized controlled trial. *Blood* **80:** 1430–1436.

Pike BL & Robinson WA (1970) Human bone marrow colony growth in agar gel. *Journal of Cell Physiology* **76:** 77–84.

Powles R, Smith C, Milan S et al (1990) Human recombinant GM-CSF in allogeneic bone-marrow transplantation for leukemia: double-blind, placebo-controlled trial. *Lancet* **336:** 1417–1420.

Rapoport AP, Abboud CN & DiPersio JF (1992) Granulocyte–macrophage colony-stimulating factor (GM-CSF) and granulocyte colony-stimulating factor (G-CSF): receptor biology, signal transduction, and neutrophil activation. *Blood Reviews* **6:** 43–57.

Rennick D, Jackson J, Yang G et al (1989) Interleukin-6 interacts with interleukin-4 and other hematopoietic growth factors to selectively enhance the growth of megakaryocytic, erythroid, myeloid and multipotential progenitor cells. *Blood* **73:** 1828–1835.

Roberts R, Gallagher J, Spooncer E et al (1988) Heparin sulfate bound growth factors: A mechanism for stromal cell mediated hemopoiesis. *Nature* **332:** 376–378.

Ruoslahti E & Yamaguchi Y (1991) Proteoglycans as modulators of growth factor activities. *Cell* **64:** 867–869.

Sakaguchi M, Kawakita M, Matsushita J et al (1987) Human erythropoietin stimulates murine megakaryocytopoiesis in serum free culture. *Experimental Hematology* **15:** 1023–1034.

Sanderson C (1992) Interleukin-5, eosinophils, and disease. *Blood* **79:** 3101–3109.

Scarffe JH (1991) Emerging clinical uses for GM-CSF. *European Journal of Cancer* **27:** 1493–1504.

Schibler KR, Yang YC & Christensen RD (1992) Effect of interleukin-11 on cycling status and clonogenic maturation of fetal and adult hematopoietic progenitors. *Blood* **80:** 900–903.

Schick BP, Walsh CJ & Jenkins-West T (1988) Sulfated proteoglycans and sulfated proteins in guinea pig megakaryocytes and platelets in vivo. *Journal of Biological Chemistry* **263:** 1052–1062.

Schuster MW, Larson RA, Thompson JA et al (1990) Granulocyte–macrophage colony-stimulating factor (GM-CSF) for myelodysplastic syndromes (MDS): results of a multi-center randomized controlled trial (abstract). *Blood* **76 (supplement 1):** 46a.

Sheridan W (1992) The use of recombinant G-CSF in autologous bone marrow transplantation— New approaches to accelerate neutrophil and platelet recovery. *Clinician* **10:** 53–60.

Sheridan W, Begley CC, Juttner CA et al (1992) Effect of peripheral-blood progenitor cells mobilised by filgrastim (G-CSF) on platelet recovery after high-dose chemotherapy. *Lancet* **339:** 640–644.

Shikama Y, Ishibashi T, Kimura H et al (1992) Transient effect of erythropoietin on thrombo-cytopoiesis in vivo in mice. *Experimental Hematology* **20:** 216–222.

Siczkowski M, Clarke D & Gordon MY (1992) Binding of primitive hematopoietic progenitor cells to marrow stromal cells involves heparan sulfate. *Blood* **80:** 912–919.

Sieff CA, Emerson SG, Donahue RE et al (1985) Human recombinant granulocyte–macrophage colony-stimulating factor: a multilineage hematopoietin. *Science* **230:** 1171–1173.

Spivak JL (1989) Erythropoietin. *Blood Reviews* **3:** 130–135.

Spooncer E, Gallagher IT, Krizsa F & Dexter TM (1983) Regulation of haematopoiesis in long-term bone marrow cultures. IV. Glycosaminoglycan synthesis and the stimulation of haemopoiesis by β-D-Xylosides. *Journal of Cell Biology* **96:** 510–514.

Stahl CP, Zucker-Franklin D, Evatt BL & Winton E (1991) Effects of human interleukin-6 on megakaryocyte development and thrombocytopoiesis in primates. *Blood* **78:** 1467–1475.

Tanaka R, Koike K, Imai T et al (1992) Stem cell factor enhances proliferation but not maturation, of murine megakaryocytic progenitors in serum-free culture. *Blood* **80:** 1743–1749.

Tepler I, Pap S, Pelaez J et al (1991) GM-CSF potentiated peripheral blood progenitor cell (PBPC) collection with or without bone marrow as hematologic support of high-dose chemotherapy—Two protocols. *Breast Cancer Research and Treatment* **20:** S25–S29.

Teppermann AD, Curtis JE & McCulloch EA (1974) Erythropoietic colonies in culture of human marrow. *Blood* **44:** 659–669.

Teramura M, Kobayashi S, Hoshino S et al (1992) Interleukin-11 enhances human mega-karyocytopoiesis in vitro. *Blood* **79:** 327–331.

Tewari A, Buhles WC & Starnes HF (1990) Preliminary report: effects of interleukin-1 on platelets. *Lancet* **336:** 712–714.

Till JE & McCulloch EA (1961) A direct measurement of the radiation sensitivity of normal mouse bone marrow cells. *Radiation Research* **14:** 213–222.

Tominaga A, Takaki S, Hitoshi Y et al (1992) Role of the interleukin 5 receptor system in hematopoiesis: Molecular basis for overlapping function of cytokines. *BioEssays* **14:** 527–533.

Tong J, Gordon MS, Srour EF et al (1993) In vivo administration of recombinant methionyl human stem cell factor expands the number of hematopoietic stem cells. *Blood* **82(3):** 784–791.

Tsukada J, Misago M, Kikuchi M et al (1992) Interaction between recombinant human erythropoietin and serum factor(s) on murine megakaryocyte colony formation. *Blood* **80:** 37–45.

Turner KJ, Fritz LJ, Temple P et al (1991) Purification, biochemical characterization, and cloning of a novel megakaryocyte stimulating factor that has megakaryocyte colony stimulating activity. *Blood* **78 (supplement):** 247a.

Ulich TR, Del Castillo J, Watson LR et al (1990) In vivo hematologic effects of recombinant human macrophage colony-stimulating factor. *Blood* **75:** 846–850.

Vadhan-Raj S, Buescher S, Broxmeyer HE et al (1988) Stimulation of myelopoiesis in patients with aplastic anemia by recombinant human granulocyte-macrophage colony-stimulating factor. *New England Journal of Medicine* **319:** 1628–1634.

Vainchenker W, Bouguet J, Guichard J & Breton-Gorius J (1979) Megakaryocyte colony formation from human bone marrow precursors. *Blood* **54:** 940–945.

Vannucchi AM, Grossi A, Rafanelli D & Ferrini R (1990) In vivo stimulation of megakaryo-cytopoiesis by recombinant murine granulocyte–macrophage colony-stimulating factor. *Blood* **76:** 1473–1480.

Wadenvik H, Kutti J, Ridell B et al (1991) The effect of α-interferon on bone marrow megakaryocytes and platelet production rate in essential thrombocythemia. *Blood* **77:** 2103–2108.

Weisbart RH, Golde DW, Clark SC et al (1985) Human granulocyte–macrophage colony-stimulating factor is a neutrophil activator. *Nature* **314:** 361–363.

Welte K, Platzer E, Lu L, Gabrilove JL et al (1985) Purification and biochemical character-ization of human pluripotent hematopoietic colony-stimulating factor. *Proceedings of the National Academy of Sciences, USA* **82:** 1526–1530.

Welte K, Zeidler C, Reiter A et al (1990) Differential effects of granulocyte–macrophage colony-stimulating factor and granulocyte colony-stimulating factor in children with severe congenital neutropenia. *Blood* **75:** 1056–1063.

Williams N, Eger RR, Jackson H & Nelson DJ (1982) Two factor requirement for mega-karyocyte colony formation. *Journal of Cell Physiology* **110:** 11–104.

Wilson EL, Rifkin DB, Kelly F et al (1991) Basic fibroblast growth factor stimulates myelo-poiesis in long-term human bone marrow cultures. *Blood* **77:** 954–960.

Withy RN, Rafied LF, Beck AK et al (1992) Growth factors produced by human embryonic kidney cells that influence megakaryopoiesis include erythropoietin, interleukin 6, and transforming growth factor-beta. *Journal of Cell Physiology* **153:** 362–372.

Wong GG, Wites JS, Temple PA et al (1985) Human GM-CSF: molecular cloning of the complementary DNA and purification of the natural and recombinant proteins. *Science* **228:** 810–815.

Wright EG & Lord BI (1992) Haemopoietic tissue. In Lord BI & Dexter TM (eds) *Baillière's Clinical Haematology* **5:** 499–507.

Wright EG & Pragell BI (1992) Stem cell proliferation inhibitors. In Lord BI & Dexter TM (eds) *Baillière's Clinical Haematology* **5:** 723–740.

Yamaguchi Y, Suda T, Suda J et al (1988) Purified interleukin 5 supports the terminal differentiation and proliferation of murine eosinophilic precursors. *Journal of Experi-mental Medicine* **163:** 43–48.

Yonemura Y, Kawakita M, Masuda T et al (1992) Synergistic effects of interleukin 3 and interleukin 11 on murine megakaryocytopoiesis in serum-free culture. *Experimental Hematology* **20:** 1011–1016.

5

The interferons in haematological malignancies

FRANCO MANDELLI
WILLIAM ARCESE
GIUSEPPE AVVISATI

The Interferons (IFNs) have been extensively evaluated as therapy for many haematological malignancies, but their role remains unclear for the majority of these diseases.

Following a brief description of the biological properties of IFNs, this review summarizes results from published clinical trials of IFNs in the management of lymphoproliferative as well as myeloproliferative malignant disorders and discusses their current role in the management of these disorders.

THE IFN FAMILY

The term IFN was originally used to identify a soluble protein factor produced by cells in response to a wide range of viruses (Isaacs and Lindemann, 1957). Three main subspecies of human IFN have now been recognized: α, β and γ—produced by leukocytes, fibroblasts and T lymphocytes, respectively (Stewart et al, 1980).

The genes coding for IFNs α and β are localized on chromosome 9 while the gene coding for IFN-γ is localized on chromosome 12. So far, at least 23 different IFN-α genes have been identified, coding for 15 functional proteins. All the IFN-α genes are closely related and clustered on chromosome 9 close to the gene for IFN-β (Balkwill, 1989). Because of the few chemical differences observed between the IFN-α subtypes and of their similar clinical activity, it is still unclear why there are so many species of IFN-α.

MECHANISMS OF ACTION

To exert their action on cells, IFNs must bind to specific cell surface membrane receptors. Two distinct IFN receptors are present on the cell membrane: the receptor for IFNs α and β, the gene of which is located on chromosome 21, and the receptor for IFN-γ, with the coding gene located on chromosome 6 (Aguet and Morgensen, 1983).

Following the binding of IFNs their specific receptors are down-regulated, while the IFN–receptor complex transmits signals to the nucleus for inducing, up-regulating or down-regulating the expression of some cellular genes. Thereafter, IFN is rapidly internalized and degraded.

Antiproliferative effect

The potent inhibitory effect of IFNs on cell proliferation has been clearly demonstrated in several laboratory studies (Gresser, 1985). Both natural and recombinant IFNs-α have shown greater control of haematopoietic cell proliferation and differentiation than IFNs β and γ (Blalock et al, 1980; Chadha and Srivastava, 1981; Borden et al, 1982). This inhibitory effect is more evident in non-cycling tumour cells and in some cases an accumulation of cells in G_0, accompanied by a decrease in transition to G_1 as well as the arrest of some cell types in G_1, has been observed (Horoszewicz et al, 1979; Creasey et al, 1980).

The mechanisms responsible for this antiproliferative effect of IFNs are unclear. The down-regulation of the proto-oncogene c-*myc* or other oncogenes (Samid et al, 1985; Kimci, 1987) as well as the induction of the two enzymes 2'-5' A synthetase and a protein kinase that inhibits protein translation (Revel et al, 1980; Senn, 1984; Bishoff and Samuel, 1985) may be involved. In particular, the 2'-5' A synthetase, by activating a latent endoribonuclease, degrades the mRNA linked to double-stranded RNA and thus inhibits RNA transcription and translation.

Immune regulation

The most important immune changes produced by IFNs appear to be the enhancement of the cytotoxic activity of NK cells and macrophages (Edwards et al, 1984), but their immunomodulatory effects may also play a role in tumour control. IFNs, as members of the cytokine network induce the secretion of other cytokines. Moreover, IFNs induce or enhance the expression of cell surface antigens for the major histocompatibility complex (MHC) and increase the expression of receptors for the Fc fragment of IgG on the surface of lymphocytes and macrophages, thus enhancing the tumoricidal activity of these cells (De Maeyer-Guinard and De Maeyer, 1985; Fertsch and Vogel, 1984).

TREATMENT OF MALIGNANT LYMPHOPROLIFERATIVE DISEASES

A lymphoproliferative malignancy is a disorder which arises from an uncontrolled ('neoplastic') proliferation of the lymphoid tissue. Distinct lymphoid malignances have been identified at virtually every step of lymphoid differentiation and IFNs have been used in the clinical management of all these disorders with a wide range of clinical results. In most cases, either natural or recombinant IFN-α has been used for treating these neoplastic disorders.

Among the lymphoproliferative disorders we can identify: (i) the leukaemias of lymphoid origin (acute, chronic and hairy cell); (ii) the lymphomas (Hodgkin and non-Hodgkin); (iii) multiple myeloma.

Leukaemias of lymphoid origin

Acute lymphocytic leukaemia (ALL)

Few studies have evaluated the role of IFNs in ALL (Ochs et al, 1986, 1991). One of the more interesting and provocative studies has been that of Meyer et al (1987) in which patients with ALL were randomized to receive IFN-α after allogeneic bone marrow transplantation. The intent was to reduce the incidence of cytomegalovirus infection and interstitial pneumonia. The results of this study were surprising as the frequency of these post-transplant complications were not affected by the administration of IFN-α, while a significant decrease in the rate of post-transplant relapses was noted in the group treated with IFN-α.

This observation needs further evaluation to clarify whether this effect of IFN-α in ALL is limited to the biological and immunological conditions that obtain after bone marrow transplantation or whether they might be extended to other more common situations such as those present during standard chemotherapeutic approaches. A randomized trial evaluating the role of IFN-α as post-remission therapy in children with ALL in second complete remission is being conducted by the Pediatric Oncology Group in the USA but no data are yet available.

Chronic lymphocytic leukaemia (CLL)

CLL is a lymphoproliferative disorder characterized by the clonal proliferation and accumulation of lymphocytes usually of B lineage. The disease is usually stable for months or years and patients are highly responsive to alkylating agents and corticosteroids.

Natural and recombinant IFNs-α have been used in advanced as well as in early disease. In advanced stages the overall response rate has been about 15% and the great majority of responses were minor. More recently, the use of IFN-α in early stage CLL has produced a reduction in circulating B lymphocytes in the majority of the treated patients. In particular, Pangalis and Griva (1988), using recombinant IFN-α2b, have observed one complete remission and 4 partial responses in 10 previously untreated patients with early-stage CLL. These data were more recently confirmed by Bussiotis and Pangalis (1991). A reduction in the number of circulating lymphocytes has also been observed by Rozman and coworkers (1988) in 10/10 stage 0 or 1 CLL patients. Using 3 MU of IFN-α2a three times a week for a total of 14 weeks, the same results have been obtained by Molica and Alberti (1990) in 11/11 previously untreated CLL patients. Finally, Ziegler-Heitbrock et al

(1989) administered IFN-α 5 MU three times a week subcutaneously, to 9 CLL patients younger than 60 years and with less than 50000 circulating lymphocytes. In all patients, a reduction in lymphocyte count was observed. Moreover, a normalization of the spleen size and an increase in IgG concentrations were observed in one and three patients, respectively.

These observations require further confirmation. Moreover, it has to be remembered that patients with early-stage CLL rarely require any kind of treatment, so that the general use of IFN-α alone in this category of patients may not be ethically appropriate. Instead its effectiveness in early-stage CLL implies that IFN-α should be further evaluated in combination with conventional chemotherapy in all CLL patients requiring treatment.

Hairy cell leukaemia (HCL)

HCL is a rare malignant lymphoproliferative disorder characterized by the neoplastic proliferation of B lymphocytes. Clinical features include the presence of splenomegaly and frequent opportunistic infections. Laboratory evaluation reveals the presence of pancytopenia and of pathognomonic cells with fine irregular filamentous cytoplasmic projection and an acid phosphatase activity resistant to preincubation with tartaric acid (TRAP). The progression of this rare disease reflects the degree of severity of cytopenia and infective deaths are very common. However, during the past decade the availability of several therapeutic options have dramatically improved the survival duration of these patients. Among these new therapeutic options, IFNs have played a major role.

The use of IFNs in HCL was first reported by Quesada et al (1984b). These investigators reported results from seven advanced HCL patients using a salvage treatment with partially purified IFN-α. All seven patients achieved normalization of the peripheral blood count and the bone marrow examination revealed a complete remission in three patients and a partial remission in the remaining four patients. Since then a large number of studies have been published using recombinant or non-recombinant IFNs, administered at standard or low dose, for a short or a long period (Jacobs et al, 1985; Foon et al, 1986; Mandelli et al, 1986; Lauria et al, 1988; Ratain et al, 1988; Moormeier et al, 1989; Thompson et al, 1989; Berman et al, 1990; Gastl et al, 1990; Golomb et al, 1991). Even though the modalities of administration and the type of IFNs have varied in the different studies, the following statements may be made:

1. The standard dose of IFN-α is 3 MU daily or 3 times per week, intramuscularly or subcutaneously, for a period of at least 12 months.
2. 90% of HCL patients will usually achieve an improvement in blood cell count with complete remission observed in 10–20%. However, 10% of patients are refractory to IFN-α treatment.
3. IFN-α has little effect on the presence of reticulin fibres in the bone marrow of HCL patients, even though TRAP activity disappears during IFN-α treatment.
4. The response rate obtained with the use of low-dose IFN-α

(0.2 MU m^{-2}, 3 times per week) is lower than that obtained with standard dose; therefore, low-dose IFN-α should not be used for remission induction even though this dosage should be evaluated as long-term maintenance treatment.

5. So far, no differences in therapeutic efficacy have been observed among the different types of IFNs-α in HCL.

6. Discontinuation of IFN-α therapy causes most patients eventually to relapse; however, they will respond to reinstitution of IFN-α therapy.

7. At present IFN-α is one of the most effective standard treatments for HCL; however, in order better to define the future therapeutic strategies in HCL, we have to keep in mind that IFN-α alone does not cure HCL.

Only a few studies have evaluated the effects of IFNs β and γ in HCL. In a patient resistant to IFN-α, IFN-β has produced a response (Michalevicz et al, 1988), while IFN-γ does not seem to be an effective agent in HCL (Quesada et al, 1988).

Lymphomas

Hodgkin disease (HD)

Thus far, there have been very few clinical studies evaluating the role of IFNs in HD. These studies have demonstrated some effect of IFN-α in reducing the tumour mass of resistant HD (Horning et al, 1985; Leavitt et al, 1987), although the responses were brief. Therefore, at present it does not seem that IFN-α is useful for treating HD.

Non-Hodgkin lymphomas (NHL)

This heterogeneous group of lymphoproliferative disorders are classified, according to the 'Working Formulation' as low, intermediate and high grade lymphomas. There is also a great heterogeneity in response to IFNs, depending on the type of NHL. In particular, in the high and intermediate grade NHL, clinical studies have demonstrated that IFN-α produces a response in 15–20% of patients with less than a 5% complete remission rate. Therefore, IFN-α alone seems to have no role in the treatment of these NHL.

In contrast, the use of IFN-α in phase I and II clinical studies has shown beneficial activity in low grade NHL with an overall response rate of about 40–50% including a 10% complete remission rate (Gutterman et al, 1980; Louie et al, 1981; Quesada et al, 1984a; Horning et al, 1985; O'Connell et al, 1986; Foon et al, 1987; Leavitt et al, 1987; Mantovani et al, 1989; Van der Molen et al, 1990). However, the median response duration was shorter than that observed with chemotherapy.

Because of the demonstrated activity of IFN-α in low grade NHL and the evidence from experimental data of a synergy between human IFN and cyclophosphamide or doxorubicin (Balkwill and Moodie, 1984), many phase III studies have evaluated the benefit of IFN-α in combination therapy in low grade NHL.

The results of four of these cooperative studies have been published:

Group d'Etude de Lymphomes Folliculaires (GELF) (Solal-Celigny et al, 1991). This study tested the m-CAVP regimen (cyclophosphamide 600 mg m^{-2}, doxorubicin 25 mg m^{-2}, vumon 26 60 mg m^{-2} and prednisone 60 mg m^{-2} every 4 weeks) versus m-CAVP plus IFN-α 5 MU three times per week for 18 months. Preliminary results showed an increased response rate, a longer disease-free survival and a longer survival for patients treated with IFN-α and m-CAVP.

British Study (Price et al, 1991). This study used, as induction treatment, chlorambucil (CB) 10 mg daily for 6 weeks, followed by three 14-day cycles given at 2-week intervals, with or without IFN-α 2 MU m^{-2} thrice weekly, subcutaneously throughout the 18 week period. Responding patients were then randomized a second time to no further therapy or to maintenance treatment with IFN-α at the above dose for a year. The preliminary results showed no difference in response rate between CB versus CB + IFN-α; however, a prolonged time to progression for patients receiving IFN-α as maintenance has been observed. Thus, from this study it seems that a prolonged exposure to IFN-α is helpful.

Eastern Cooperative Oncology Group (ECOG) (Smalley et al, 1992). This study, published very recently, tested the COPA regimen (cyclophosphamide 600 mg m^{-2} day 1 doxorubicin 50 mg m^{-2} day 1, and prednisone 100 mg m^{-2} days 1–5 every 28 days for 8–10 cycles) versus COPA plus IFN-α (6 MU m^{-2} intramuscularly on days 22–26 of each 28-day cycle) in clinically aggressive low grade NHL and certain histological variants of intermediate grade NHL. 147 patients were assigned to the COPA regimen and 144 to the COPA–IFN-α regimen.

The published results show comparable objective responses for both regimens, but that including IFN-α had a greater effect in prolonging the time to treatment failure ($p < 0.001$) and the duration of complete response ($p = 0.03$).

According to multivariant analysis, an age of less than 65 years ($p = 0.01$), IFN-α treatment ($p = 0.014$), female sex ($p = 0.015$), low grade tumour hystology ($p = 0.015$) and the absence of B symptoms ($p = 0.021$) were all associated with improved survival.

EORTC study (Hagenbeek et al, 1992). The objective of this study was to test at random the role of IFN-α as maintenance treatment versus no maintenance in patients with low grade NHL responding to induction treatment with: CVP (cyclophosphamide 300 mg m^{-2} per os, days 1–5; vincristine 1.4 mg m^{-2} i.v. day 1, prednisone 40 mg m^{-2} per os, days 1–5). As of May 1992, 331 patients were registered and 248 were evaluable for response to CVP. 231 patients have been randomized: 116 to IFN, 115 to no further treatment. When the two arms are compared, the progression-free survival in the IFN-α arm is 135 weeks versus 86 weeks observed in the control group ($p = 0.02$). All these data indicate that IFN-α has a role in the treatment of low grade NHL either combined with conventional induction treatment or as maintenance treatment.

Cutaneous T-cell lymphomas (CTCL)

The CTCL, including mycosis fungoides (MF) and Sezary's syndrome (SS) are indolent NHL which may remain confined to the skin for several years but which eventually involve the peripheral blood, lymph nodes and other organs.

The use of IFN-α as single therapeutic agent in CTCL has proved to be highly effective with an overall response rate ranging from 60–80% of patients (Bunn et al, 1986; Tura et al, 1987; Nicolas et al, 1989; Olsen et al, 1989; Rinne et al, 1989; Papa et al, 1991). However, the optimal dose of IFN for CTCL is not yet known.

Moreover, despite the high rate of response observed in CTCL patients treated with IFN-α, they eventually relapse, even though the relapse occurs more frequently in patients with advanced or refractory disease. Thus, because IFN-α seems to be very effective as single agent in early stages of the disease, further studies are needed to better define the role of this agent in the treatment of CTCL.

Multiple myeloma (MM)

MM is a haematological malignancy originating from the uncontrolled proliferation of a single clone of plasma cells, which in the great majority of the cases secretes large quantities of monoclonal immunoglobulins and/or light chains and frequently produces bone destruction, bone marrow failure, malignant hypercalcaemia and recurrent infections.

Despite the substantial progress observed in recent years in understanding the biology of MM, the disease is still incurable even though many new therapeutic approaches are under evaluation. Among these new therapeutic modalities, the IFNs have acquired a prominent role (Mellsted et al, 1979; Avvisati and Mandelli, 1992). The best results have been obtained combining IFN-α with conventional chemotherapy for induction treatment in newly diagnosed MM patients or using IFN-α as maintenance treatment in those who have already responded to conventional induction therapy.

In a pilot study of the Eastern Cooperative Oncology Group (ECOG) a combination of VBMCP with alternating cycles of recombinant IFN-α2b administered to 54 evaluable patients with previously untreated MM produced an 80% objective response rate. Moreover, 30% of the patients had a complete response (CR) defined as disappearance of the monoclonal immunoglobulin and absence of plasma cells from the bone marrow. The median survival was 40 months (Oken et al, 1990).

Recently, the preliminary results of a randomized study comparing melphalan and prednisone (MP) to MP plus IFN-α2a in 50 previously untreated MM patients have shown that 95% of the patients receiving MP plus IFN-α2a have responded to therapy as opposed to 68% of the patients receiving MP alone ($p < 0.05$). The response duration was longer in the MP plus IFN-α2a group than in the MP group ($p < 0.025$). The median survival was 80 weeks in the MP group while in the MP plus IFN-α2a group 93% of patients were still alive after 90 weeks ($p < 0.025$) (Montuoro et al, 1990). However, it must be recognized that the follow-up of this study is too short to permit any definitive conclusion.

A partial confirmation of this study is given by the results obtained in the last trial of the Myeloma Group of Central Sweden (MGCS) (Mellstedt, 1991). In this study, patients were randomized to receive natural IFN-α in addition to MP therapy during the induction and maintenance treatment. A total of 133 patients entered the MP/IFN-α group and 134 the MP group. The response rate was 65% in the MP/IFN-α group and 43% in the MP group ($p < 0.01$). The total survival curves did not differ between the two arms. However, for stage II patients, the median survival duration from response was significantly longer in the MP/IFN-α group than in the MP group, 40 months vs. 22 months respectively ($p < 0.05$). It should be noted, however, that the two other randomized trials comparing melphalan and prednisone with or without IFN-α in newly diagnosed MM patients failed to show any differences in response rate, progression-free survival or overall survival (Cooper et al, 1990; Corrado et al, 1991).

The rationale for using IFN-α as maintenance treatment in MM patients responding to conventional induction chemotherapy was given by the in vitro evidence that at the end of the induction treatment the myeloma cells of the responding patients are in a 'plateau phase' similar to the G_0 phase of the cell cycle (Durie et al, 1980). Therefore, considering the antiproliferative effects of IFNs and that IFN-α markedly reduces the self-renewal capacity of myeloma-forming cells (Bergsagel et al, 1986), it appears more appropriate to utilize IFN-α as an agent for maintaining the response obtained with conventional induction treatments.

At present the results of four randomized studies dealing with the use of IFN-α are available in the medical literature; these studies have been conducted in different parts of the world: three in Europe (Italy, Sweden, Germany) and one in USA by the South West Oncology cooperative Group (SWOG).

Italian study (Mandelli et al, 1990). This was the first published study in which IFN-α was described as an agent for maintaining the response already obtained with conventional therapy rather than as an agent for inducing a response. During a period of 3 years, 101 MM patients responding to year long courses of traditional first-line induction chemotherapy were randomized to receive ($n = 50$) recombinant IFN-α2b as maintenance treatment; the remaining 51 patients were randomized to the control group which did not receive maintenance treatment.

The overall results of the study were as follows: the median duration of response (from the time of randomization to maintenance treatment) was 26 months in the patients given IFN and 14 months in the untreated patients ($p = 0.0002$), while the median duration of survival (from the time of randomization to maintenance therapy) was 52 months in the IFN group and 39 months in the control group ($p = 0.0526$). However, among the patients who had an objective response to induction chemotherapy the difference in survival was statistically significant ($p = 0.0352$).

Swedish study (Westin et al, 1991). In this study, following the MP induction treatment 120/308 evaluable patients achieved a 'plateau phase' defined as response ($>50\%$ reduction of monoclonal component) lasting 4 months. These patients in the plateau phase were randomized to receive ($n = 59$ patients) or not ($n = 61$ patients) IFN-α2b at the dose of 5 MU three times per week subcutaneously until relapse. After a median observation time from randomization of 20 months, an interim analysis of the study was performed. The analysis revealed a highly significant difference in the duration of the plateau phase between the two treatments arms ($p < 0.001$). In particular, the median duration of plateau was 59 weeks in the IFN arm and 26 weeks in the no therapy arm. Because of the short follow-up, data on survival duration are not yet available. This well designed study indicates that the use of IFN-α as maintenance treatment, in MM patients responding to initial induction treatment and achieving a 'true' plateau phase, can significantly prolong the response duration and therefore partially confirms the results of the Italian study.

German study (Peest et al, 1990). In this study 71/140 MM patients having obtained a stable disease after the induction chemotherapies, were randomized to receive IFN-α2b as maintenance treatment. The published results revealed no differences in relapse rate between the two randomized groups and the median response duration was 7 months in both groups. No data on the overall survival duration of both groups are so far available. However, in this study the absence of benefit in the group maintained on IFN-α may be due to the presence of some differences in the modalities of randomization respect to the other studies such as: (i) the absence of a stratification for the induction treatment before the randomization to the maintenance arm; (ii) the shorter duration of the plateau phase when compared to the longer duration of the plateau phase of other studies.

SWOG study (Salmon and Crowley, 1992). This is the most recent study on the use of IFN-α as maintenance treatment for newly diagnosed MM patients responding to the conventional induction chemotherapies VMCP/VBAP or VAD or VMCPP/VBAPP. Patients achieving a response, defined as 75% of myeloma mass regression, were randomizsed to receive ($n = 106$) or not ($n = 104$) IFN-α2b until relapse. After a median follow-up of 12 months from the start of maintenance treatment, no differences in response or overall survival duration for patients receiving IFN have been observed.

These data do not confirm the results of the Italian and Swedish studies. However, some differences among the SWOG and the Italian and Swedish studies may be responsible for the different results. First, in the SWOG study the responding patients are only those with a reduction of at least 75% of myeloma mass while in the Italian and Swedish studies the cut-off for response is a reduction of at least 50% of myeloma mass. Second, the patient population with stage III myeloma is higher in the SWOG than in the Italian and Swedish studies. Consequently the population of high-risk myeloma is higher in the SWOG study. Third, the number of stage I myeloma is lower in the SWOG study. Encouraging results have been obtained by the same group using IFN-α + dexamethasone in those patients with a lower reduction (<75%) of myeloma mass after induction chemotherapy.

As far as IFN-β and IFN-γ are concerned, to date there are only a few negative published reports in which these type of IFNs have been used as salvage treatment with an overall response rate of less than 5% (Avvisati and Mandelli, 1992). Therefore, at present it does not seem that IFNs β and γ have a role in MM therapy.

TREATMENT OF MYELOPROLIFERATIVE DISEASES

The term myeloproliferative disease (MPD) includes a heterogeneous group of malignant haematological disorders that share common characteristics, consisting of a clonal haematopoietic stem-cell proliferation with subsequent overproduction of one or more cell lineages. Early in the course of the disease, cell differentiation seems likely to be normal, but the malignant clone is unstable and retains variable propensity to evolve into a more aggressive acute disorder. The MPD are usually identified by the predominant cell line involved in the haematological disorder (Zuckerman et al, 1992).

Advances in our understanding of the mechanisms of cell growth regulation and differentiation are providing insights into the pathophysiology of some myeloproliferative diseases. Therefore, in line with the experiences arising from Chronic Myeloid Leukaemia (CML), we can assume that in future, cytogenetic and molecular studies might allow each MPD to be identified through their pathognomonic alteration.

Interferon is being used increasingly in the treatment of CML and its therapeutic efficacy on essential thrombocythaemia (ET) and polycythaemia vera (PV) is now widely confirmed. However, the role of IFN in the management of myelofibrosis with myeloid metaplasia (MMM) is still controversial. In this report a review on the IFN therapy in these four MPD is presented. At present, there are insufficient data to extend the survey to the other myeloproliferative disorders.

Chronic myeloid leukaemia

Philadelphia-positive (Ph+) CML is a clonal disease of an early haematopoietic pluripotent cell and is characterized by an excessive cellular proliferation with myeloid mass expansion. The abnormal Philadelphia chromosome is unique to the disease and occurs in more than 95% of the cases. It is due to a reciprocal translocation, between chromosome 9 and 22 t(9;22) (q34; q11). By this translocation, the ABL proto-oncogene from chromosome 9 is inserted into the BCR gene on chromosome 22 with generation of the bcr/abl hybrid gene.

Neither conventional cytotoxic therapy (Champlin et al, 1985) nor more aggressive intensive chemotherapy (Kantarjian et al, 1985) have substantially modified the natural history of the disease, which invariably evolves from a more benign chronic phase towards a fatal blast crisis with a median time of about 4 years. At present, only through allogeneic bone marrow transplantation can the malignant clone be eradicated and patient cure achieved (Goldman et al, 1988). However patient age and the need for an HLA compatible donor limit this therapeutic approach to a minority of patients.

Interferon therapy in Philadelphia-positive CML

After the first experiences reported by Talpaz et al (1983, 1986), IFN is widely used in the treatment of CML patients. Various kinds of IFN-α (2a, 2b, 2c), IFN-γ or, more recently, a combination of both have been employed at doses ranging from 3–10 MU m^{-2} in several clinical trials and complete haematological remission has been obtained in 55–75% of treated patients.

Cytogenetic response of any degree including complete cytogenetic remission (CCR) has been observed in about 50% of patients given IFN during the first year of chronic phase and in 20% of those treated more than 1 year from diagnosis.

A detailed analysis of these results is given in a comprehensive review recently published by Morra et al (1992). In this chapter, an update of the most recent acquisitions on the IFN therapy in Ph+ CML is reported.

Predicting factors for karyotypic response to IFN therapy

From the Italian Cooperative CML study group in a prospective study including 218 patients treated by IFN-α2b at starting dose of 9 MU per day, a major karyotypic response (KR) (Ph− metaphases >66%) has been observed in 36 out of 180 (20%) evaluable patients (Fiacchini, 1992). The karyotypic response was significantly correlated with a platelet count of <500 vs. 500–1000 vs. >1000 PLTS × 10^9 l^{-1}: 32% vs. 13% vs. 0.0% KRs, respectively; ($p = 0.001$) and circulating blast cells of <2% vs. >2%: 29% vs. 8% KRs; ($p = 0.0004$). Karyotypic response also correlated with the Sokal prognostic risk (Sokal et al, 1984) although to a lesser extent. Indeed, a cytogenetic response was attained in 28%, 15% and 13% of patients at low, intermediate and high risk, respectively. From this study, patients with a normal platelet count without blast cells in the peripheral blood and at low risk by Sokal seem likely to be the likeliest candidates to obtain a major karyotypic response.

At the M.D. Anderson Cancer Center, 134 patients were studied for correlation between cytogenetic response to IFN-α and the bcr/abl splicing patterns (Lee et al, 1992). A complete cytogenetic response was achieved in 55% of 51 patients with b2/a2 splicing pattern, in 24% of 70 patients with b3/a2 splicing pattern and in none of 13 patients with both messages ($p < 0.0001$). No association was found between splicing patterns and time required to achieve CCR or its duration. Finally, all patients in CCR showed persistent PCR positivity for residual bcr/abl transcripts. This last observation had been reported in 10 patients in CCR after therapy with IFN-α2b alone or in combination with IFN-γ (Opalka et al, 1991).

Interferon therapy and survival

Confirming data reported by Talpaz et al (1991), the Italian Cooperative Study Group in a prospective trial including the 218 patients mentioned above, found a significant correlation between cytogenetic response and survival. At 4 years, 94% of patients with minor and major cytogenetic response are surviving versus 56% of the others. The presence of circulating blast cells and survival were also correlated, while Sokal's prognostic risk index was not significantly predictive for survival. However the CALGB was not able to find any significant difference between 31 patients who experienced partial or complete response and 49 non-responders at cytogenetic level for a median survival of 5 years (Ozer et al, 1992).

In a further prospective study conducted by the Italian Cooperative Study Group, 322 patients were stratified by the Sokal risk and randomized to receive IFN-α2a or hydroxyurea in a 2:1 ratio. In each risk subgroup of patients, the 4-year survival was significantly higher in IFN-treated patients (Zuffa, 1992).

So far, 624 patients in the German CML study and 500 patients in the UK–MRC study have been enrolled into prospective trials randomized for IFN versus conventional therapy. However, patient follow-up is still too short to permit evaluation of the effects on survival.

Interferon as combination therapy

Interferon seems to be less effective when administered to patients in late chronic phase or in at an advanced stage of disease. Combinations of IFN with cytotoxic drugs have therefore been tried, such as hydroxyurea (Alimena et al, 1990), ARA-C (Guilhot et al, 1991) or intensive chemotherapy (Kantarjian et al, 1986; Burke et al, 1990). The proportion of patients achieving some degree of Ph chromosome suppression with these treatments compares favourably with that observed in similar subsets of patients receiving IFN alone. Another approach is to follow IFN administration with autologous bone marrow transplantation; the results, although promising, are still too preliminary (Meloni et al, 1989; McGlave et al, 1990; Reiffers et al, 1991).

Finally, IFN-α given to patients who relapse after T-cell depleted or unmanipulated allogeneic BMT has been shown effective in containing disease progression and eventually in restoring donor cell haematopoiesis (Arcese et al, 1990; Higano et al, 1992). These experiences indicate the post-transplantation use of IFN to prevent relapse, particularly in patients at higher risk of recurrence. To test this proposal the European Bone Marrow Transplantation Group is conducting a prospective randomized study.

Side-effects and resistance

IFN therapy gives rise to several side-effects. The earliest such as flu-like syndrome, are usually transient, manageable with antipyretic or analgesic agents and not dose-limiting. Conversely, the late side-effects related to long-lasting IFN administration and consisting of muscle pain, fatigue, depression, insomnia and neurotoxicity, are responsible for dose reduction in 10–30% of cases. In 5–10% of patients temporary or permanent IFN discontinuation is required. The response to IFN depends on the dose of the drug actually administered. Thus the maximum tolerated dose may be below the dose required for maximum therapeutic efficacy.

The role played by anti-IFN neutralizing antibodies in inducing resistance to therapy is controversial. In some series, only a few patients were positive for anti-IFN antibodies (Dianzani et al, 1989; Aitchison et al, 1991), but from two other reports (Itri et al, 1989; Freund et al, 1991) anti-IFN antibodies developed in 25% and 30% of patients, respectively. The presence of anti-IFN antibodies had no prognostic significance in the former, while it was claimed to be responsible for therapeutic failure in the latter. Natural IFN-α overcame resistance in some cases.

Essential thrombocythaemia (ET)

ET is a clonal myeloproliferative disorder (Fialkow et al, 1981) characterized by an increasing number of morphologically and functionally abnormal platelets. Its diagnosis is mainly based upon exclusion of the other myeloproliferative diseases; diagnostic criteria established by the Polycythaemia Vera Study Group are generally applied (Murphy et al, 1986). Frequent and sometimes fatal complications in the course of the disease include thromboembolic episodes and/or haemorrhage (Pearson, 1991). Despite the high morbidity rate, a long survival in most patients has been reported (Balduini, 1992).

In symptomatic patients conventional treatment consisting of alkylating agents (Case, 1984) or antimetabolites (Mazzucconi et al, 1986; Löfwenberg and Wahlin, 1988) has been shown to be effective in reducing platelet count and clinical complications. However, the need for long-term maintenance therapy leads to an increasing risk of leukaemia related to cytotoxic drug administration and to possible impairment of gonadal function.

The antiplatelet effect induced by IFN therapy in patients with other myeloproliferative disorders or with thrombocytosis related to non-haematological disease suggested extending the use of IFN to ET. Furthermore, experimental studies showing the capacity of IFN-α and γ to inhibit in vitro megakaryocyte colony growth (Ganser et al, 1987; Gugliotta et al, 1989) provided the biological rationale for such a therapeutic approach.

Various kinds of IFN-α have been administered at doses ranging from 1–10 MU subcutaneously on a daily schedule in the majority of patients. A complete response with normalization of platelet count and disappearance of clinical symptoms has been achieved in 84% of all patients within a median of 2 months. The IFN-related side-effects were generally well tolerated, but dose reduction or discontinuation was required in 20–30% of patients given IFN at higher dosage.

From the analysis of experience from several centres, it can be concluded that in ET an effective therapeutic response may be obtained even for slightly lower doses of IFN (Gugliotta et al, 1989; Lazzarino et al, 1989). Interestingly, some patients, who were previously resistant to cytotoxic agents showed restored sensitivity to these drugs after discontinuation of IFN therapy (Lazzarino et al, 1989).

In accord with in vitro data, IFN reduces the platelet production rate and peripheral blood count in ET mainly through an antiproliferative action on the megakaryocytes and to a considerably lesser degree by shortening platelet mean lifespan (Wadenvik et al, 1991). The latter observation could explain the early therapeutic response frequently noted.

Although a continuous remission after withdrawing IFN has been recently reported (Kasparu et al, 1992), an increasing platelet count usually follows IFN discontinuation. Therefore, IFN at minimum effective dosage should be maintained indefinitely (Giles et al, 1990; Gisslinger et al, 1991).

More recently, anagrelide has been introduced as an alternative approach for treating thrombocythaemic patients (Silverstein et al, 1988) and has been highly effective in reducing thrombocytosis and maintaining normal platelet count (Anagrelide Study Group, 1992). Anagrelide seems to exert its therapeutic action by slowing down megakaryocyte maturation without inhibiting cell proliferation (Mazur et al, 1989). However, part of its effect in reducing platelet count may relate to enhanced splenic macrophage function with subsequent reduction of platelet survival (Gilbert et al, 1989). Therefore IFN and Anagrelide retain distinct mechanisms of activity with likely equivalent therapeutic efficacy.

In order to find the best therapeutic schedule for the patients with ET, IFN and anagrelide, alone and combined should be compared prospectively.

Polycythaemia vera (PV)

The main characteristic of the clonal myeloproliferative disease PV consists of an excessive expansion of the erythroid mass (Adamson et al, 1976; Murphy et al, 1986). Nevertheless, as usually observed in other MPD, a granulocytopoietic and megakaryocytopoietic hyperplasia is frequently associated with the disease. A marked hypersensitivity of the progenitor cells to IL-3 and GM-CSF seems to be involved in the pathogenesis of the disease (Dai et al, 1992).

Although PV is normally a long-lasting disease, the slow progression towards myelofibrosis and the possible leukaemic evolution are two well known features of the disease. To reduce the circulating red cell mass, phlebotomy has been regularly used for patients with PV. However, its use produces an increased risk of thrombosis, particularly in more aged patients (Berk et al, 1986). The risk of leukaemia in PV was found to be enhanced by the prolonged administration of alkylating agents (Berk et al, 1981). Their use should be avoided, therefore, particularly in younger patients.

On the basis of these considerations and in line with clinical experience in other MPD, the therapeutic effect of IFN has been evaluated in PV. Five patients pre-treated by phlebotomy were given IFN-α subcutaneously at the starting dose of 3 MU, three times a week (Silver, 1990). An early therapeutic response was observed in two patients, for whom the IFN dose was progressively tapered to 0.45 MU, three times a week. However, to obtain a therapeutic response the IFN dose was increased up to 5 MU 5 times a week in the other three patients. The red cell mass was contained in all five patients and four of them also experienced a regression of spleen size, which was not observed in the fifth patient because of a previously documented portal vein thrombosis. IFN was well tolerated during both the induction and maintenance phase of therapy. However, marrow fibrosis and cellularity remained unchanged in all patients. A dramatic improvement of severe clinical symptoms including pain, itching, fever and sweating observed in one patient haematologically responding to hydroxyurea has been attributed to IFN therapy (Ariad and Bezwoda, 1991). Finally, a complete or partial response was achieved within 4 months in seven of 11 pretreated patients receiving IFN-α at dose of 3 MU per day (Turri et al, 1991). Interestingly a complete response was also obtained in three patients who had been resistant to hydroxyurea.

The preliminary results of IFN therapy in PV seem to be particularly promising. However, they need to be confirmed in a larger patient series and with longer follow-up to permit a cost/benefit evaluation of IFN therapy in preventing marrow fibrosis and leukaemic progression.

Myelofibrosis with myeloid methaplasia (MMM)

Marrow fibrosis is frequently detected in MPD. However, it is a particular feature of MMM, a clonal disease of the haematopoietic stem cell (Sato et al, 1986). Furthermore, the MMM is characterized by anisopokilocytosis and leukoerythroblastosis in the peripheral blood and by extramedullary haematopoiesis with hepatosplenomegaly (Gilbert, 1984). In MMM, marrow fibrosis is a reactive process mediated by platelet-derived growth factor (PDGF) and platelet-factor IV (Groopman, 1980; McCarthy, 1985). The disease is invariably fatal because of haemorrhagic and infectious complications related to progressive cytopenia, hepatic failure, siderochromatosis and leukaemic evolution. The median survival is about 5 years and it has not been substantially modified by the current therapeutic approaches, such as splenectomy, androgens and chemotherapeutic agents (Manoharan, 1988).

The therapeutic efficacy of IFN in other MPD and the experimental studies showing the ability of IFN α, β and γ to inhibit the in vitro growth of the megakaryocyte colonies (Ganser et al, 1987), involved in disease pathogenesis, provided the rationale for the clinical use of IFN. IFN-α, administered at a mean dose of 3 MU per day, has usually been employed in clinical trials. Experience is limited and only a few patients have been treated at each stage of the disease. None the less, we can draw the conclusion that IFN-α has little therapeutic impact on MMM (Parmeggiani et al, 1987; Wickramashinghe et al, 1987; Bevan and Bateman, 1988; Gastl et al, 1988; Seewann et al, 1988; Barosi et al, 1989; Craig et al, 1991; McCarthy et al, 1991). A transient reduction of splenomegaly has been reported in only 25% of patients, while the degree of marrow fibrosis was not substantially modified in any case. Moreover, the clinical and haematological tolerance to IFN was very low, particularly in cytopenic patients. Platelet counts frequently decreased further on therapy and such an observation would suggest a higher effectiveness of IFN-α during the hyperproliferative phase of disease.

Human platelets have specific receptors for IFN-γ, but not for IFNs α and β (Molinas et al, 1987) and IFN-γ can inhibit fibrononectin synthesis in vitro (Duncan and Berman, 1985). On this basis, Martyrè et al (1991) have administered recombinant human IFN-γ subcutaneously at dose of 20 MU per day to four patients over 6 months. In all patients erythropoiesis improved without a reduction in platelet count. It is worth noting that platelet levels of PDGF and TGF-β, which were significantly increased before treatment, returned to the normal range. The therapeutic potential of IFN-γ should be more extensively explored.

In conclusion, among the myeloproliferative diseases, MMM is the least responsive to IFN-α therapy. However, better patient selection, the search for combination therapy of IFN and cytotoxic drugs and the use of IFN-γ may better define the real therapeutic impact of IFN on MMM.

SUMMARY

Interferons (IFNs) are a family of biological response modifiers with a broad spectrum of action on cellular proliferation as well as immunoregulation. In the last decade, these properties have prompted several investigations of the effect of IFNs on various haematological malignancies. IFNs-α have been used most extensively.

The response rate is dependent on the type of the disease. The most striking effects have been observed in hairy cell leukaemia and chronic myeloid leukaemia. In both these malignancies the results are well consolidated and indicate that IFNs-α have modified the natural history of the disease. Results of IFN therapy in low grade lymphoma, cutaneous T-cell lymphoma and multiple myeloma suggest a beneficial role of IFNs-α in the induction, as well as the maintenance, phase. The efficacy of IFNs is now widely confirmed in treating patients with essential thrombocythaemia or polycythaemia vera. However, the role of IFNs in the management of chronic lymphocytic leukaemia and myelofibrosis with myeloid metaplasia is still controversial.

Acknowledgement

The authors thank Miss Francesca Di Giorgio for the excellent assistance in preparing the manuscript.

REFERENCES

Adamson JW, Fialkow PJ, Murphy S et al (1976) Polycytemia Vera: stem cell and probable clonal origin of the disease. *The New England Journal of Medicine* **295:** 913–916.

Aguet M & Morgensen KE (1983) Interferon receptors. *Interferon* **3:** 1–22.

Aitchison R, Allen P, Schey S et al (1991) Anti-interferon antibodies in α interferon treated patients with chronic myeloid leukaemia. *British Journal of Haematology* **78:** 465–466.

Alimena G, Morra E, Lazzarino M et al (1990) Interferon α 2b as therapy for patients with Ph1 positive chronic myelogenous leukemia. *European Journal of Hematology* **45 (supplement 52):** 25–28.

Anagrelide Study Group (1992) Anagrelide, a therapy for thrombocythemic states: experience in 577 patients. *American Journal of Medicine* **92:** 69–76.

Arcese W, Mauro F, Alimena G et al (1990) Interferon therapy for Ph1 positive CML patients relapsing after T-cell depleted allogeneic BMT. *Bone Marrow Transplantation* **5:** 309–315.

Ariad S & Bezwoda WR (1991) Alpha-interferon for polycythemia vera. *Blood* **77:** 670.

Avvisati G & Mandelli F (1992) Interferon treatment of multiple myeloma: an emerging dilemma for the 1990s. In Talpaz M, Kurzrock R & Gutterman JU (eds) *Biological Response Modifiers in the Treatment of Hematopoietic Neoplasia*, pp 43–55. New York: Marcel Dekker.

Balduini CL (1992) Primary thrombocythaemia: new drugs for an evolving disease. *Haematologica* **77:** 297–301.

Balkwill FR (1989) Interferons. *Lancet* **i:** 1060–1063.

Barosi G, Liberato LN, Costa A & Ascari E (1989) Cytoreductive effects of recombinant alpha interferon in patients with myeloid metaplasia. *Blut* **58:** 271–274.

Bergsagel DE, Haas RH & Messner HA (1986) Interferon alfa-2b in the treatment of chronic granulocytic leukemia. *Seminars in Oncology* **13 (supplement 2):** 29–34.

Berk PD, Goldberg JD, Silverstein MN et al (1981) Increased incidence of acute leukaemia in polycythemia vera associated with chlorambucil therapy. *New England Journal of Medicine* **304:** 441–447.

Berk PD, Goldberg JD, Donovan PB et al (1986) Therapeutic recommendations in polycytemia vera based on polycythemia vera study group protocols. *Seminars in Haematology* **23:** 132–143.

Berman E, Heller G, Kempin S et al (1990) Incidence of response and long term follow-up in patients with hairy cell leukemia treated with recombinant interferon alfa-2a. *Blood* **75:** 839–845.

Bevan PC & Bateman CJT (1988) Interferon α for idiopathic myelofibrosis. *Lancet* **i:** 766.

Bishoff JR & Samuel CE (1985) Mechanism of interferon action. *Journal of Biological Chemistry* **260:** 8237–8239.

Blalock J, Georgiades JE, Langford MP et al (1980) Purified human immune interferon has more potent anticellular activity than fibroblast or leukocyte interferon. *Cellular Immunology* **49:** 390–394.

Borden EC, Hogan TF & Voelkel JG (1982) Comparative antiproliferative activity in vitro of natural interferons alpha and beta for diploid and transformed human cells. *Cancer Research* **42:** 4948–4953.

Bunn PA Jr, Ihde DC & Foon KA (1986) The role of recombinant interferon alpha-2a in the therapy of cutaneous T-cell lymphomas. *Cancer* **57:** 1685–1689.

Burke PJ & Rowley SD (1990) Remission of aggressive phase chronic myelocytic leukemia (CML) with timed sequential therapy (TST) and interferon (I) given in aplasia. *Blood* **78 (supplement 1):** 258a.

Bussiotis VA & Pangalis GA (1991) Interferon alfa-2b therapy in untreated early stage, B-chronic lymphocytic leukemia patients: one-year follow-up. *British Journal of Haematology* **79 (supplement 1):** 30–33.

Case DC (1984) Therapy of essential thrombocythemia with thiotepa and chlorambucil. *Blood* **63:** 51–54.

Chadha KC & Srivastava BI (1981) Comparison of the antiproliferative effects of human fibroblast and leukocyte interferons on various leukemic cell lines. *Journal of Clinical Hematology Oncology* **11:** 55–60.

Champlin RE & Golde DW (1985) Chronic myelogenous leukaemia: recent advances. *Blood* **65:** 1039–1047.

Cooper MR, Dear K, McIntyre et al (1990) A randomized study comparing melphalan/ prednisone (M/P) with or without Alpha 2b interferon (M/P/I) in newly diagnosed multiple myeloma. *Blood* **76 (supplement 1):** 345a (abstract 1371).

Corrado C, Flores A, Pavlovsky S et al (1991) Randomized trial of melphalan (L-PAM)- prednisone (PRED) with or without recombinant alpha2 interferon (r α2 IFN) in multiple myeloma. *Proceedings of the American Society of Clinical Oncology* **10:** 304 (abstract 1064).

Craig JIO, Anthony RS & Parker AC (1991) Circulating progenitor cells in myelofibrosis: the effect of recombinant α-2b interferon in vivo and in vitro. *British Journal of Haematology* **78:** 155–160.

Creasey AA, Bartholomew JC & Merigan TC (1980) Role of G_0–G_1 arrest in the inhibition of tumor cell growth by interferon. *Proceedings of the National Academy of Sciences, USA* **77:** 1471–1475.

Dai CH, Krantz SB, Dessypris EN et al (1992) Polycythemia Vera. II. Hypersensitivity of bone marrow erythroid, granulocyte–macrophage, and megacaryocyte progenitor cells to interleukin-3 and granulocyte-macrophage colony-stimulating factor. *Blood* **80:** 891–899.

De Maeyer-Guinard J & De Maeyer E (1985) Immunomodulation by interferons: recent developments. *Interferon* **6:** 69–86.

Dianzani F, Antonelli P, Amicucci P et al (1989) Low incidence of neutralising antibody formation to Interferon α-2b in human recipients. *Journal of Interferon Research* **9 (supplement 1):** 33–36.

Duncan MR & Berman B (1985) γ-interferon is the lymphokine and β-interferon the monokine responsible for inhibition of fibroblast collagen production and late but not early fibroblast proliferation. *Journal of Experimental Medicine* **162:** 516–527.

Durie BGM, Russel DH & Salmon SE (1980) Reappraisal of plateau phase in myeloma. *Lancet* **ii:** 65–67.

Edwards BS, Hawkins MJ & Borden EC (1984) Comparative in vivo and in vitro action of human NK cells by two recombinant α-interferons differing in antiviral activity. *Cancer Research* **44:** 3135–3139.

Fertsch D & Vogel SN (1984) Recombinant interferons increase macrophage Fc receptor capacity. *Journal of Immunology* **132:** 2436–2439.

Fiacchini M & Italian Cooperative Study Group on Chronic Myeloid Leukemia (1992) Prognostic study of α-interferon (IFN) treated chronic myeloid leukaemia (CML) patients. Predicting karyotypic response. *2nd International Conference on Chronic Myeloid Leukemia*, Bologna, Italy (abstract 99).

Fialkow PJ, Faguet GB, Jacobson RJ et al (1981) Evidence that essential thrombocythemia is a clonal disorder with origin in multipotent stem cell. *Blood* **58:** 916–919.

Foon KA, Malnish AE, Abrams PG et al (1986) Recombinant leukocyte A interferon therapy for advanced hairy cell leukemia. *American Journal of Medicine* **80:** 351–356.

Foon KA, Roth MS & Bunn PA (1987) Interferon therapy of non-Hodgkin's lymphoma. *Cancer* **59:** 601–604.

Freund M, von Wussow P, Dietrich H et al (1989) Recombinant human interferon (IFN) alpha-2b in chronic myelogenous leukaemia: dose dependency of response and frequency of neutralizing anti interferon antibodies. *British Journal of Hematology* **72:** 350–356.

Ganser A, Carlo-Stella C, Greher J et al (1987) Effect of recombinant interferons alpha and gamma on human bone marrow-derived megacaryocytic progenitor cells. *Blood* **70:** 1173–1179.

Gastl G, Lang A, Huber C et al (1988) Interferon alpha for idiopathic myelofibrosis. *Lancet* **i:** 765–766.

Gastl G, Aulitsky W, Tilg H et al (1990) Minimal interferon-alpha doses for hairy cell leukemia. *Blood* **75:** 812–813.

Gilbert HS (1984) Myelofibrosis revisited: characterization and classification of myelofibrosis in the setting of myeloproliferative disease. In Berk PD, Castro-Malaspina H & Wasserman LR (eds) *Myelofibrosis and biology of connective tissue*, pp 3–17. New York: Alan R Liss.

Gilbert HS, Vallabhajousula S, Phillips V et al (1989) Correction of functional asplenia in myeloproliferative disease during treatment of thrombocythemia with anagrelide. *Blood* **74 (supplement 1):** 157.

Giles FJ, Anderson CC, Grant IR et al (1990) Recombinant alpha 2a interferon an effective maintenance agent in essential thrombocythemia. *Leukemia and Lymphoma* 3: 103–107.

Gisslinger H, Chott A, Scheithauer W et al (1991) Interferon in essential thrombocythaemia. *British Journal of Haematology* 79 (supplement 1): 42–47.

Goldman JM, Gale RP, Horowitz MM et al (1988) Bone marrow transplantation for chronic myelogenous leukaemia in chronic phase: increased risk of relapse associated with T-cell depletion. *Annals of Internal Medicine* 108: 806–814.

Golomb HM, Fefer A, Golde DW et al (1991) Survival experience of 195 patients with hairy cell leukemia treated in a multi-institutional study with interferon-alfa. *Leukemia and Lymphoma* 4: 99–102.

Gresser I (1985) How does interferon inhibit tumor growth? *Interferon* 6: 93–126.

Groopman JE (1980) The pathogenesis of myelofibrosis in myeloproliferative disorders. *Annals of Internal Medicine* 92: 857–858.

Gugliotta L, Bagnara GP, Catani L et al (1988) In vivo and in vitro inhibitory effect of α-interferon on megakaryocyte colony growth in essential thrombocythemia. *British Journal of Haematology* 71: 177–181.

Guilhot F, Dreyfus B, Brizard A et al (1991) Cytogenetic remission in chronic myelogenous leukemia using interferon α 2a and hydroxyurea with or without low-dose cytosine arabinoside. *Leukemia and Lymphoma* 4: 49–55.

Gutterman JU, Blumenschein GR, Alexanian R et al (1980) Leukocyte interferon-induced tumor regression in human metastatic breast cancer, multiple myeloma, and malignant lymphoma. *Annals of Internal Medicine* 93: 399–406.

Hagenbeek A, Carde P, Somers R et al (1992) Maintenance of remission with human recombinant alpha-2 interferon (Roferon-A) in patients with stages III and IV low grade malignant non-Hodgkin's lymphoma. Results from a prospective, randomised phase III clinical trial in 331 patients. *Blood* 80 (supplement 1): 74a (abstract 288).

Hasselbach H (1988) Interferon in myelofibrosis. *Lancet* i: 355.

Higano CS, Raskind W, Singer JW et al (1992) Use of α interferon for the treatment of relapse of chronic myelogenous leukemia in chronic phase after allogeneic bone marrow transplantation. *Blood* 80: 1437–1442.

Horning SJ, Merigan TC, Krown SE et al (1985) Human interferon alpha in malignant lymphoma and Hodgkin's disease: results of the American Cancer Society trial. *Cancer* 56: 1305–1310.

Horoszewicz JS, Leong SS & Carter WS (1979) Non cycling tumor cells are sensitive targets for the antiproliferative activity of human interferon. *Science* 206: 1091–1093.

Isaacs A & Lindemann J (1957) Virus interference: The interferon. *Proceedings of the Royal Society of London (Biology)* 147: 259–267.

Itri LM, Sherman MI, Palleroni AV et al (1989) Incidence and clinical severity of neutralizing antibodies in patients receiving recombinant interferon-alpha 2a. *Journal of Interferon Research* 9 (supplement 1): 9–15.

Jacobs AD, Champlin RE & Golde DW (1985) Recombinant α-2-interferon for hairy cell leukemia. *Blood* 65: 1017–1020.

Kantarjian HM, Vellekoop L, McCredie KB et al (1985) Intensive combination chemotherapy (ROAP 10) and splenectomy in the management of chronic granulocytic leukaemia. *Journal of Clinical Oncology* 3: 192–200.

Kantarjian HM, Talpaz M, Keating M et al (1986) Therapy of philadelphia chromosome positive chronic myelogenous leukemia (CML) with initial intensive chemotherapy (DOAP) followed by maintenance with human leukocyte α interferon. *Blood* 68: 224.

Kasparu H, Bernhart M, Krieger O & Lutz D (1992) Remission may continue after termination of rIFNα-2b treatment for essential thrombocythemia. *European Journal of Haematology* 48: 33–36.

Kimci A (1987) Autocrine interferon and the suppression of the c-myc nuclear oncogene. *Interferon* 8: 86–110.

Lauria F, Foa R, Raspadori D et al (1988) Treatment of hairy cell leukemia with α interferon (α-IFN). *European Journal of Cancer and Clinical Oncology* 24: 195–200.

Lazzarino M, Vitale A, Morra E et al (1989) Interferon alpha2b as treatment for philadelphia-negative chronic myeloproliferative disorders with excessive thrombocytosis. *British Journal of Haematology* 72: 173–177.

Leavitt J, Ratanathathorn V, Ozer H et al (1987) Alfa-2b interferon in the treatment of Hodgkin's disease and non-Hodgkin's lymphoma. *Seminars in Oncology* **14** (supplement 2): 18–23.

Lee M, Kantarjian HM, Talpaz M et al (1992) Association of the responsiveness to interferon α (α-IFN) therapy with the BCR/ABL splicing patterns in philadelphia chromosome (Ph)-positive chronic myelogenous leukaemia. *Blood* **80** (supplement 1): 210a (abstract 831).

Löfwenberg E & Wahlin A (1988) Management of polycythemia vera, essential thrombocythemia and myelofibrosis with hydroxyurea. *European Journal of Hematology* **41**: 375–381.

Louie AC, Gallagher JG, Sikora K et al (1981) Follow-up observations on the effect of human leukocyte interferon in non-Hodgkin's lymphoma. *Blood* **58**: 712–718.

Mandelli F, Annino L, Cafolla A et al (1986) Hairy cell leukemia: preliminary results with alpha 2 (r) interferon. *Tumori* **72**: 153–156.

Mandelli F, Avvisati G, Amadori S et al (1990) Maintenance treatment with recombinant interferon alfa-2b in patients with multiple myeloma responding to conventional induction chemotherapy. *New England Journal of Medicine* **322**: 1430–1434.

Manoharan A (1988) Myelofibrosis: prognostic factors and treatment. *British Journal of Haematology* **69**: 295–298.

Mantovani L, Guglielmi C, Martelli M et al (1989) Recombinant alpha interferon in the treatment of low-grade non-Hodgkin's lymphoma: results of a cooperative phase II trial in 31 patients. *Haematologica* **74**: 571–575.

Martyrè MC, Magdelenat H & Calvo F (1991) Interferon-γ in vivo reverses the increased platelet levels of platelet-derived growth factor and transforming growth factor-β in patients with myelofibrosis with myeloid metaplasia. *British Journal of Haematology* **77**: 431–435.

Mazur EM, Sohl P, Newton J et al (1989) Mechanism of Anagrelide induced thrombocytopenia. *Blood* **74** (supplement 1): 32.

Mazzucconi MG, Francesconi M, Chistolini A et al (1986) Pipobroman therapy of essential thrombocythemia. *Scandinavian Journal of Haematology* **37**: 306–309.

McCarthy DM (1985) Fibrosis of the bone marrow: content and causes. *British Journal of Haematology* **59**: 1–7.

McCarthy DM, Clark J & Giles F (1991) The treatment of myelofibrosis with α-interferon. *British Journal of Haematology* **78**: 590–591.

McGlave PB, Arthur D, Miller WJ et al (1990) Autologous Transplantation for CML using marrow treated ex vivo with recombinant human Interferon-γ. *Bone Marrow Transplantation* **6**: 115–120.

Mellstedt H for the Myeloma Group of Central Sweden (MGCS) (1991) MP/α/IFN in the induction of multiple myeloma and as maintenance therapy. A randomized trial from MGCS. *Abstract of the 3rd International Workshop on Multiple Myeloma: from Biology to Therapy*. Torino, Italy: 115–116.

Mellstedt H, Ahre A, Björkholm M et al (1979) Interferon therapy in myelomatosis. *Lancet* i: 245–247.

Meloni G, De Fabritiis P, Alimena G et al (1989) Autologous bone marrow or peripheral blood stem cell transplantation for patients with chronic myelogenous leukaemia in chronic phase. *Bone Marrow Transplantation* **4** (supplement 4): 92–94.

Meyer JD, Flournay N, Sanders JE et al (1987) Prophylactic use of human leukocyte interferon after allogeneic marrow transplantation. *Annals of Internal Medicine* **107**: 809–816.

Michalevicz R, Aderka D, Frisch B & Revel M (1988) Interferon-beta induced remission in a hairy cell leukemia patient resistant to interferon-alpha. *Leukemia Research* **12**: 845–851.

Molica S & Alberti A (1990) Recombinant alpha-2a interferon in treatment of B chronic lymphocytic leukemia. A preliminary report with emphasis on previously untreated patients in early stage of disease. *Haematologica* **75**: 75–78.

Molinas FC, Wietzerbin J & Falcoff E (1987) Human platelets possess receptors for a limphokine: demonstration of high specific receptors for Hu IFN-γ. *Journal of Immunology* **138**: 802–806.

Montuoro A, De Rosa L, De Blasio A et al (1990) Alpha 2a interferon-melphalan/prednisone versus melphalan/prednisone in previously untreated patients with multiple myeloma. *British Journal of Haematology* **76**: 365–368.

Moormeier J, Ratain MJ, Westbrook CA et al (1989) Low dose interferon in the treatment of hairy cell leukemia. *Journal of the National Cancer Institute* **81**: 1172–1174.

Morra E, Lazzarino M, Alimena G et al (1992) The role of Interferon in the treatment of chronic myelogenous leukaemia: results and prospects. *Leukemia and Lymphoma* **6:** 305–315.

Murphy S, Iland H, Rosenthal D et al (1986) Essential thrombocythemia: an interim report from the Polycytemia Vera Study Group. *Seminars in Hematology* **23:** 177–182.

Nicolas JF, Balblanc JC, Frappaz A et al (1989) Treatment of cutaneouis T-cell lymphoma with intermediate doses of interferon alpha-2a. *Dermatologica* **179:** 34–37.

O'Connell MJ, Colgan JP, Oken MM et al (1986) Clinical trial of recombinant leukocyte A interferon as initial therapy for favorable histology non-Hodgkin's lymphomas and chronic lymphocytic leukemia: an Eastern Cooperative Oncology Group pilot study. *Journal of Clinical Oncology* **4:** 128–136.

Ochs J, Abromowitch M, Rudnick S & Murphy SB (1986) Phase I-II study of recombinant alpha-2 interferon against advanced leukemia and lymphoma in children. *Journal of Clinical Oncology* **4:** 883–887.

Ochs J, Brecher ML, Mahoney D et al (1991) Recombinant interferon alfa given before and in combination with standard chemotherapy in children with acute lymphoblastic leukemia in first marrow relapse: a Pediatric Oncology Group pilot study. *Journal of Clinical Oncology* **9:** 777–782.

Oken MM, Kyle RA, Greipp PR et al (1990) Chemotherapy plus interferon (r IFN a2) in the treatment of multiple myeloma. *Proceedings of the American Society of Clinical Oncology* **9:** 288 (abstract 1116).

Olsen EA, Rosen ST, Vollmer RT et al (1989) Interferon alpha-2a in the treatment of cutaneous T-cell lymphoma. *Journal of the American Academy of Dermatology* **20:** 395–407.

Opalka B, Wandl UB, Becher R et al (1991) Minimal residual disease in patients with chronic myelogenous leukaemia undergoing long-term treatment with recombinant Interferon α-2b alone or in combination with Interferon-γ. *Blood* **78:** 2188–2193.

Ozer H, George S, Pettenati M et al (1992) Subcutaneous α-interferon (α-IFN) in untreated chronic phase philadelphia chromosome positive (Ph+) chronic myelogenous leukemia (CML): no evidence for significant improvement in response duration or survival (CALGB 8583). *Blood* **80 (supplement 1):** 358a (abstract 1422).

Pangalis GA & Griva E (1988) Recombinant alfa-2b-interferon therapy in untreated, stages A and B chronic lymphocytic leukemia. *Cancer* **61:** 869–872.

Papa G, Tura S, Mandelli F et al (1991) Is interferon alpha in cutaneous T-cell lymphoma a treatment of choice? *British Journal of Haematology* **79 (supplement 1):** 48–51.

Parmeggiani L, Ferrant A, Rodhain J et al (1987) Alpha-interferon in the treatment of symptomatic myelofibrosis with myeloid metaplasia. *European Journal of Haematology* **39:** 228–232.

Pearson TC (1991) Primary thrombocythaemia: diagnosis and management. *British Journal of Haematology* **78:** 145–148.

Peest D, Deicher H, Coldewey R et al (1990) Melphalan and prednisone (MP) versus vincristine, BCNU, adriamycin, melphalan and dexamethasone (VBAMDex) induction chemotherapy and interferon maintenance treatment in multiple myeloma. Current results of a multicenter trial. *Onkologie* **13:** 458–460.

Price CGA, Rohatiner AZS & Steward W (1991) Interferon-a2b in the treatment of follicular lymphoma: preliminary results of a trial in progress. *Annals of Oncology* **2 (supplement 2):** 141–145.

Quesada JR, Hawkins M, Hornig S et al (1984a) Collaborative phase I-II study of recombinant DNA-produced leukocyte interferon (clone A) in metastatic breast cancer, malignant lymphoma, and multiple myeloma. *American Journal of Medicine* **77:** 427–432.

Quesada JR, Reuben J, Manning JT et al (1984b) Alpha-interferon for induction of remission in hairy cell leukemia. *New England Journal of Medicine* **310:** 15–18.

Quesada JR, Alexanian R, Kurzrock R et al (1988) Recombinant interferon gamma in hairy cell leukemia, multiple myeloma, and Waldenström's macroglobulinemia. *American Journal of Hematology* **29:** 1–4.

Ratain MJ, Golomb HM, Vardiman JW et al (1988) Relapse after interferon alpha-2b therapy for hairy cell leukemia: analysis of prognostic variables. *Journal of Clinical Oncology* **6:** 1714–1721.

Reiffers J, Trouette T, Marit G et al (1991) Autologous blood stem cell transplantation for chronic granulocytic leukemia in transformation: a report of 47 cases. *British Journal of Haematology* **77:** 339–345.

Revel M, Kimci A & Shulman L (1980) Role of interferon-induced enzymes in the antiviral and antimitogenic effects of interferon. *Annals of the New York Academy of Sciences* **350:** 459–473.

Rinne E, Forstrom L & Lassus A (1989) Interferon alpha-2a in the treatment of six patients of cutaneous T-cell lymphoma. *Journal of Investigative Dermatology* **93:** 572–573.

Rozman C, Montserrat E, Viñolas N et al (1988) Recombinant α2-interferon in treatment of B chronic lymphocytic leukemia in early stages. *Blood* **71:** 1295–1298.

Salmon SE & Crowley J (1992) Impact of glucocorticoids (GC) and interferon (IFN) on outcome in multiple myeloma. *Proceedings of the American Society of Clinical Oncology* **11:** 316 (abstract 1069).

Samid D, Chang EH & Friedman RM (1985) Development of transformed phenotype induced by a human RAS oncogene is inhibited by interferon. *Biochemical and Biophysical Research Communications* **126:** 509–516.

Sato Y, Suda T, Suda J et al (1986) Multilineage expression of haematopoietic precursors with an abnormal clone in idiopathic myelofibrosis. *British Journal of Haematology* **64:** 657–667.

Seewann HL, Gastl G, Lang A et al (1988) Interferon alpha 2 in the treatment of idiopathic myelofibrosis. *Blut* **56:** 161–163.

Senn CC (1984) Biochemical pathways in interferon action. *Pharmacology and Therapeutic* **24:** 235–257.

Silver RT (1990) A new treatment for polycythemia vera: recombinant interferon alpha. *Blood* **76:** 664–665.

Silverstein MN, Petitt RM, Solberg LA et al (1988) Anagrelide: a new drug for treating thrombocytosis. *New England Journal of Medicine* **318:** 1292–1294.

Smalley RV, Andersen JW, Hawkins MJ et al (1992) Interferon alfa combined with cytotoxic chemotherapy for patients with non-Hodgkin's lymphoma. *New England Journal of Medicine* **327:** 1336–1341.

Sokal JE, Baccarani M, Tura S et al (1984) Prognostic discrimination in good-risk chronic granulocytic leukemia. *Blood* **63:** 789–799.

Solal-Celigny P, Le Page E, Brousse N et al (1991) Alpha-interferon (IF) and chemotherapy in patients (pts) with high-tumor burden follicular lymphoma (FL): preliminary results of the 'Groupe d'Etude des Lymphomas Folliculaires' (GELF). *Proceedings of the American Society of Clinical Oncology* **10:** 275 (abstract 955).

Stewart WE II, Blalock JE, Burke DC et al (1980) Interferon nomenclature. *Journal of Immunology* **125:** 2353.

Talpaz M, McCredie B, Mavligit GM et al (1983) Leucocyte interferon induced myeloid cytoreduction in chronic myelogenous leukaemia. *Blood* **62:** 689–692.

Talpaz M, Kantarjian H, McCredie K et al (1986) Hematologic remission and cytogenetic improvement induced by recombinant human Interferon α a in chronic myelogenous leukaemia. *New England Journal of Medicine* **314:** 1065–1069.

Talpaz M, Kantarjian H, Kurzrock R et al (1991) Interferon α produces substained cytogenetic responses in chronic myelogenous leukemia philadelphia chromosome positive patients. *Annals of Internal Medicine* **114:** 532–538.

Thompson JA, Kidd P, Rubin E & Fefer A (1989) Very low dose alpha-2b interferon for the treatment of hairy cell leukemia. *Blood* **73:** 1440–1443.

Tura S, Mazza P, Zinzani PL et al (1987) Alpha recombinant interferon in the treatment of mycosis fungoides. *Haematologica* **72:** 337–340.

Turri D, Mitra ME, Di Trapani R et al (1991) Alpha-interferon in polycythemia vera and essential thrombocytemia. *Haematologica* **76:** 75–77.

Van der Molen LA, Steis RG, Duffey PL et al (1990) Low- versus high-dose interferon alfa-2a in relapsed indolent non-Hodgkin's lymphoma. *Journal of the National Cancer Institute* **82:** 235–238.

Wadenvik H, Kutti J, Börje R et al (1991) The effect of α-interferon on bone marrow megakaryocytes and platelet production rate in essential thrombocythemia. *Blood* **77:** 2103–2108.

Westin J, Cortelezzi A, Hjort M et al (1991) Interferon therapy during the plateau phase of multiple myeloma: an update of a Swedish multicenter study. *3rd International Workshop on Multiple Myeloma: 'From Biology to Therapy'*, Torino, Italy (abstract 113–114).

Wickramashinghe SN, Peart S & Gill DS (1987) Alpha interferon in primary idiopathic myelofibrosis. *Lancet* **ii:** 1524–1525.

Ziegler-Heitbrock HWL, Schlag R, Flieger D & Thiel E (1989) Favorable response of early stage B CLL patients to treatment with IFN-α_2. *Blood* **73:** 1426–1430.

Zuckerman KS, Bagby GC Jr, Emanuel PD & Shafer AI (1992) Myeloprolipherative disorders. In McArthur JR & Menitove JE (eds) Hematology 1992. Education Program American Society of Hematology, pp 7–17.

Zuffa E and the Italian Cooperative Study Group on Chronic Myeloid Leukemia (1992) The Italian prospective study of Interferon-α (Roferon A) vs chemotherapy: karyotypic response and survival at 4 years. *2nd International Conference on Chronic Myeloid Leukemia*, Bologna, Italy (abstract 163).

6

Haematological applications of interleukin-2
and other immunostimulatory cytokines

MALCOLM K. BRENNER

INTRODUCTION

Although almost every cytokine described to date may directly or indirectly
stimulate part or all of the immune system, this chapter will focus on IL-2, IL-4
and IL-12, which have attracted the greatest clinical interest for their
immunostimulatory properties. These cytokines may benefit haematological
practice in a number of ways. They may enhance or induce host defences
against malignancy, and may restore immune function after ablative procedures such as bone marrow transplantation, thereby reducing morbidity
and mortality from infection. They may also serve as carrier molecules that
guide cytotoxins to malignant cells bearing cytokine receptors. Finally,
current data suggest that at least one of these immunostimulatory cytokines
can directly impair leukaemic blast cell survival.

Until recently, the therapeutic effects of these cytokines could be
analysed in vivo only by administering the recombinant proteins. In recent
gene transfer studies, however, effector lymphocytes or tumour cells are
transduced ex vivo with cytokine genes and reinfused. This novel approach
is discussed in detail in Chapter 7; this chapter will address only the clinical
applications of immunostimulatory cytokine infusion. We will begin by
discussing the evidence that immunostimulation can be of value in haematological disease.

Evidence that the immune system may control haematological malignancy

In a number of animal models, major histocompatibility complex (MHC)-
restricted antigen-specific T lymphocytes have provided protection against
transplantable leukaemias (Cheever et al, 1986). However, these effects
may not be clinically relevant to human leukaemia unless the leukaemic cells
universally express unique antigens. In addition, these antigens should also
be critical to the leukaemic behaviour of the cell, otherwise clonal escape
from specific cytotoxic T cells might occur. Over the past few years, a
substantial proportion of leukaemias and lymphomas have been found to
produce proteins which are both unique and apparently important in the
leukaemic process. These include the fusion proteins formed by trans-
located genes and the abnormal oncogenes produced following point

116   M. K. BRENNER

mutations in the encoding genes (Table 1) (Ben-Neriah et al, 1986; Chan et
al, 1987; Moller et al, 1988; Browett and Norton, 1989; de The et al, 1990;
Ridge et al, 1990; Platsoucas, 1991). Both types of protein contain unique
peptide sequences that could potentially be recognized by antigen-specific T
lymphocyte clones, but only if these peptides were processed and presented
by leukaemic cells.

Table 1. Fusion proteins and mutant oncogenes as immune targets.

(a) *Fusion proteins*

Lymphoid	Translocation	Fusion protein
B-lineage ALL	t(9;22)(q34;q11)	*bcr-abl*
	t(1;19)(q23;p13)	E2A-PBX1
	t(4;11)(q23;p13)	ALL1-AF4
	t(11;19)(q23;p13)	ENL-ALL1
	t(8;14)(p24;q32.3)	IgH-*c-myc*
T-lineage ALL	t(1;14)(q34;q11)	*tal*-TCR delta
	t(10;14)(q24;q11)	TCL1-TCR delta
	t(11;14)(p13;q11)	T-ALL^bcr^-TCR delta
NHL	Ins(2;2)(p13;p11.2–14)	REL/NRG

Myeloid	Translocation	Fusion protein
AML/CML	t(9;22) CML	bcr-abl
	t(8;21) AML M2	AML1/ETO
	t(15;17) AML M3	RAR/MYL
	t(6;9) AML	dek/can
	t(3;5) AML	NPM/ARC

(b) *Mutant oncogenes*

Lymphoid, myeloid

ras
FMS
p53

Data from Sosman et al (1989) suggest that leukaemia-specific antigens
may indeed appear on leukaemia cell surfaces, since it is possible to generate
CD3+, CD4+ T-cell clones that react with allogeneic ALL cells but not with
remission lymphocytes from the same patient. These clones appear to
recognize an antigen expressed on leukaemic but not on normal cells.
Certainly, if such mutant proteins are presented by leukaemic cells, data
from animal models demonstrate that they can be distinguished from the
wild type products by antigen-specific T cells. For example, ras-derived
peptides have been synthesized in which valine or arginine was substituted
for glycine at residue 12, a substitution associated with transforming ability
in the intact protein. MHC-restricted CD4+ T-cell lines generated in vivo
and in vitro proliferated in response to mutant peptide but had no response
to wild-type peptide (Jung and Schluesner, 1991; Peace et al, 1991). Using a

similar approach, the bcr-abl junctional peptide has subsequently been shown to recruit specific T cells when injected into mice.

A second immune-mediated anti-leukaemia mechanism (Karre et al, 1980) involves natural killer (NK) cells, lymphocytes which may be T-cell receptor (CD3) positive or negative, but which are not MHC-restricted in their cytotoxic activity (Herberman and Ortaldo, 1981). These cells are particularly numerous and active as activated killer (AK) cells during the first few weeks following autologous or allogeneic BMT (Karre et al, 1980; Brenner et al, 1986) or following administration of cytokines such as IL-2 (Anderson et al, 1988; Rosenberg et al, 1988; Smith, 1988; Gottlieb et al, 1989). In vitro, they can be shown to selectively inhibit leukaemic clonal growth, while sparing normal progenitor cells. This selection may occur through recognition of differences in cellular superantigen expression by the CD3+ subset of NK/AK cells (Fisch et al, 1990a,b), or because of differences in expression of the cell adhesion molecules necessary for effector-target cell interaction (Davignon et al, 1981; Simmons et al, 1988; Timonen, 1990; Oblakowski et al, 1991). As we learn more about other cell surface molecules targeted by NK cells, we may well discern other differences in expression between normal and malignant cells, which permit selective recognition and killing (Ciccone et al, 1990a,b).

Regardless of the effector mechanisms used, there is now no doubt that the immune system has the potential to eradicate residual leukaemia and lymphoma in humans. This potential is demonstrated by the readily detectable graft-versus-leukemia (GVL) effect exerted by allogeneic bone marrow following transplantation. GVL activity has been shown in three ways (Bortin et al, 1979; Barrett et al, 1989; International Bone Marrow Transplant Registry, 1989; Horowitz et al, 1990): (i) patients who suffer from graft-versus-host disease (GVHD) are less likely than others to relapse (Weiden et al, 1979, 1981; Weisdorf et al, 1987; Apperley et al, 1988; Horowitz et al, 1990; Ferrara et al, 1991); (ii) patients receiving a T-lymphocyte depleted bone marrow transplant—in whom the risk of GVHD is very low—may have a higher risk of relapse (Goldman et al, 1988; Horowitz et al, 1990); (iii) recipients of syngeneic (identical twin) allograft have a higher risk of relapse than recipients of HLA-identical sibling grafts (International Bone Marrow Transplant Registry, 1989; Horowitz et al, 1990).

Taken together, these data indicate that the immune system can contribute to the eradication of haematological malignancy in man, and they support the further exploration of immunomodulatory agents in this setting.

Immunostimulation after ablative therapy

Ablative therapy is always followed by a degree of cellular and humoral immunocompromise. Infections resulting from this state are a major cause of BMT failure. Full recovery of immune function may be delayed a year or more after transplantation of MHC-identical sibling marrow, while recipients of MHC mismatched or unrelated donor transplants suffer from an even more prolonged and profound immunosuppression. Up to 40% of these patients die from intercurrent viral infection. As unrelated/mismatched donor bone marrow transplantation becomes more widespread, the search for agents that will accelerate immune recovery becomes ever more urgent. It is likely that the cytokines described in this chapter will make a significant contribution.

INTERLEUKIN-2 (IL-2)

Pre-clinical studies

Effects on the immune system

IL-2 was originally described as a growth factor for MHC-restricted, antigen-specific T lymphocytes. It also enhances non-specific cytotoxic mechanisms mediated by MHC-unrestricted NK lymphocytes (Rosenberg, 1988, 1991) and monocytes (Malkovsky et al, 1987), induces these cells to proliferate, and also directly modifies the growth and development of B lymphocytes. In addition to these direct effects, IL-2 induces the release of a large number of secondary cytokines (Heslop et al, 1989, 1991) from T lymphocytes and NK cells. All of these mechanisms affect the overall impact of IL-2 administration on normal and malignant haematopoietic tissue and have been extensively documented elsewhere (Rosenberg et al, 1988).

Effects on normal haematopoiesis

In vitro, IL-2 demonstrates a number of different and apparently opposing effects on normal haematopoiesis. These effects may be mediated directly or indirectly.

Direct effects. Unlike lymphoid cells, most haematopoietic progenitor cells do not express IL-2 receptors and have generally not been found to proliferate in response to IL-2 (Burdach and Levitt, 1987; Burdach et al, 1987). However, it has been reported that the earlier GEMM precursor cells are positive for IL-2 receptor β chain (p55) and proliferate in response to IL-2; the contribution of secondary cytokines to this effect has not been fully excluded (Michalevicz et al, 1988). In contrast to this stimulatory effect, IL-2 in vitro may directly inhibit the growth of marrow fibroblasts (MacDonald et al, 1990), an action that would tend to impair progenitor cell growth.

Indirect effects via lymphoid cells. IL-2 activates T cells and NK cells and stimulates their expansion. Both cellular subsets can support or impair the growth of haematopoietic progenitor cells in vitro, depending on the culture system used. Growth is modulated not only by direct cell contact, but also by the release of cytokines (see below) (Gottlieb et al, 1989; Savary and Lotzova, 1990).

Indirect effects via secondary cytokine release. IL-2 induces the release of cytokines that stimulate (IL-3, IL-5, GM-CSF) or inhibit (TNF, IFN-γ) haematopoiesis in vitro (Heslop et al, 1989, 1991; Gottlieb et al, 1989; Savary and Lotzova, 1990). Because the net effect of these cytokines depends entirely on the precise characteristics of the model system used, the in vivo responses of any given patient group cannot be predicted on the basis of these studies.

Effects on haemopoietic malignancy

IL-2, like other immunostimulatory cytokines, may have both beneficial and adverse effects on tumour cell growth in vitro. These effects may be mediated directly by induction of a cellular immune response, or indirectly by induction of secondary cytokine release (Figure 1).

Beneficial effects. IL-2 increases antigen-specific T-cell and NK/AK-cell cytotoxic effector function. Cells activated in this way can directly kill or inhibit the growth of leukaemic blast cells (Farrar et al, 1982; Oshimi et al, 1986; Adler et al, 1988; Heslop et al, 1989; Savary and Lotzova, 1990). Amongst the secondary cytokines induced by IL-2 are TNF and IFN-γ. These secondary cytokines have three effects. They have a direct cytotoxic and anti-proliferative effect on leukaemic cells (Heslop et al, 1989a,b); they activate NK and AK effector cells (Heslop et al, 1989a,b); and finally they render tumour cells more susceptible to AK/NK killing, in part by enhancing expression of cell adhesion molecules (Heslop et al, 1989; Stotter et al, 1989; Olive et al, 1991).

Adverse effects. The possible benefits of IL-2 could be neutralized if the agent itself, or the cytokines it induced, were able to act as growth factors for leukaemic cells. To demonstrate that IL-2 is a direct growth factor requires that two criteria be met. The first is that receptors for the cytokine should be present on the malignant cell, and the second is that the cell should proliferate in the presence of the factor, or at least enter the cell cycle. There seems little doubt that a proportion of patients with acute lymphoblastic leukaemia (ALL) and lymphoma have malignant clones whose progeny fulfil both these requirements, although the precise proportion remains controversial (Foa et al, 1990). For acute myeloblastic leukaemia (AML), there is much less certainty. While cells from some patients, particularly those with the FAB M4/5 subtypes, have been shown to express either the low-affinity p55 (Armitage et al, 1986) or the intermediate-affinity p75 (Rosolen et al, 1989) component of the IL-2 receptor, there is no convincing evidence that AML blasts express both IL-2 receptor chains. Since both chains are required to form a high-affinity binding site, it is unlikely that AML blasts would effectively compete for IL-2 at the low systemic concentrations achieved during infusion. None the less, in vitro some AML blasts undergo a degree of DNA synthesis in the presence of IL-2 at high concentrations (Carron and Cawley, 1990; Tanaka, 1991). Even in these cases, much of the apparent response may be explained by lymphocyte contamination. Of more potential concern is the ability of IL-2 to induce myeloid

1. Direct

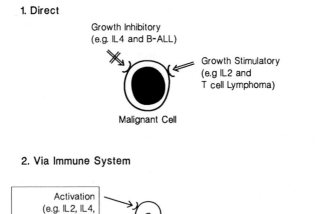

2. Via Immune System

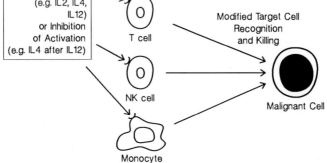

3. Via Secondary Cytokines

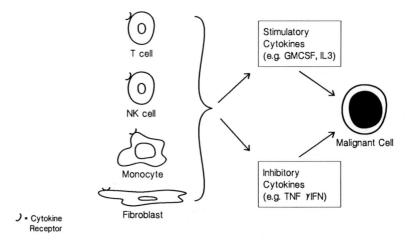

Figure 1. Examples of effects of immunostimulatory cytokines on malignant cells.

growth factor secretion by T cells. These myeloid factors include IL-3, GM-CSF and IL-5, all of which may promote the growth of myeloid leukaemias (Delwel et al, 1988).

These concerns notwithstanding, IL-2 has shown significant anti-neoplastic activity in a wide variety of murine leukaemia and lymphoma models (Talmadge et al, 1987; Foa et al, 1990; Slavin et al, 1990), supporting its use in human clinical studies.

Clinical uses of IL-2 in malignant haematological disease

Conventional investigation of anti-neoplastic drugs follows an established routine. It begins with phase I dose escalation studies in a range of advanced cancers, to determine a maximum tolerated dose (MTD). In a phase II study, this fixed dose is given to patients with a more restricted range of conditions and evidence of response is sought. In a phase III study, the responses of a larger number of patients may be compared in a randomized trial with those of a group receiving an alternative therapy. This routine was used to study the effects of IL-2 in solid tumours, but for a variety of reasons may be inappropriate for investigation of immunomodulators in general and IL-2 in particular. First, the effects of immunomodulators may depend on duration of administration as much as on the dose given; a maximum tolerated dose may be far beyond the dose of drug that produces maximum immunomodulation, and may only be tolerable in courses too short for the immune system to produce its optimum long-term benefits. Second, the anti-neoplastic activity of IL-2 is almost certainly contingent on its immunomodulatory capacity. In patients with bulky cancer, the immune system will be at a numerical disadvantage compared to malignant cells. Finally, in patients who have extensive disease and who have received intensive prior treatment, cytotoxic effector cells may be impaired in their ability to respond to IL-2 (Foa et al, 1991).

Recent interest, particularly in haematological malignancy, has therefore focused on the use of IL-2 in the setting of minimal residual disease (MRD), in which IL-2 is often given for longer periods in lower doses. In the case of MRD, the ratio of effector lymphocytes to malignant targets would most favour the effector cells, providing the optimum setting for a successful immunological assault. However, in MRD it is considerably harder to study the efficacy of any putative anti-neoplastic drug. Because there is no measurable disease, there can be no immediate assessment of the effect of different doses or dose regimens; large, randomized, long-term studies are required to demonstrate any beneficial effects with certainty. An additional concern about using IL-2 in MRD is that patients will have recently received high-dose chemotherapy. IL-2 infused at immunomodulatory doses is toxic to many of the same organs damaged by preparative regimens for BMT (Rosenberg et al, 1988; Smith, 1988), and therefore may cause unacceptable toxicity in conjunction with BMT/intensive chemotherapy. Because of this uncertainty about the optimum timing and dosage of IL-2 administration, the drug has been used in a variety of treatment regimens, both for relapsed and minimal residual disease states.

122   M. K. BRENNER

Bulky disease

Acute lymphoblastic leukaemia. Although patients with relapsed ALL have been treated with high-dose IL-2, there are no published reports of any responses.

Acute myeloblastic leukaemia. Responses have been observed in two patients with AML in early relapse who had less than 15% blasts in the marrow (Foa et al, 1990). Maraninchi et al (1991) reported marrow responses (2 complete, 1 partial) to IL-2 infusion in 3 of 10 relapsed patients. In all three, however, the response was brief. Interestingly, blast cells in the peripheral blood were affected more profoundly, and in a higher proportion of patients, then were marrow blasts.

Myeloma. High serum levels of IL-2 predict prolonged survival in multiple myeloma (Cimino et al, 1990) and IL-2-activated lymphocytes can kill autologous myeloma cells (Bianchi et al, 1989; Peest et al, 1989). Although no large series of myeloma patients has been reported, a number of early phase I studies of IL-2 administration have included myeloma patients. Gottlieb et al (1990) reported that of four myeloma patients who received IL-2 after autologous BMT, two had measurable disease and in both patients, the disease remained stable for more than 2 years after IL-2 treatment.

Non-Hodgkin lymphoma. Even though many patients' non-Hodgkin lymphoma cells express IL-2 receptors, there have been a number of phase I/II studies of IL-2, with or without LAK cells, in advanced disease. These studies have included patients with HIV-related lymphoma (Malkovska and Sondel, 1990; Rubin et al, 1990; Bernstein et al, 1991; Duggan et al, 1992; Mazza et al, 1992). Responses have been poor overall, with fewer than 10% of patients achieving complete remission, and about 20% showing partial response or disease stabilization. It has been suggested that the combination of IL-2 and LAK cell therapy is more effective than IL-2 alone, but the numbers of treated patients are too small to allow conclusions. Efforts have been made to reduce the toxicity of IL-2 infusions by using endolymphatic delivery of the drug, but it is too early to assess the value of this approach (Galvani et al, 1992).

Hodgkin lymphoma. Fewer patients with Hodgkin than with non-Hodgkin lymphoma have responded significantly to IL-2 +/- LAK cell infusion. Overall there is a 10–20% partial response rate, usually followed by rapid tumour regrowth (Paciucci et al, 1989; Bernstein et al, 1991; Tourani et al, 1991; Gisselbrecht et al, 1992). Despite this limited success, interest in using IL-2 to treat Hodgkin lymphoma has been rekindled by the detection of Epstein–Barr virus (EBV) proteins and DNA in the Reed–Sternberg cells of this disease. If EBV contributes significantly to this disease, then malignant cells that express EBV antigens may be a readily recognizable target for IL-2 stimulated cytotoxic T lymphocytes (Young and Rowe, 1992; Deacon et al, 1993). As yet, no clinical data are available.

Minimal residual disease

IL-2 administration has been studied most often in haematological malignancies to treat minimal residual disease following chemotherapy or autologous bone marrow transplantation. Attempts have been made to use high-dose IL-2, after **allogeneic** BMT, to increase the potency of any graft versus leukaemia activity. These have been constrained by a concern that IL-2 might augment the growth of alloreactive donor T lymphocytes and so exacerbate graft vs. host disease (GVHD) (Gottlieb et al, 1989a,b; Blaise et al, 1990).

The first studies of IL-2 in minimal residual leukaemia began in early 1987. In a phase I–II trial, escalating doses of IL-2 were given to patients with AML in remission after chemotherapy or autologous BMT. The aim was to see whether the drug could be tolerated in doses which would produce measurable immunomodulation.

Toxicity. In general, IL-2 was well tolerated when given as three 5-day courses at doses between 200 and $800\,\mu g\,m^{-2}$ per day (Gottlieb et al, 1989a,b). Almost all patients developed fever $> 38°C$ and nausea, and about half become significantly but transiently hypotensive. No patient needed treatment on an intensive therapy unit. However, the first two patients received 10-day infusions which were poorly tolerated. Both patients developed hypotension; one developed severe bronchospasm, and the other developed an interstitial pneumonitis that progressed to a fatal outcome despite withdrawal of the IL-2.

Effects on the immune system. At the above doses, IL-2 produced a high level of immune modulation characterized by increased numbers of CD56+, CD16+ or CD8+ AK cells (Gottlieb et al, 1989a,b). There was increased direct cytotoxicity to EBV-infected cells, but not to target cells infected with CMV, another herpes virus (Duncombe et al, 1992). More importantly, perhaps, there was a substantial increase in the number and activity of cells able to inhibit the clonogenic growth of leukaemic blasts (Gottlieb et al, 1989a,b). Leukaemic colony and cluster formation were inhibited by up to 95%. It was also possible to augment production of the anti-leukaemic/anti-viral cytokines TNF and IFN-γ (Heslop et al, 1989a). Serum levels of IFN-γ rose sharply during infusion of IL-2, and although a rise in serum TNF could not be detected, CD16+ and CD3+ lymphocytes obtained from these patients during IL-2 infusion showed a greatly increased production of TNF in culture.

Effect of IL-2 infusion on normal haematopoiesis. One residual concern about IL-2 infusion was that the cytokines induced, particularly TNF and IFN-γ would damage the engrafting normal progenitor cells as well as inhibit the growth of malignant myeloid progenitor cells. In fact, the neutrophil count rose significantly during IL-2 infusion, an effect that could not be attributed entirely to demargination. IL-2 also induced haematopoietic growth factors, so that IL-3 and GM-CSF could both be detected in circulating lymphoid cells as transcripts and as proteins. There was also a rise in serum GM-CSF during infusion (Heslop et al, 1991). Despite production of IL-3, however, platelet levels fell during IL-2 infusion, perhaps due to increased consumption mediated by the effects of TNF on vascular endothelium (Bauer et al, 1989).

Effect on outcome. At follow-up (Hamon et al, 1993), six of seven patients who received IL-2 after autologous BMT were disease free at 21–58 months. This early phase I study obviously contains too few patients to allow firm conclusions, but the results are at least encouraging.

Other MRD studies. More recent trials of IL-2 infusions in haematological malignancy have produced safety and immunological efficacy data comparable to those described above (Blaise et al, 1990; Foa et al, 1991; Higuchi et al, 1991; Lotzova et al, 1991; MacDonald et al, 1991; Olive et al, 1991; Soiffer et al, 1992). Only in those studies in which IL-2 was given in higher doses immediately after BMT was there an unacceptably high level of toxicity. For example, Higuchi et al (1991) gave escalating induction doses of IL-2 for 5 days followed by fixed maintenance doses for 10 days. They treated 16 patients who had received autologous BMT for AML, ALL, lymphoma or myelomatosis 14–91 days previously. The maximum tolerated induction dose was $3 \times 10^6 \, U \, m^{-2}$ per day, with hypotension and thrombocytopenia as the dose-limiting toxicities. All patients tolerated the maintenance dose well and the desired increases in CD16+, CD56+ NK and AK cell numbers and activity were observed. Similarly, Blaise et al (1993) gave IL-2 to 16 patients with AML and 28 with ALL following autologous bone marrow transplantation. The IL-2 was given over a 2-month period up to a total mean dose of $120 \, U \, m^{-2}$ per patient. Five of the 16 AML patients (27%) and 15 of the 28 ALL patients (52%) have relapsed at 2 years.

Low dose IL-2 in MRD. Because the effects of IL-2 may depend on the duration of administration as well as on the dose intensity, the effects of long-term, low-dose IL-2 have been studied. At $2 \times 10^5 \, U \, m^{-2}$ per day, IL-2 was well tolerated as a 90-day continuous infusion through a Hickman catheter (Soiffer et al, 1992). There was mild impairment of platelet recovery but no effect on neutrophils or haemoglobin levels. A five- to fortyfold increase in NK cells, which phenotypically were predominantly CD56+, CD13+ and CD3−, was observed. Related studies using low-dose subcutaneous IL-2 administration after high-dose IL-2 infusion (Higuchi et al, 1991) have produced similar results. Importantly, low-dose IL-2 therapy was well tolerated after allogeneic BMT in these studies (Soiffer et al, 1992) and did not induce GVHD. Long-term, low-dose administration of IL-2 may therefore allow the potentially beneficial effects of IL-2 to be produced and maintained with minimal adverse effects (see also 'Cytokine combinations', below).

IL-2 and LAK cells in MRD patients. Attempts have also been made to combine IL-2 infusion with LAK cell therapy (Benyunes et al, 1993) immediately after BMT or chemotherapy. Unfortunately, the approach has proved technically difficult since preparation of adequate numbers of LAK cells by apheresis produces severe thrombocytopenia.

Use of IL-2 as purging agent. In most studies of IL-2 in minimal residual leukaemia, the drug has been administered to the patients; however, efforts have also been made to use the cytokine to treat marrow ex vivo as a form of immunological purging (Charak et al, 1991; Gambacorti-Passerini et al, 1991). In a study by Klingemann et al (1993), 12 patients with AML in remission received marrow purged by culturing for 8 days in the presence of $1000\,\mathrm{IU\,m^{-1}}$ IL-2. The marrow was then re-infused, and the patients received subcutaneous IL-2 (2–$6 \times 10^5\,\mathrm{U\,m^{-2}}$) for 7 days, in an attempt to maintain the activity of the transferred cytotoxic effector cells. The therapy was well tolerated, but delayed engraftment—particularly of platelets—was a major adverse event (ANC $<0.5 \times 10^9 \mathrm{l}^{-1}$ mean 49 days, range 20–71: Platelets $<20 \times 10^9 \mathrm{l}^{-1}$ mean 98 days, range 58–>380). This problem may be overcome by including peripheral blood stem cells with the infused marrow. Two patients have relapsed and eight remain well at up to 22 months.

Can IL-2 promote leukaemic cell growth?

Because of reports that IL-2 may induce leukaemic cell growth either directly or through the induction of secondary cytokines (Armitage et al, 1986; Delwel et al, 1988; Carron et al, 1990; Foa et al, 1990a; Tanaka, 1991) there has been concern that therapy may promote relapse. MacDonald et al (1990) reported that in one study, four of nine patients with AML M4/5 subsequently relapsed with cells expressing the low affinity (β chain) IL-2 receptor. Overall, however, there has been no evidence to support the contention that IL-2 has a leukaemia-promoting action.

Need for randomized studies

The phase I–II studies to date have shown that IL-2 can be given safely after autologous BMT and will induce or enhance effector mechanisms that are predicted to exert an antineoplastic effect. Although none of these studies were designed to provide firm conclusions about clinical benefit, the results in ALL and AML have been sufficiently encouraging to foster a multicentre randomized study to determine definitively whether IL-2 can reduce relapse risk. By mid-1993, 101 AML and 69 ALL patients had been randomized on this study to receive IL-2 or no further therapy following autologous BMT. At this two-year point, investigation of ALL patients has stopped, since no discernible advantage was detected. Accrual of AML patients, however, will continue.

Additional applications of IL-2 in haematological disease

Use of IL-2 to induce tolerance after BMT

If lethally irradiated mice receiving allogeneic T-cell-replete BMT are given IL-2 after engraftment, then GVHD is accelerated and intensified

(Malkovsky et al, 1986). But if the mice are simultaneously given syngeneic T-cell-depleted marrow, then GVHD is absent—even when donor and recipient are MHC disparate, and even though there is full donor engraftment (Sykes et al, 1990a). Moreover, the new graft retains 'GVL' activity since it can eradicate leukaemic cells given at the same time (Sykes et al, 1990b). Although the mechanism for this effect has not been established, it is likely that the proliferating mature donor T cells are anergized by exposure to recipient immune system cells and high doses of IL-2. That this anergy is specific is demonstrated by the capacity of T cells in the incoming immune system to prevent engraftment of a transplantable leukaemia.

If this approach can be demonstrated to be safe and effective in larger animals it is reasonable to hope that we may be able to use IL-2 to prevent GVHD even after MHC non-identical BMT and yet retain or even enhance both the MHC restricted and non-restricted GVL effects described previously.

Use of IL-2 to enhance immune recovery

It had been hoped that IL-2 would accelerate the recovery of a functional immune system after ablative therapies (Bosly et al, 1992). However, while IL-2 may increase the number and activity of MHC unrestricted effector cells, there are no data to suggest that there is an equivalent effect on the recovery of MHC restricted, antigen-specific T-cell responses, whether these are mediated by CD4+ (helper) or CD8+ (cytotoxic) T lymphocytes. Indeed, there is evidence suggesting that administration of IL-2 may actually impede T-helper cell function. Thus, IL-2 infusion may abrogate T-cell-dependent B-cell antibody responses to immunogens (Gottlieb et al, 1992). Since IL-2 also impairs neutrophil chemotaxis (Klempner et al, 1990), it is not surprising that IL-2 administration may actually be associated with an increased risk of infection in marrow-ablated patients.

Use of IL-2–toxin conjugates

Antibodies to the P55 component of the IL-2 receptor have long been suggested as potential effector molecules for treating leukaemias and lymphomas which express this receptor. More recently, attempts have been made to use the IL-2 molecule itself to carry a toxic moiety to receptor-bearing neoplastic cells. Perhaps the most advanced of these systems uses a genetically engineered diphtheria A-chain toxin–IL-2 chimera (LeMaistre et al, 1992). In this molecule (DAB486IL-2), the native receptor-binding domain of diphtheria toxin has been replaced with human IL-2. In a phase I study, this chimeric molecule was well tolerated, with skin rashes and transient elevation of hepatic transaminases being the dominant adverse effects. Even in this phase I dose escalation study, three of 18 patients entered remissions which lasted 5 to 18-plus months. Another example of an IL-2 toxin, the pseudomonas-IL-2 hybrid, is very effective at killing murine leukaemia cells but appears to have no cytotoxic effect on human T cell leukaemia (FitzGerald et al, 1993).

One concern associated with the use of any IL-2 toxin conjugate is that an immune response generated to the chimeric model will be cross-reactive to native IL-2. The resulting auto-immune response could have devastating consequences for the immune system. Although this problem has not yet been encountered, the possibility will be considered in future studies (Strom et al, 1993).

INTERLEUKIN-4

Because IL-4 has been shown to increase both T-cell and natural killer cell proliferation and to induce tumour cell regression in animal models (Lotze et al, 1992), it was anticipated that IL-4 would act as an important immuno-modulatory agent in neoplasia and immune deficiency. Unfortunately, studies at NIH showed no tumour responses in any patient receiving IL-4 (Lotze et al, 1992). The combination of IL-4 and IL-2 had been said to be synergistic for LAK and tumour infiltrating lymphocyte (TIL) growth and activity, but the same NIH study showed no apparent increase in the response rates of patients receiving IL-4 in addition to IL-2 (Lotze et al, 1992).

Despite this disappointment, interest in the use of IL-4 as an immuno-modulator has begun to recover as a number of new observations have been made. For example, IL-4 gene-modified cancer cells appear to behave as potent tumour vaccines in a number of different models (see Chapter 7), and IL-4 antagonists may be valuable for enhancing IL-2-mediated effector function in vivo (see 'Cytokine combinations' below). Most recently, it has been shown that IL-4 induces apoptotic death in B-ALL blasts. This appears to be a direct effect, which is confined to early normal and malignant B-cell progenitors (Manabe et al, 1993). A phase I study of IL-4 in patients with relapsed ALL has begun at St Jude Children's Research Hospital, but response data are not yet available.

INTERLEUKIN-12 (NATURAL KILLER CELL STIMULATORY FACTOR)

Like IL-2, IL-12 can enhance the cytolytic activity of CD56+ natural killer cells and increase their release of cytokines such as IFN-γ. Again like IL-2, IL-12 induces CD3+ antigen-specific T cells to proliferate. However, unlike IL-2, IL-12 alone does not induce significant CD56 cell proliferation. It will induce T cells to proliferate only if they have received a co-stimulatory signal, for example after occupation of the antigen-specific T-cell receptor (Bertagnolli et al, 1992; Robertson et al, 1992; Tripp et al, 1993). In other words, IL-12 acts as an initiation cytokine for cell-mediated immunity (Scott, 1993), and in animal models appears to have a critical role in producing an effective immune response against a range of pathogens and tumour cell lines (Heinzel et al, 1993; Hsieh et al, 1993). Interest in IL-12 has therefore focused on its use in treating patients with neoplasms with profound immune deficiency. It seems likely that the first clinical trials of this agent will be phase I studies in cancer patients, but that once a safe immunomodulatory dose has been found, attention will shift to AIDS patients. Judging from the significant interactions of IL-12 with IL-2 and IL-4 (see below), it may be reasonable to predict that the true value of this agent—in haematology, as in other settings—will only become evident when it can be included in studies of cytokine combinations.

CYTOKINE COMBINATIONS

Physiologically, cytokine action occurs as part of a complex interactive network, so that the overall effect is dependent on the precise composition and temporal organization of the network. As discussed in Chapters 3 and 4, individual cytokine agents can therefore never be expected to produce optimal effects; to paraphrase Dr Johnson, the wonder is not that an individual cytokine works poorly, but rather that it works at all! The limitation applies equally well to the three immunomodulatory cytokines discussed in this chapter. The next few years will see continued exploration of cytokine combinations which may produce results unobtainable with any single agent.

Examples of combinations

IL-2 and IL-4

Even though the clinical efficacy of IL-2 is not yet established, attempts to maximize its immunological efficacy and minimize its toxicity are worthwhile. One approach is to manipulate those mechanisms responsible for the down-regulation of IL-2-induced lymphocyte activation. While IL-4 induces cytotoxic effector function in its own right, its most important effect physiologically may be to produce homeostasis of IL-2 action. Thus, if endogenous IL-4 activity is neutralized by monoclonal antibody during IL-2 infusion, then the half-life of AK function is greatly prolonged in patients receiving IL-2 (Bello-Fernandez et al, 1991). Moreover, neutralization of endogenous IL-4 augments secretion of anti-leukaemic/anti-viral cytokines such as TNF and IFN-γ by 100-fold or more. It might therefore be possible to reduce IL-2 dosage and simplify IL-2 treatment regimens by combining infusion of IL-2 with injection of antibody to IL-4 or its receptors. This approach is being investigated.

IL-2, IL-4 and IL-12

IL-4 and IL-12 can act as co-stimulators and produce markedly enhanced CD56+ NK cell proliferation and activation (Naume et al, 1992). IL-2 and IL-12 given sequentially can produce synergistic effects on CTL and CD56+ cell proliferation and activation (Robertson et al, 1992). Once IL-12 has been studied as a single agent in the clinic, combination trials with IL-4 and IL-2 will likely follow.

IL-2 and interferons

Optimism about cytokine combinations must be tempered with caution, since the only clinical trials of immunomodulatory cytokine combinations to date have not been favourable. For example, patients with myeloma or solid tumours who receive combinations of IL-2 and IFN-α or -β (Duggan et al, 1992; Morecki et al, 1992; Schneekloth et al, 1993) have shown no greater immunomodulation or tumour responses than patients receiving IL-2 alone. More recently, IL-2 has been combined with IFN-γ in patients after ABMT for haematological disease. The regimen was well tolerated, but there was no apparent reduction in relapse rates (Baumgarten et al, 1993).

CONCLUSIONS

Immunostimulatory cytokines may have a significant contribution to make, both in the therapy of haematological malignancy and in the amelioration of the consequences of conventional therapy for haematological diseases. It is likely that cytokine combinations will be required for therapeutic benefit. The almost complete absence of randomized efficacy studies, however, means that the value of these agents remains to be established.

REFERENCES

Adler A, Chervenic PA, Whiteside TL et al (1988) Interleukin 2 induction of lymphokine activated killer activity (LAK) in the peripheral blood and bone marrow of acute leukaemia patients. I. Feasibility of LAK generation in adult patients with active disease and in remission. *Blood* **71:** 709.

Anderson PM, Bach FH & Ochoa AC (1988) Augmentation of cell number and LAK activity in peripheral blood mononuclear cells activated with anti-CD3 and interleukin-2. Preliminary results in children with acute lymphocytic leukemia and neuroblastoma. *Cancer Immunology and Immunotherapy* **27:** 82–88.

Apperley JF, Mauro FR & Goldman JM (1988) Bone marrow transplantation for chronic myeloid leukemia in first chronic phase: importance of a graft versus leukemia effect. *British Journal of Haematology* **69:** 239–245.

Armitage RJ, Lai AP, Roberts PJ & Cawley JC (1986) Certain myeloid cells possess receptors for interleukin-2. *British Journal of Haematology* **64:** 799–807.

Barrett AJ, Horowitz MM & Gale RP (1989) Marrow transplantation for acute lymphoblastic leukemia: Factors affecting relapse and survival. *Blood* **74:** 862–871.

Bauer KA, ten Cate H & Barzegar S (1989) Tumor necrosis infusions have a procoagulant effect on the hemostatic mechanism of humans. *Blood* **74:** 165–172.

Baumgarten E, Schmid H, Pohl U et al (1993) Low dose natural interleukin-2 and recombinant interferon-gamma following autologous bone marrow grafts in pediatric patients with high risk acute leukemia. *Leukemia*, in press.

Bello-Fernandez C, Bird, Heslop HE et al (1991) Homeostatic action of interleukin 4 on endogenous and rIL2 induced activated killer cell function. *Blood* **77:** 1283–1289.

Ben-Neriah Y, Daley GQ, Mes-Massom AM et al (1986) The chronic myelogenous leukemia specific P210 protein is the product of the bcl/abl hybrid gene. *Science* **233:** 212–214.

Benyunes MC, Massumoto C, York A et al (1993) Interleukin-2 with or without lymphokine-activated killer cells as consolidative immunotherapy after autologous bone marrow transplantation for acute myelogenous leukemia. *Bone Marrow Transplantation* **12:** 159–163.

Bernstein ZP, Vaickus L, Friedman N et al (1991) Interleukin-2 lymphokine-activated killer cell therapy of non-Hodgkin's lymphoma and Hodgkin's disease. *Journal of Immunotherapy* **10:** 141–146.

Bertagnolli MM, Lin BY, Young D & Herrmann SH (1992) IL-12 augments antigen-dependent proliferation of activated T lymphocytes. *Journal of Immunology* **149:** 3778–3783.

Bianchi AC, Heslop HE, Veys P et al (1989) Enhancement of monoclonal antibody dependent cell mediated cytotoxicity by IL-2 and GM-CSF. *British Journal of Haematology* **73:** 468–474.

Blaise D, Olive D, Stoppa AM et al (1990) Hematologic and immunologic effects of recombinant Interleukin-2 after autologous bone marrow transplantation. *Blood* **76:** 1092–1097.

Blaise D, Stoppa AM, Olive D et al (1993) Auto BMT followed by recombinant IL2 (rIL2) in 41 patients with CR1 acute leukemia. *Experimental Hematology* **21:** 1115 (abstract).

Bortin MJ, Truitt RL, Rimm AA & Bach FH (1979) Graft-versus-leukemia reactivity induced by alloimmunisation without augmentation of graft-versus-host reactivity. *Nature* **281:** 490–491.

Bosly A, Guillaume T, Brice P et al (1992) Effects of escalating doses of recombinant human interleukin-2 in correcting functional T-cell defects following autologous bone marrow transplantation for lymphomas and solid tumors. *Experimental Hematology* **20(8):** 962–968.

Brenner MK, Reittie JE, Grob J-P et al (1986) The contribution of large granular lymphocytes to B cell activation and differentiation after T cell depleted allogeneic bone marrow transplantation. *Transplantation* **42:** 257–261.

Browett PJ & Norton JD (1989) Analysis of ras gene mutations and methylation state in human leukemias. *Oncogene* **4:** 1029–1036.

Burdach SEG & Levitt LJ (1987) Receptor specific inhibition of bone marrow erythropoiesis by recombinant DNA-derived interleukin 2. *Blood* **69:** 1368–1375.

Burdach S, Shatsky M, Wagenhorst B & Levitt L (1987) Receptor specific modulation of myelopoiesis by recombinant DNA-derived interleukin 2. *Journal of Immunology* **139:** 452–458.

Carron JA & Cawley JC (1990) IL2 and myelopoiesis: IL2 induces blast cell proliferation in some cases of acute myeloid leukemia. *British Journal of Haematology* **73:** 168–172.

Chan LC, Karhi KK & Rayter SI (1987) A novel abl protein expressed in Philadelphia chromosome positive acute lymphoblastic leukemia. *Nature* **325:** 635–637.

Charak BS, Agah R, Gray D & Mazumder A (1991) Interaction of various cytokines with interleukin 2 in the generation of killer cells from human bone marrow: application in purging of leukemia. *Leukemia Research* **15:** 801–810.

Cheever MA, Britzmann Thompson D, Klarnet JP et al (1986) Antigen driven long term-cultured T cells proliferate in vivo, distribute widely, mediate specific tumor therapy, and persist long-term as functional memory T cells. *Journal of Experimental Medicine* **163:** 1100–1112.

Ciccone E, Colonna M, Viale O et al (1990a) Susceptibility or resistance to lysis by alloreactive natural killer cells is governed by a gene in the human major histocompatibility complex between BF and HLA-A. *Proceedings of the National Academy of Sciences, USA* **87:** 9794.

Ciccone E, Pende D, Viale O et al (1990b) Specific recognition of human CD3− CD16+ natural killer cells requires the expression of an autosomic recessive gene on target cells. *Journal of Experimental Medicine* **172:** 47.

Cimino G, Avvisati G, Amadori S et al (1990) High serum IL-2 levels are predictive of prolonged survival in multiple myeloma. *British Journal of Haematology* **75:** 373–377.

Davignon D, Martz E, Reynolds T et al (1981) Lymphocyte function-associated antigen 1 (LFA-1): A surface antigen distinct from Lyt 2,3 that participates in T lymphocyte-mediated killing. *Proceedings of the National Academy of Sciences, USA* **78:** 4535–4539.

de The H, Chomienne C, Lanotte M et al (1990) The t(15;17) translocation of acute pro-myelocytic leukaemia fuses the retinoic acid receptor alpha gene to a novel transcribed locus. *Nature* **347:** 558–561.

Deacon EM, Pallesen G, Niedobitek G et al (1993) Epstein–Barr virus and Hodgkin's disease: transcriptional analysis of virus latency in the malignant cells. *Journal of Experimental Medicine* **177(2):** 339–349.

Delwel R, Salem M, Pellens C et al (1988) Growth regulation of human acute myeloid leukemia: effects of five recombinant growth factors in a serum free culture system. *Blood* **72:** 1944–1949.

Duggan DB, Santarelli MT, Zomkoff K et al (1992) A phase II study of recombinant interleukin-2 with or without recombinant interferon-beta in non-Hodgkin's lymphoma. A study of the Cancer and Leukemia Group B. *Journal of Immunotherapy* **12(2);** 115–122.

Duncombe AS, Grundy JE, Oblakowski P et al (1992) Bone marrow transplant recipients have defective MHC-unrestricted cytotoxic responses against cytomegalovirus in comparison with Epstein–Barr virus: the importance of target cell expression of lymphocyte function-associated antigen 1 (LFA1). *Blood* **79:** 3059–3066.

Farrar JJ, Benjamin WR, Hilfiker ML et al (1982) The biochemistry, biology and role of interleukin 2 in the induction of cytotoxic T cell and antibody-forming B cell responses. *Immunological Reviews* **63:** 129–166.

Ferrara JLM & Deeg HG (1991) Graft-versus-host disease. *New England Journal of Medicine* **324:** 667–674.

Fisch P, Malkowsky M, Kovats S et al (1990a) Recognition by human V9 and V2 T cell of a GroEL Homolog on Daudi Burkitt's lymphoma cells. *Science* **250:** 1269–1273.

Fisch P, Weil-Hillman G, Uppenkamp M et al (1990b) Antigen-specific recognition of autologous leukemia cells and allogeneic Class-I MHC antigens by IL-2-activated cytotoxic T cells from a patient with acute T-cell leukemia. *Blood* **74:** 343–353.

FitzGerald D, Kreitman RJ & Pastan I (1993) Recombinant immunotoxins for cancer treatment. *Experimental Hematology* **21:** 1012 (abstract 15).

Foa R, Caretto P, Fierro MT et al (1990a) Interleukin 2 does not promote the in vitro and in vivo proliferation and growth of human acute leukemia cells of myeloid and lymphoid origin. *British Journal of Haematology* **75:** 34–40.

Foa R, Fierro MT, Tosti S et al (1990b) Induction and persistence of complete remission in a resistant acute myeloid leukemia patient after treatment with recombinant interleukin-2. *Leukemia and Lymphoma* **1:** 113–117.

Foa R, Fierro MT, Cesano A et al (1991a) Defective lymphokine-activated killer cell generation and activity in acute leukemia patients with active disease. *Blood* **78:** 1041–1046.

Foa R, Guarini A, Gillio TA et al (1991b) Peripheral blood and bone marrow immuno-phenotypic and functional modifications induced in acute leukemia patients treated with interleukin 2: evidence of in vivo lymphokine activated killer cell generation. *Cancer Research* **51:** 964–968.

Galvani DW, Walton S, Davies JM et al (1992) Endolymphatic delivery of IL2 in patients with melanoma and lymphoma. *Biotherapy* **4(4):** 251–255.

Gambacorti-Passerini C, Rivoltini L, Fizzotti M et al (1991) Selective purging by human interleukin-2 activated lymphocytes of bone marrows contaminated with a lymphoma line or autologous leukaemic cells. *British Journal of Haematology* **78:** 197–205.

Gisselbrecht C, Maraninchi D, Pico JL et al (1992) Interleukin-2 (IL-2) in lymphoma: A phase II multicenter study. *Proceedings of the Annual Meeting of the American Association of Cancer Research* **33:** (abstract 1360).

Goldman JM, Gale RP, Horowitz MM et al (1988) Bone marrow transplantation for chronic myelogenous leukemia in chronic phase. Increased risk for relapse associated with T-cell depletion. *Annals of Internal Medicine* **108:** 806–814.

Gottlieb DJ, Brenner MK, Heslop HE et al (1989a) A phase I trial of recombinant interleukin 2 following high dose chemoradiotherapy for haematological malignancy: applicability to the elimination of minimal residual disease. *British Journal of Cancer* **60:** 610–615.

Gottlieb DJ, Prentice HG, Heslop HE et al (1989b) Effects of recombinant interleukin 2 administration on cytotoxic effector function following intensive chemoradiotherapy. *Blood* **74:** 2335–2342.

Gottlieb DJ, Prentice HG, Mehta AB et al (1990) Malignant plasma cells are sensitive to MHC unrestricted lysis: preclinical and clinical studies of interleukin-2 in the treatment of multiple myeloma. *British Journal of Haematology* **75:** 499–505.

Gottlieb DJ, Prentice HG, Heslop HE et al (1992) IL-2 infusion abrogates humoral immune responses in humans. *Clinical Experimental Immunology* **87:** 493–498. .

Hamon MD, Prentice HG, Gottlieb DJ et al (1993) Immunotherapy with interleukin 2 after ABMT in AML. *Bone Marrow Transplantation* **11(5):** 399–401.

Heinzel FP, Schoenhaut DS, Rerko RM et al (1993) Recombinant interleukin 12 cures mice infected with Leishmania major. *Journal of Experimental Medicine* **177(5):** 1505–1509.

Herberman RB & Ortaldo JR (1981) Natural killer cells: their role in defenses against disease. *Science* **214:** 24–30.

Heslop HE, Gottlieb DJ, Bianchi ACM et al (1989a) In vivo induction of gamma interferon and tumour necrosis factor by interleukin 2 infusion following intensive chemotherapy or autologous marrow transplantation. *Blood* **74:** 1374–1380.

Heslop HE, Gottlieb DJ, Reittie JE et al (1989b) Spontaneous and interleukin 2 induced secretion of tumour necrosis factor and gamma interferon following autologous marrow transplantation or chemotherapy. *British Journal of Haematology* **72:** 122–126.

Heslop HE, Duncombe AS, Reittie JE et al (1991a) Interleukin 2 infusion induces haemo-poietic growth factors and modifies marrow regeneration after chemotherapy or autologous marrow transplantation. *British Journal of Haematology* **77:** 237–244.

Heslop HE, Duncombe AS, Reittie JE et al (1991b) Interleukin 2 infusion after autologous bone marrow transplantation accelerates hemopoietic regeneration. *Transplantation Proceedings* **23:** 1704–1705.

Higuchi CM, Thompson JA, Petersen et al (1991) Toxicity and immunomodulatory effects of interleukin-2 after autologous bone marrow transplantation for hematologic malignancies. *Blood* **77:** 2561–2268.

Horowitz MM, Gale RP & Sondel PM (1990) Graft-versus-leukemia reactions after bone marrow transplantation. *Blood* **75:** 555–562.

Hsieh CS, Macatonia SE, Tripp CS et al (1993) Development of TH1 CD4+ T cells through IL-12 produced by Listeria-induced macrophages. *Science* **260:** 547–549.

International Bone Marrow Transplant Registry (1989) Transplant or chemotherapy in acute myelogenous leukemia. *Lancet* **i:** 1119–1122.

Jung S & Schluesner HJ (1991) Human T lymphocytes recognize a peptide of single point-mutated, oncogenic ras proteins. *Journal of Experimental Medicine* **173:** 273–276.

Karre K, Klein GO, Kiessling R et al (1980) Low natural in vivo resistance to syngeneic leukemias in natural killer-deficient mice. *Nature* **284:** 624–626.

Klempner MS, Noring R, Mier JW & Atkins MB (1990) An acquired defect in neutrophils from patients receiving interleukin-2 immunotherapy. *New England Journal of Medicine* **322:** 959–965.

Klingemann HG, Eaves CJ, Barnett MJ et al (1993) Transplantation of patients with high risk acute myeloid leukemia in first remission with autologous marrow cultured in interleukin-2 followed by interleukin-2 administration. *Blood*, in press.

LeMaistre CF, Meneghetti C, Rosenblum M et al (1992) Phase I trial of an interleukin-2 (IL-2) fusion toxin (DAB486IL-2) in hematologic malignancies expressing the IL-2 receptor. *Blood* **79(10):** 2547–2554.

Lotze MT, Zeh HJ, Elder EM et al (1992) Use of T-cell growth factors (interleukins 2, 4, 7, 10, and 12) in the evaluation of T-cell reactivity of melanoma. *Journal of Immunotherapy* **12:** 212–217.

Lotzova E, Savary CA, Schachner JR et al (1991) Generation of cytotoxic NK cells in peripheral blood and bone marrow of patients with acute myelogenous leukemia after continuous infusion with recombinant interleukin-2. *American Journal of Hematology* **37:** 88–99.

MacDonald D, Adams JA, McCarthy D & Barrett AJ (1990) Interleukin-2 inhibits growth of fibroblasts derived from human bone marrow. *Acta Haematologica* **83:** 26–30.

MacDonald D, Jiang YZ, Swirsky D et al (1991) Acute myeloid leukaemia relapsing following interleukin-2 treatment expresses the alpha chain of the interleukin-2 receptor. *British Journal of Haematology* **77:** 43–49.

Malkovska V & Sondel PM (1990) Prospects for interleukin 2 therapy in hematologic malignant neoplasms. *Journal of the National Cancer Institute Monographs* **10:** 69–72.

Malkovsky M, Loveland B, North M et al (1987) Recombinant interleukin 2 directly augments the cytotoxicity of human monocytes. *Nature* **325:** 262.

Malkovsky M, Brenner MK, Hunt R et al (1986) T-cell depletion of allogeneic bone marrow prevents acceleration of graft-versus-host disease induced by exogenous interleukin 2. *Cellular Immunology* **103:** 476–480.

Manabe A, Coustan-Smith E, Kumagai M et al (1993) Interleukin-4 (IL-4) induces pro-grammed cell death (apoptosis) in human B cell progenitors. *Blood*, in press (abstract).

Maraninchi D, Blaise D, Viens P et al (1991) High-dose recombinant interleukin-2 and acute myeloid leukemias in relapse. *Blood* **78:** 2182–2187.

Mazza P, Bocchia M, Tumietto F et al (1992) Recombinant interleukin-2 (IL-2) in acquired immune deficiency syndrome (AIDS): preliminary report in patients with lymphoma associated with HIV infection. *European Journal of Haematology* **49(1):** 1–6.

Michalevicz R, Campana D, Katz F et al (1988) Recombinant interleukin 2 and anti-Tac influence the growth of enriched multipotent hemopoietic progenitors: proposed hypotheses for different responses in early and late progenitors. *Leukemia Research* **12:** 113–121.

Moller DR, Konishi K, Kirby M et al (1988) Bias toward use of a specific T cell receptor beta-chain variable region in a subgroup of individuals with sarcoidosis. *Journal of Clinical Investigations* **82:** 1183–1191.

Morecki S, Revel-Vilk S, Nabet C et al (1992) Immunological evaluation of patients with hematological malignancies receiving ambulatory cytokine-mediated immunotherapy with recombinant human interferon-alpha 2a and interleukin-2. *Cancer Immunology and Immunotherapy* **35(6):** 401–411.

Naume B, Gately M & Espevik T (1992) A comparative study of IL-12 (cytotoxic lymphocyte maturation factor)-, IL-2-, and IL-7-induced effects on immunomagnetically purified CD56+ NK cells. *Journal of Immunology* **148:** 2429–2436.

Oblakowski P, Bello-Fernandez C, Reittie JE et al (1991) Possible mechanisms of selective killing of myeloid leukaemic blast cells by lymphokine-activated killer cells. *Blood* **77:** 1996–2001.

Olive D, Lopez M, Blaise D et al (1991) Cell surface expression of ICAM-1 (CD54) and LFA-3 (CD58), two adhesion molecules, is up-regulated on bone marrow leukemic blasts after in vivo administration of high-dose recombinant interleukin-2. *Journal of Immunotherapy* **10:** 412–417.

Oshimi K, Oshimi Y, Atutusu M et al (1986) Cytotoxicity of interleukin 2 activated lympho-cytes for leukemia and lymphoma cells. *Blood* **68:** 938–948.

Paciucci PA, Holland JF, Glidewell O & Odchimar R (1989) Recombinant interleukin-2 by continuous infusion and adoptive transfer of recombinant interleukin-2-activated cells in patients with advanced cancer. *Journal of Clinical Oncology* **7:** 869–878.

Peace DJ, Chen W, Nelson H & Cheever MA (1991) T cell recognition of transforming proteins encoded by mutated ras proto-oncogenes. *Journal of Immunology* **146:** 2059–2065.

Peest D, de Vries I, Holscher R et al (1989) Effect of interleukin-2 on the ex vivo growth of human myeloma cells. *Cancer Immunology and Immunotherapy* **30:** 227–232.

Platsoucas CD (1991) Human autologous tumor-specific T cells in malignant melanoma. *Cancer Metastasis Review* **10:** 151–176.

Ridge SA, Worwood M, Oscier D et al (1990) FMS mutations in myelodysplastic, leukemic, and normal subjects. *Proceedings of the National Academy of Sciences, USA* **87:** 1377–1380.

Robertson MJ, Soiffer RJ, Wolf SF et al (1992) Response of human natural killer (NK) cells to NK cell stimulatory factor (NKSF): cytolytic activity and proliferation of NK cells are differentially regulated by NKSF. *Journal of Experimental Medicine* **175:** 779–788.

Rosenberg SA (1988) Immunotherapy of cancer using IL-2: current status and future prospects. *Immunology Today* **9(2):** 58–62.

Rosenberg SA (1991) Development of adoptive cellular immunotherapies for the treatment of cancer. In Broder S (ed.) *Molecular Foundation of Oncology*, pp 153–193. Baltimore: Williams and Wilkins.

Rosenberg SA, Lotze MT & Mule JJ (1988) New approaches to the immunotherapy of cancer using Interleukin-2. *Annals of Internal Medicine* **108:** 853–864.

Rosolen A, Nakanishi M, Poplack DG et al (1989) Expression of interleukin-2 receptor B subunit in hematopoietic malignancies. *Blood* **73:** 1968–1972.

Rubin JT, Rosenberg SA & Lotze MT (1990) The efficacy of high dose recombinant interleukin-2 based immunotherapy in man. In Rees RC (ed.) *The Biology and Clinical Applications of Interleukin-2*, p 139. Oxford: IRL Press.

Savary CA & Lotzova E (1990) Inhibition of human bone marrow and myeloid progenitors by interleukin 2 activated lymphocytes. *Experimental Hematology* **18:** 1083–1089.

Schneekloth C, Korfer A, Hadam M et al (1993) Low-dose interleukin-2 in combination with interferon-alpha effectively modulates biological response in vivo. *Acta Haematological* **89(1):** 13–21.

Scott P (1993) IL-12: initiation cytokine for cell-mediated immunity. *Science* **260:** 496–497.

Simmons D, Makgoba MW & Seed B (1988) ICAM, an adhesion ligand of LFA-1, is homologous to the neural cell adhesion molecule NCAM. *Nature* **331:** 624–627.

Slavin S, Ackerstein A, Naparstek E et al (1990) The graft versus leukaemia (GVL) phenomenon: is GVL separable from GVHD? *Bone Marrow Transplantation* **5:** 155.

Smith KA (1988) Interleukin-2: inception, impact and implications. *Science* **240:** 1169–1176.

Soiffer RJ, Murray C, Cochran K et al (1992) Clinical and immunologic effects of prolonged infusion of low-dose recombinant interleukin-2 after autologous and T-cell-depleted allogeneic bone marrow transplantation. *Blood* **79:** 517–526.

Sosman JA, Oettel KR, Hank JA et al (1989) Specific recognition of human leukemic cells by allogeneic T cell lines. *Transplantation* **48:** 486–495.

Stotter H, Weibke EA, Tomita S et al (1989) Cytokines alter target cell susceptibility to lysis: II. Evaluation of tumor infiltrating lymphocytes. *Journal of Immunology* **142:** 1767–1773.

Strom TB, Kelley VR, Murphy JR et al (1993) Interleukin-2 receptor-directed therapies: antibody- or cytokine-based targeting molecules. *Annual Reviews of Medicine* **44:** 343–353.

Sykes M, Romick ML, Hoyles KA & Sachs DH (1990a) In vivo administration of interleukin 2 plus T cell-depleted syngeneic marrow prevents graft-versus-host disease mortality and permits alloengraftment. *Journal of Experimental Medicine* **171:** 645–658.

Sykes M, Romick ML & Sachs DH (1990b) Interleukin 2 prevents graft-versus-host disease while preserving the graft-versus-leukemia effect of allogeneic T cells. *Proceedings of the National Academy of Sciences, USA* **87:** 5633–5637.

Talmadge JE, Philips H & Schindler J (1987) Systematic preclinical study on the therapeutic properties of recombinant human interleukin 2 for the treatment of metastatic disease. *Cancer Research* **47:** 5725.

Tanaka M (1991) Growth of certain myeloid leukemic cells can be stimulated by interleukin-2. *Growth Factors* **5:** 191–199.

Timonen T (1990) Characteristics of surface proteins involved in binding and triggering of human natural killer cells. In Schmidt RE (ed.) *Natural Killer Cells: Biology and Clinical Application. 6th Int. Natural Killer Cell Workshop, Goslar*, pp 18–23. Basel: Karger.

Tourani JM, Levy V, Briere J et al (1991) Interleukin-2 therapy for refractory and relapsing lymphomas. *European Journal of Cancer* **27:** 1676–1680.

Tripp CS, Wolf SF & Unanue ER (1993) Interleukin 2 and tumor necrosis factor alpha are costimulators of interferon gamma production by natural killer cells in severe combined immunodeficiency mice with listeriosis, and interleukin 10 is a physiologic antagonist. *Proceedings of the National Academy of Sciences, USA* **90(8):** 3725–3729.

Weiden PL, Flournoy N, Thomas ED et al (1979) Antileukemic effect of graft-versus-host disease in human recipients of allogeneic-marrow grafts. *New England Journal of Medicine* **300:** 1068–1073.

Weiden PL, Sullivan KM, Flournoy N et al & Seattle Marrow Transplant Team (1981) Antileukemic effect of chronic graft-versus-host disease. Contribution to improved survival after allogeneic marrow transplantation. *New England Journal of Medicine* **304:** 1529–1533.

Weisdorf DJ, Nesbit ME, Ramsay NKC et al (1987) Allogeneic bone marrow transplantation for acute lymphoblastic leukemia in remission: prolonged survival associated with acute graft-versus-host disease. *Journal of Clinical Oncology* **5:** 1348–1355.

Young LS & Rowe M (1992) Epstein–Barr virus, lymphomas and Hodgkin's disease. *Seminars in Cancer Biology* **3(5):** 273–284.

7

Cytokine gene transfer in the therapy of malignancy

HELEN E. HESLOP

It is a basic tenet of tumour immunology that enhancement of the immune response may facilitate the eradication of weakly immunogenic tumours. Thus, when recombinant cytokines became available, one of the initial clinical applications was to administer these agents in an attempt to enhance immune function directed against malignant cells. Although several cytokines have been shown to have anti-tumour activity in biological assays in vitro, initial clinical trials of cytokine therapy in vivo in patients with malignancy have, with a few exceptions, proved disappointing. Significant systemic toxicity has been associated with minimal therapeutic benefit. For example, TNF causes regression of murine tumours, but has shown little beneficial effect in human trials. Similarly, high-dose IL-2 regularly causes regression of tumours in murine models, but does so only sporadically in humans (Rosenberg, 1991, 1992a).

One potential reason for this discrepancy may be that systemic toxicity occurs at lower doses in humans than in mice, and that this has prevented administration of these agents at doses comparable to those causing tumour regression in murine models. In addition, under physiological conditions cytokines act locally as short-range mediators between cells and levels attained with systemic dosage in humans will be much lower than the levels attained locally when cytokines are produced in particular microenvironments.

One approach to overcoming the problems arising from systemic administration is to transduce cytokine genes into either immune system effector cells or tumour cells in order to produce high local levels that may enhance anti-tumour function. This Chapter describes haematopoietic and immune system effectors that may mediate anti-tumour effects and experimental strategies for cytokine gene transfer to malignant cells or immune system effector cells. The results of such transfer in animal models and the early results of clinical trials in humans are also discussed.

THE ANTI-TUMOUR RESPONSE

Several arms of the antigen non-specific and specific host response may potentially mediate anti-tumour activity. Non-specific effectors include

Baillière's Clinical Haematology—
Vol. 7, No. 1, March 1994
ISBN 0–7020–1819–8

macrophages, neutrophils and eosinophils. They recognize targets both via Fc receptors which bind to antibody on the target cell surface and by the interaction of cell adhesion molecules and ligands on the tumour cell surface. In addition, macrophages may enhance antigen presentation and facilitate recruitment of antigen-specific responses. Other non-specific effectors include MHC-unrestricted NK cells which may also recognize malignant cells. The ligands for such recognition are not well defined, but here too it is likely that cell adhesion molecules play a role in target–effector cell interactions.

The antigen-specific limb of the host effector response is mediated by MHC-restricted cytotoxic T lymphocytes (CTL). These cells recognize internal cellular proteins as short fragments of processed peptide presented on the cell surface in conjunction with MHC molecules (Townsend and Bodmer, 1989). Any internal protein may therefore be processed and presented so as to be a target for such T-cell recognition. A number of human malignancies contain unique fusion proteins or proto-oncogenes which may be processed, presented and recognized as tumour-specific antigens (Brenner and Heslop, 1991; Jung and Schluesner, 1991; Peace et al, 1991; Chen et al, 1992b).

Failure of the host to recognize a tumour may result from a paucity or lack of tumour-specific antigens or from insufficient anti-tumour effector activation.

USE OF CYTOKINE GENE TRANSFER TO ENHANCE HOST RESPONSES

Malignant cell

Non-specific responses can be augmented directly by modifying the malignant cell so that it secretes cytokines which directly activate or recruit non-specific effectors. Alternatively, tumour cells can be modified to increase their ability to recruit an efficient *specific* immune response which in turn will recruit non-specific effector cells.

Host defence

Similarly, the activity of the specific arm of the host anti-tumour response can be increased by a number of routes. Recognition of a tumour by specific CTL requires several criteria to be met: (i) the tumour must contain unique proteins capable of being a target for specific immune responses; (ii) presentation of the relevant peptides on a tumour cell must occur with sufficient frequency to induce immune responses; (iii) the peptide–MHC complex must be within the immunological repertoire of the individual; (iv) it must be possible to amplify the response by exogenous help from either accessory immune system cells or co-stimulatory signals. This exogenous help is required because CD8 cytotoxic effector T cells do not normally produce IL-2 in sufficient quantity on activation to induce expansion, which is produced instead by CD4+ cells. All these processes can be influenced by cytokines, either by transducing them into the tumour cell itself or into the

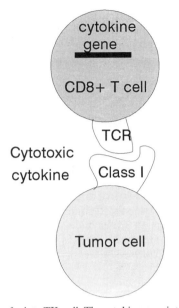

Figure 1. Cytokine gene transfer into TIL cell. The cytokine gene is transduced into the TIL cell which is then selected in G418. Transduced cells are then administered to the patient and home to the site of the tumour where high levels of cytokine are released locally. The cytokine may be directly toxic to the tumour cell or recruit additional effectors.

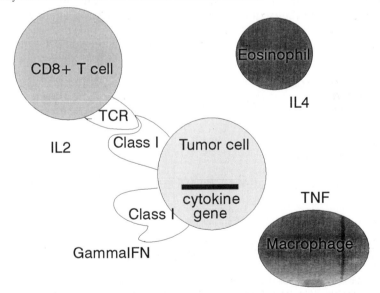

Figure 2. Cytokine gene transfer into tumour cell. The cytokine is transduced into the tumour cell which is then reinoculated after selection in G418. Local secretion of cytokine protein may enhance the anti-tumour reactivity by a number of mechanisms. Examples shown in this figure include recruitment of CTLs by IL-2, eosinophils by IL-4, and macrophages by TNF and increase in class I expression with IFN-γ. All these effects may induce rejection of tumour locally but only some effectors will eradicate distant tumour deposits.

effector T lymphocytes. The potential strategies are illustrated in Figures 1 and 2 and are described in more detail below. As will become apparent, most of the strategies adopted modify both the specific and the non-specific components of the host response to tumour.

DELIVERY SYSTEMS

An obvious prerequisite for cytokine gene therapy, is the efficient transfer of the appropriate cytokine gene into target cells. A number of techniques have been used for in vitro gene transfer including physical methods, such as calcium phosphate transfer, lipofusion or electroporation. These methods are generally of low efficiency; they may also result in integration of multiple copies in one cell and a higher risk of insertional mutagenesis. Because of the need for higher efficiency transfer in clinical studies and to minimize the risk of insertional mutagenesis, the most widely used clinical delivery system has been replication-incompetent retroviruses. The effects of other viruses and of lipofusion are being explored.

Retroviral vectors

The normal retroviral genome contains coding sequences for viral genes and an encapsidation sequence (psi) necessary for packaging and production of infectious particles (Figure 3). The genome is flanked by two long terminal repeats (LTRs) which contain promoter/enhancer regions and are required for integration and subsequent expression of viral genes. When retroviruses are used as delivery systems for gene transfer, viral genes are deleted and replaced by the gene of interest. The resulting retroviral vector is replication

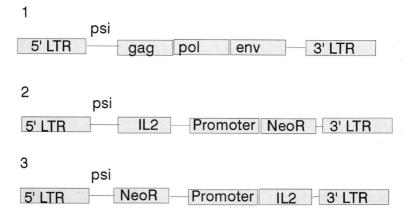

Figure 3. Retroviral vectors. Vector 1 is the moloney murine leukaemia virus from which many retroviral vectors used in clinical trials are derived. This vector contains LTRs, an encapsidation sequence (psi) and the viral genes gag, pol and env. These viral genes are deleted in retroviral vectors in clinical use, but the psi sequence remains. Vector 2 contains a cytokine gene expressed from the LTR and a neomycin resistance gene expressed from an internal promoter. In vector 3 the neomycin resistance gene is expressed from the LTR and the cytokine gene from the internal promoter.

defective and cannot produce infectious particles as it lacks the viral genes necessary for virion formation (Miller, 1990; Cornetta et al, 1991). Transfection of the vector into a packaging cell line which contains viral genes in *trans* but lacks encapsidation sequence allows virions containing the vector RNA to be packaged and the supernatant therefrom to be used for transfection of target cells. These virions produced in the supernatant of the packaging cell line can infect cells but not replicate. Recombination between the retroviral vector and helper virus sequences may produce replication-competent retrovirus (RCR), but a number of modifications reduce this possibility to a low, albeit measurable frequency.

Following infection of a cell with retrovirus, RNA is converted to DNA by the enzyme reverse transcriptase, and DNA then integrates randomly into the genome. This integration step represents another potential hazard since insertional mutagenesis may occur at a site where an oncogene is activated or a tumour suppressor gene inactivated. As the vector inserts almost at random, and such genes comprise only a minute fraction of the genome, and several such events would be needed for transformation this possibility is low (Gutierrez et al, 1992). It reaches significance only if the vector is contaminated by RCR (Donahue et al, 1992).

Retroviral vectors used for cytokine gene transfer generally contain the cytokine gene and a selectable marker gene such as the neomycin resistance gene, with one gene expressed from the LTR and the other from an internal promoter (Figure 3). Some vectors do not contain a selectable marker in order to obtain higher expression of the desired cytokine. The efficiency of gene transfer, as measured by cytokine secretion in resulting clones, varies with the construction of the vector, the integration site in an individual clone and the type of cell transfected.

One disadvantage of this methodology when it is applied to tumour cell transduction is that the cells to be transduced must be grown in vitro, selected and then reinoculated. In most clinical settings transduced tumour would comprise only a small portion of the overall tumour burden and eradication of untransduced tumour would require generation of immune system effectors able to circulate and mediate activity against distant tumour deposits. This problem could be overcome if vectors could be administered in vivo and targeted to malignant cells. Such vectors would have to recognize the malignant cell and be capable of accessing all tumour deposits (Russell, 1990). Safety concerns with retroviruses currently militate against this strategy. Moreover, retroviral vectors will only integrate and function in dividing cells and are inactivated by human complement. However, if viral vectors such as adeno-associated virus or lipofusion are shown to be safe and effective this strategy may become feasible.

AUGMENTING EFFECTOR CELL FUNCTION BY GENE TRANSFER INTO TIL CELLS

One approach to increasing local cytokine levels and enhancement of immune function is to transduce cytokine genes into tumour-infiltrating lymphocytes (TILs) which have been cultured ex vivo and are then returned to the patient. TILs are lymphocytes derived from tumour biopsies that can be expanded ex vivo by culture with IL-2 (Rosenberg et al, 1986). TIL cell lines can be grown from a number of human cancers and may recognize malignant cells in an HLA-restricted manner. While some of the action of TILs may be due to direct cytotoxicity, there is also evidence that part of the observed cytotoxic activity may be mediated by secondary cytokines such as TNF and gamma interferon (IFN-γ) (Barth et al, 1991). A number of studies have shown that administration of TILs in conjunction with systemic IL-2 results in responses in a significant number of patients. Nevertheless, while responses do occur, prolonged remissions or cures are rare.

In an attempt to enhance the efficacy of this approach, several studies are exploring the effect of transducing cytokine genes into TIL cell lines. The rationale for this approach is that such cells will home to the vicinity of the tumour and release high amounts of cytokine locally. Protocols using TNF-transduced TILs were approved by the FDA in 1991. The retroviral vector used in these studies contains the human TNF gene expressed from the retroviral LTR and the neomycin resistance gene expressed from the SV40 promoter. Cells are transduced, and high-secreting clones are selected by G418 resistance conferred by the neomycin resistance gene. One problem with this strategy is that although it is feasible to transduce TILs efficiently with the neomycin resistance gene (Culver et al, 1991), it has been difficult to achieve consistently high expression of TNF from TIL cells (Anderson, 1992). This may be due to the presence of regulatory factors for cytokine gene expression which distinguish lymphocytes from other cell types or to poor expression in the retroviral construct employed.

A second potential problem with this strategy is that the transduced cytokine may act as an autocrine growth factor for the TILs resulting in uncontrolled growth. One possible method of dealing with this problem is to co-express a 'suicide gene' in TILs so that cell death may be induced if adverse effects occur. For example, vectors encoding the thymidine kinase gene render host cells sensitive to the cytotoxic effects of nucleotide analogues such as gancyclovir. For significant protection to be conveyed, a high proportion of cells would need to express the transferred gene, so selection of transduced cells would be mandatory. In addition, expression would need to be maintained, and this may be especially problematic in TIL cells.

The first patients to receive such therapy were treated at the NIH in January 1991. This is a phase I dose escalation study and patients initially receive TNF-transduced TILs alone in doses from 10^8 to 3×10^{11} cells. Since TIL cell survival and growth is IL-2 dependent, subsequently IL-2 will be administered in conjunction with TNF-transduced TILs in the hope of further augmenting activity. The results from the first six patients treated with such therapy have been reported and few side-effects have been seen (Rosenberg, 1992a,b). Three received TNF-transduced TILs alone and no responses were seen; three received TNF-transduced TILs in conjunction with IL-2 and one patient had a sustained response (Rosenberg, 1992b).

AUGMENTING TUMOUR CELL RECRUITMENT OF HOST RESPONSE BY CYTOKINE GENE TRANSFER INTO MALIGNANT CELLS

The rationale for this strategy is that failure of tumour cells to be eradicated by the immune system may be due to poor immunogenicity of the tumour. This may result from either a paucity of immunogenic determinants on tumour cells or from insufficient activation of host effector cells capable of destroying tumour target cells. In an attempt to enhance recognition, several investigators have used animal models to evaluate the effect of transducing tumour cells with cytokine genes. Transfection of tumour cell lines with a number of cytokine genes has augmented immunogenicity to the extent that injection of neoplastic cells in doses that would normally establish a tumour, instead result in recruitment of effector cells and eradication of injected tumour cells. In many cases the animal is then resistant to challenges by further injections of non-transduced parental tumour. The transduced tumour has therefore acted like a vaccine. This strategy has the additional advantage that the cytokine secretion ceases when the transduced tumour cells have been eliminated.

A number of preclinical studies have evaluated transfer and expression of cytokine genes in tumour cells. These studies have aimed to delineate which cytokines have anti-tumour activity, and which tumours are susceptible to this immunomodulation approach. The mechanisms of response have also been examined and the effector cells from the immune and haematopoietic system characterized. The results of these studies are summarized below and in Table 1. Cytokines which stimulate either the immune and haemato-poietic systems have been shown to have an effect.

Interleukin-2 (IL-2)

In most cases, transfer of IL-2 into weakly immunogenic murine tumour cell lines results in suppression of growth when the tumour is administered to animals in vivo, although the degree of suppression varies with different tumours. Fearon et al (1990) found that transfection of a weakly immuno-genic colon cancer line, CT26, with the IL-2 gene resulted in much greater suppression than was observed when the poorly immunogenic B16 melanoma line was transduced with the same vector. Gansbacher et al (1990b) found that the degree of tumour suppression correlates with the amount of IL-2 produced by transfected tumour cells. Such responses appear to be mediated by CD8+ cells as the effect can be observed in mice lacking CD4 but not CD8 cells, and the effect is blocked by antibodies to CD8 or class I molecules. Both of these investigators were also able to detect tumour-specific CTLs in the spleens of vaccinated animals. It therefore appears that help from CD4 cells is not required when IL-2 is produced by tumour cells. Fearon et al (1990) have hypothesized that failure to produce an effective immune response in vivo may relate to paralysis of T-cell help due to the absence of appropriate co-stimulatory signals, rather than an absence of tumour-specific CTLs.

Table 1. Cytokine gene insertion in murine models.

Gene	Tumour	Local inhibition	Systemic immunity	Mediator	Reference
IL-2	Murine colon cancer	Yes	Yes	CD8 T cells	Fearon et al (1990)
	Murine melanoma	Yes	Yes	CD8 T cells	Fearon et al (1990)
	Murine fibrosarcoma	Yes	Yes	CD8 T cells	Gansbacher et al (1990)
	Rat sarcoma	Yes	Yes	CD8 T cells	Russell et al (1991)
	Murine mastocytoma	Yes	Yes	CTL	Ley et al (1991)
	Human renal cell	Yes		Macrophages	Gastl et al (1992)
	Human renal cell	Yes		Macrophages	Belldegrun et al (1993)
IL-4	Murine plasmacytoma	Yes		Macrophages Eosinophils	Tepper et al (1989)
	Murine renal cell	Yes	Yes	CD8 T cell	Golumbek et al (1991)
	Murine plasmacytoma	Yes			Li et al (1990)
TNF	Murine sarcoma	Yes		CD4 and CD8 cells	Asher et al (1991)
	Murine plasmacytoma	Yes		CR3+ cells	Blankenstein et al (1991)
	Murine skin tumour	Yes			Teng et al (1991)
IFN-γ	Murine fibrosarcoma	Yes	Yes	CD8 T cells	Gansbacher et al (1990)
	Murine sarcoma	Yes	Yes	CD8 T cells	Restifo et al (1992)
	Murine neuroblastoma	Yes	Yes	CD8 T cells	Watanabe et al (1989)
G-CSF	Murine colon cancer	Yes		Granulocytes	Colombo et al (1991)
IL-7	Murine plasmacytoma	Yes		CD4 T cells CR3+ cells	Hock et al (1991)
	Murine mammary adenocarcinoma	Yes			
	Murine glioma	Yes	Yes	CD8 T cells	Aoki et al (1992)
GM-CSF	Murine melanoma (irradiated)	Yes	Yes	CD4 and CD8 T cells	Dranoff et al (1993)
TGF-β	Murine fibrosarcoma	No			Torre-Amione et al (1990)

In both these studies (Fearon et al, 1990; Gansbacher et al, 1990b) tumour-specific immunity developed so that subsequent re-challenge with a dose of non-transfected cells normally capable of causing tumour formation, failed to generate a tumour. Induction of tumour-specific immunity required several days, because parental non-transduced cells injected at the same time at another site induced tumour formation (Fearon et al, 1990). Furthermore, tumour-specific CTLs were not detected until 1 week after vaccination. In one study immunity was not prolonged, as re-challenge at 4 weeks induced a tumour in 50% of mice (Fearon et al, 1990). Gansbacher et al (1990b) however found no development of tumours when a tumorigenic dose was injected 6 weeks after vaccination. It therefore appears possible to induce an immune response that persists and has at least short-term memory.

Two recent studies have evaluated the effects of transfer of the IL-2 gene to human renal cancer cell lines (Gastl et al, 1992; Belldegrun et al, 1993). Transfection with the IL-2 gene increased the susceptibility of these cells to killing by peripheral blood lymphocytes in vitro (Belldegrun et al, 1993) and in both studies transfer of transduced cells to nude mice led to rejection associated with an infiltrate of macrophages.

Interleukin-4 (IL-4)

Expression of the IL-4 gene in malignant cells also results in suppression of tumour growth, but different effector cells are responsible for the anti-tumour activity. Tepper et al (1989) transduced IL-4 into the J558L BALB/c plasmacytoma line and the K485 mammary cancer line. Transduced tumours reinoculated into mice showed reduced tumorigenicity, and the effect was also seen when transduced and non-transduced cells were admixed and inoculated simultaneously. Inhibition of non-transduced cells was not, however, seen when non-transduced cells were inoculated at separate sites. Inhibition of tumour growth correlated with secretion of IL-4, and considerable infiltration of macrophages and eosinophils was seen at the site. Tumour rejection occurred even when antibodies that specifically block the accumulation of granulocytes were administered and eosinophils were found to be an important mediator of the anti-tumour effect (Tepper et al, 1992). The observation that distant tumour was not eliminated by these effectors suggests that cytokines which recruit such non-immune effectors may not prove as useful clinically as cytokines that recruit more specific and longer-lived cells such as CTLs.

Not all anti-tumour activity is cell-mediated. Secondary cytokines may also be involved in the response, as TNF, IFN-γ and IL-5 are all detected in peritoneal infiltrates in mice receiving intraperitoneal injection of IL-4-transduced CHO cells (Platzer et al, 1992). IFN-γ appears to be especially important in mediating the observed effects, as the anti-tumour effect of IL-4 transduction can be abrogated by injection of IL-4-transduced cells in conjunction with anti-IFN-γ antibody.

Golumbek et al also found that transfection of IL-4 into a renal cancer cell line resulted in tumour suppression, again associated with macrophage and neutrophil infiltration (Golumbek et al, 1991). These investigators also found evidence for involvement of T cells in a later response. T cells were found in the infiltrate at the tumour site by 2 weeks after inoculation, and immunized mice were protected from re-challenge with parental cells, suggesting that systemic immunity had been induced. Tumour growth occurred if CD8 cells were depleted prior to re-challenge. Furthermore, inoculation of tumour into nude or SCID mice resulted in delayed growth of tumour. Li et al also found that in clones producing low amounts of IL-4, tumour growth was more delayed in normal animals than in nude mice suggesting a role for T cells in suppressing tumour growth (Li et al, 1990).

Tumour necrosis factor (TNF)

Transfection of TNF into a plasmacytoma cell line does not change growth characteristics in vitro but does result in strong suppression of growth in vivo (Blankenstein et al, 1991). This effect is mediated by neutrophils, macrophages and NK cells, and is blocked by antibody to TNF protein, and also by administration of an antibody to CR3 which prevents migration of inflammatory cells (Blankenstein et al, 1991). By contrast, transfection of IL-6 into the same tumour line gave rise to no suppression, and perhaps even to stimulation of growth. These observations suggest that in this model TNF mediates its anti-tumour activity by recruiting inflammatory cells such as macrophages. T cells may also be involved in tumour suppression, as complete inhibition occurs in T-replete mice, whereas slow tumour growth is seen in nude mice (Blankenstein et al, 1991; Teng et al, 1991).

Transfection of TNF into a sarcoma cell line resulted in tumours that grew to several millimeters in size and then regressed (Asher et al, 1991). Regression was abolished if antibodies to either CD4 or CD8 were administered. Interestingly, while transfection of TNF cDNA results in inhibition of tumour growth, transfection with a modified vector which produces only membrane-bound TNF (due to deletion of a segment that normally induces release) does not result in inhibition of tumour growth (Karp et al, 1992). It therefore appears that secretion of TNF is needed to recruit immune effectors.

Granulocyte colony-stimulating factor (G-CSF)

Transfection of the G-CSF gene into a colon cell line produced inhibition of tumour growth that could be abrogated by anti-G-CSF antibodies (Colombo et al, 1991). This response appears to be mediated by neutrophils which are recruited to the tumour site by the chemotactic effects of G-CSF and inhibition is also seen in nude mice.

Granulocyte–macrophage colony-stimulating factor (GM-CSF)

It would be predicted that GM-CSF would exert its anti-tumour function predominantly by recruitment of non-specific effector mechanisms. Experimental findings, however, suggest a greater complexity. When ten cytokines were assessed in the B16 melanoma model for ability to induce tumour-specific immunity, only IL-2-transduced tumours were rejected and GM-CSF-transduced tumours produced substantial toxicity due to leukocytosis. However if transduced tumour cells were irradiated prior to inoculation into the recipient GM-CSF-transduced cells provoked the most potent response (Dranoff et al, 1993). Furthermore, immunity persisted for longer than observed when IL-2-transduced tumour was injected. This was a surprising finding as GM-CSF has no direct effect on T-cell function and the investigators postulate that the benefits may relate to its effect in enhancing the function of antigen-presenting cells (Dranoff et al, 1993).

Interferon-γ (IFN-γ)

Introduction of the IFN-γ gene into a weakly immunogenic fibrosarcoma cell line also results in inhibition of growth (Gansbacher et al, 1990a). The transduced cells express increased number of class I molecules compared to the parental cells, and are more susceptible than parental cells in vitro to CTL activity. In vivo tumorigenicity of the cell line is abrogated by transfection with IFN-γ, and a persistent immune response against subsequent challenge with untransduced cells is induced. This effect appears to be T-cell-mediated as it is not seen in nude mice.

INN-γ transfection of a non-immunogenic sarcoma cell line which cannot normally be used to generate TILs results in clones with increased expression of class I molecules which are able to generate TILs (Restifo et al, 1992). Increased expression of class I molecules cannot be the sole mechanism for this effect however, as the TIL generated are subsequently able to mediate activity against established pulmonary metastases derived from non-transduced parental cells. Similar effects are seen in a model in which IFN-γ is transduced into a murine neuroblastoma cell line C1300 (Watanabe et al, 1989). Cell lines producing high amounts of IFN-γ failed to grow in vivo and tumour suppression was prevented by antibodies to IFN-γ or T lymphocytes.

Interleukin-7 (IL-7)

Expression of the IL-7 gene in the plasmacytoma line J558L also results in suppression of tumour growth in vivo (Hock et al, 1991). T cells appeared to play a major role in this suppression, because it was not observed in nude mice. Rejection was accompanied by an infiltrate of CD4+ and CD8+ T cells as well as cells expressing the type 3 complement receptor CR3, and was abrogated by depletion of either CR3+ cells or CD4+ cells, but not CD8+ cells. The mechanism of rejection therefore differs from that observed with IFN-γ and IL-2, where CD8+ CTLs appear to be the most important effectors. The authors hypothesized that CD4+ cells may mediate their effect via recruitment of CR3+ macrophages.

Transduction of IL-7 into a murine glioma line also produces inhibition of tumour growth (Aoki et al, 1992). In this case the effect is mediated by CD8+ cells as the tumour is not rejected in animals depleted of CD8+ cells but is rejected in animals depleted of CD4+ cells.

Transforming growth factor-β (TGF-β)

In contrast to studies with the other cytokines detailed above, transfection of a highly immunogenic murine tumour with TGF-β did not result in stimulation of CTL responses in vitro and TGF-β producing tumours continued to grow in transiently immunosuppressed mice (Torre-Amione et al, 1990). Transfection with this cytokine may therefore allow the tumour to escape from immune surveillance.

Conclusions from murine studies

The studies outlined above have shown that this approach can result in inhibition of tumour growth in models using a number of tumour cell lines and several cytokines. The observation that non-transduced tumour cells inoculated at the same site are also inhibited, shows that it is possible to achieve local activation of the immune response. One caveat, however, is that with some models non-transduced tumours at distant sites are not eradicated. This may reflect the fact that the effectors induced with these cytokines are inflammatory cells with short half-lives and no memory, which are recruited locally by chemotaxis, and would only be expected to act locally. Moreover, while it is possible to detect tumour-specific CTLs in models where cytotoxic T cells are induced, long-term memory is not consistently produced. This may reflect inadequate survival of CD8+ cells in the absence of CD4+ cells or systemic IL-2. Certainly culture with IL-2-transduced tumour cells does induce the generation of specific CTLs that have a wider range of activity than those induced by culture with the parental tumour alone (Fearon et al, 1990; Gansbacher et al, 1990). Expansion of these cells ex vivo or administration of IL-2 systemically may potentially result in enhanced survival and eradication of distal tumour.

POTENTIAL PROBLEMS WITH ADAPTING THIS APPROACH TO HUMANS

All the above results were obtained in murine models. While the results are tantalizing, a number of immunomodulatory strategies that have been efficacious in murine models have not produced any clinical benefit in humans. There are several potential problems in relation to performing comparable studies in humans, although clinical value could only be assessed by doing so.

Risks of transducing tumour cells with cytokine genes

One risk is that the transferred growth factor may act as an autocrine growth factor for tumour cells. This is certainly the case in some murine models; for example, expression of the IL-2 gene in a murine T cell line results in autocrine growth in vitro and tumorigenicity in vivo in immunodeficient mice (Yamada et al, 1987). In other settings, however, the recruitment of immune effectors induced by cytokine secretion outweighs the induction of autocrine growth. Thus, while transfection of IL-4 to a cell line results in autocrine growth in vitro, stimulatory effects on immune system effectors in vivo predominate and the tumour is rejected (Blankenstein et al, 1990). These divergent observations underscore the importance of evaluating in vitro and in vivo effects with each potential cytokine/tumour combination. This problem may potentially be overcome by expressing a 'suicide gene' in transduced tumour cells.

Feasibility of transduction

Because of the low efficiency of most transduction methods, it is necessary to transduce the patient's malignant cells and then to select for modified cells using a selectable marker such as G418 resistance conferred by the neomycin resistance gene. Otherwise only a minority of the cells will be gene modified and the stimulatory effects may not occur. It is therefore essential to be able to grow the patient's malignant cells ex vivo, so this approach is currently limited to tumours which can be grown in such a fashion. This requirement may be circumvented in the future if methodology can be developed to produce high transfer efficiency and ideally to target vectors to malignant cells in vivo, or by using transduced cell lines which share MHC antigens with the host (Gansbacher et al, 1990b). As detailed above development of vectors which will selectively infect malignant cells in vivo is under way.

Requirement for 'memory' cells

Any clinical benefit of this tumour response modification is more likely to be seen in the setting of minimal residual disease than in patients with advanced malignancy. Therefore if the initial phase I trials show that this approach is safe, and if subsequent phase II trials show efficacy, 'vaccination' could then be moved up to times when patients at high risk of failure were in remission. In this setting of a low tumour burden, however, prolonged immune activation would probably be required to eradicate residual malignant cells. Therefore, transfection with cytokine genes which induce short-lived responses, such as those mediated by neutrophils, eosinophils and macrophages, may be of less benefit than those which induce more protracted responses. In addition, long-term rather than short-term memory in the CTL subset will probably be required.

CLINICAL TRIALS

As of August 1993, four groups have begun clinical trials incorporating cytokine gene transfer into malignant cells (Table 2) and more protocols are pending approval by regulatory agencies. Preliminary information is available from two trials. The NIH group has clinical protocols approved for the use of cytokine gene transfer in melanoma, kidney cancer and colorectal cancer. In these studies patients will receive subcutaneous or intradermal injection of 2×10^8 tumour cells transduced with either the IL-2 or TNF

148 H. E. HESLOP

Table 2. Clinical trials of cytokine gene insertion in human cancers.

Gene	Tumour	Institution
Approved protocols		
IL-2	Colon cancer Melanoma Renal	NIH, Bethesda, MD
TNF	Colon cancer Melanoma Renal	NIH, Bethesda, MD
IL-2	Neuroblastoma	St Jude Children's Research Hospital, Memphis TN
IL-2	Melanoma Renal	Memorial Sloan Kettering Cancer Center, New York NY
IL-2	Malignant melanoma	University Hospital, Leiden, The Netherlands
IL-4	Melanoma	University of Pittsburgh, PA
IFN-γ	Melanoma	Duke University, Durham NC
GM-CSF	Renal (irradiated)	Johns Hopkins Oncology Center, Baltimore MD

gene. Three weeks later the area is excised and lymphocytes obtained from draining lymph nodes expanded in culture and infused with IL-2. Three patients with melanoma have been treated so far with TNF-transduced tumour (Rosenberg, 1992). In all cases local erythema and induration occurred at the injection site and at the time of local excision no tumour was found.

A similar approach is being explored at St Jude Children's Research Hospital using neuroblastoma as a model (Brenner et al, 1992). In this study patients receive subcutaneous injections of IL-2-transduced neuroblastoma cells in a dose-escalation study. Neuroblastoma is a tumour which should be susceptible to immune modulation for a number of reasons: (i) the tumour often remits spontaneously, especially in infants; (ii) it is derived from neuroectodermal tissue, so may present tumour specific antigens; (iii) neuroblastoma cells are sensitive to immune system effectors and in vitro cytotoxic activity can be enhanced if neuroblastoma cells are transduced with IL-2 (Leimig et al, 1993). Two patients have been treated so far, who have developed induration and erythema at the injection site. Skin biopsy performed at 2 weeks showed T-cell infiltrates, but no residual neuroblastoma cells.

FUTURE DIRECTIONS

Current studies aim to delineate whether this approach is useful in humans, and to define cytokine/tumour combinations. If clinical benefit is obtained, possible extensions of cytokine gene therapy include more specific targeting of cytokine to tumour cells. It has been shown that a genetically engineered fusion protein, consisting of a chimeric anti-GD2 antibody and IL-2, enhances killing of GD2 expressing melanoma cells by TIL lines (Gillies et al, 1992). Furthermore the enhancement is greater than that mediated by equivalent concentrations of free IL-2.

In addition greater benefit may be seen if tumour cells are co-transfected with cytokine combinations: for example a cytokine which enhances antigen-presenting cell function such as GM-CSF, in conjunction with a cytokine such as IL-2 which activates and expands CTLs. Finally, transfer of cytokine genes together with other co-stimulatory molecules such as B7, or with foreign MHC antigens (Chen et al, 1992a; Townsend and Allison, 1993), may result in enhancement of the immune response.

SUMMARY

Failure to eradicate tumour may be due to insufficient activation of host effector cells. Attempts to enhance such effector function by administration of high doses of cytokines systemically has produced little therapeutic benefit and considerable toxicity. An alternative approach is to provide cytokines locally at sites of tumour deposits. One method for achieving this is to transduce cytokine genes into TIL cells which will then home to sites of tumour. An alternative strategy is to transduce cytokine genes into tumour cells to enhance haematopoietic and immune system defence against tumour. In murine models transfection of tumour cells with cytokine genes has resulted in eradication of local tumour in models using several tumour types and several cytokines. The mechanism by which anti-tumour activity is produced varies with the transduced cytokine and the haematopoietic and immune effector cells recruited. Mechanisms include generation of CTLs which specifically recognize tumour cells, enhancement of antigen present-ation, and recruitment of non-specific cytotoxic cells such as eosinophils and neutrophils. With some combinations systemic immunity is induced so the animal is resistant to rechallenge at a distant site with non-transduced parental tumour and the transduced tumour has acted like a vaccine. Both these strategies are currently being evaluated in phase I trials in human tumours.

Acknowledgements

This work was supported in part by NIH grant CA21765 (CORE) and by American Lebanese Syrian Associated Charities (ALSAC).

REFERENCES

Anderson C (1992) Gene therapy researcher under fire over controversial cancer trials. *Nature* **360:** 399–400.
Aoki T, Tashiro K, Miyatake S et al (1992) Expression of murine interleukin 7 in a murine glioma cell line results in reduced tumorigenicity in vivo. *Proceedings of the National Academy of Sciences, USA* **89:** 3850–3854.
Asher AL, Mule JJ, Kasid A et al (1991) Murine tumor cells transduced with the gene for tumor necrosis factor alpha. *Journal of Immunology* **146:** 3227–3234.
Barth RJ, Mule JJ, Spiess PJ & Rosenberg SA (1991) Interferon gamma and tumor necrosis

150 H. E. HESLOP

factor have a role in tumor regressions mediated by murine CD8+ tumor infiltrating lymphocytes. *Journal of Experimental Medicine* **173**: 647–658.

Belldegrun A, Tso C-L, Sakata T et al (1993) Human renal carcinoma line transfected with interleukin-2 and/or interferon alpha gene(s): implications for live cancer vaccines. *Journal of the National Cancer Institute* **85**: 207–216.

Blankenstein T, Li W, Muller W & Diamantstein T (1990) Retroviral interleukin 4 gene transfer into an interleukin 4-dependent cell line results in autocrine growth but not in tumorigenicity. *European Journal of Immunology* **20**: 935–938.

Blankenstein T, Qin Z, Uberla K et al (1991a) Tumor suppression after tumor cell-targeted tumor necrosis factor alpha gene transfer. *Journal of Experimental Medicine* **173**: 1047–1052.

Blankenstein T, Rowley DA & Schreiber H (1991b) Cytokines and cancer: experimental systems. *Current Opinion in Immunology* **3**: 694–698.

Brenner MK & Heslop HE (1991) Graft-versus-host reactions and bone marrow transplantation. *Current Opinion in Immunology* **3**: 752–757.

Brenner MK, Furman WL, Santana V et al (1992) Phase I study of cytokine-gene modified autologous or allogeneic neuroblastoma cells for treatment of relapsed/refractory neuroblastoma. *Human Gene Therapy* **3**: 665–677.

Chen L, Ashe S, Brady WA et al (1992a) Costimulation of antitumor immunity by the B7 counterreceptor for the T lymphocyte molecules CD28 and CTLA-4. *Cell* **71**: 1093–1102.

Chen W, Peace DJ, Rovira DK et al (1992b) T-cell immunity to the joining region of p210BCR-ABL protein. *Proceedings of the National Academy of Sciences, USA* **89**: 1468–1472.

Colombo MP, Ferrari G, Stoppacciaro A et al (1991) Granulocyte colony-stimulating factor gene transfer suppresses tumorigenicity of a murine adenocarcinoma in vivo. *Journal of Experimental Medicine* **173**: 889–897.

Cornetta K, Morgan RA & Anderson WF (1991) Safety issues related to retrovirus-mediated gene transfer in humans. *Human Gene Therapy* **2**: 5–14.

Culver K, Cornetta K, Morgan R et al (1991) Lymphocytes as cellular vehicles for gene therapy in mouse and man. *Proceedings of the National Academy of Sciences, USA* **88**: 3155–3159.

Donahue RE, Kessler SW, Bodine D et al (1992) Helper virus induced T cell lymphoma in nonhuman primates after retroviral mediated gene transfer. *Journal of Experimental Medicine* **176**: 1125–1135.

Dranoff G, Jaffee E, Lazenby A et al (1993) Vaccination with irradiated tumor cells engineered to secrete murine GM-CSF stimulates potent, specific, and long lasting anti-tumor immunity. *Proceedings of the National Academy of Sciences, USA*, in press.

Fearon ER, Pardoe DM, Itaya T et al (1990) Interleukin-2 production by tumor cells bypasses T helper function in the generation of an antitumor response. *Cell* **60**: 397–403.

Gansbacher B, Bannerji R, Daniels B et al (1990a) Retroviral vector-mediated gamma-interferon gene transfer into tumor cells generates potent and long lasting antitumor immunity. *Cancer Research* **50**: 7820–7825.

Gansbacher B, Zier K, Daniels B et al (1990b) Interleukin 2 gene transfer into tumor cells abrogates tumorigenicity and induces protective immunity. *Journal of Experimental Medicine* **172**: 1217–1224.

Gastl G, Finstad CL, Guarini A et al (1992) Retroviral vector-mediated lymphokine gene transfer into human renal cancer cells. *Cancer Research* **52**: 6229–6236.

Gillies SD, Reilly EB, Lo K-M & Reisfeld RA (1992) Antibody-targeted interleukin 2 stimulates T-cell killing of autologous tumor cells. *Proceedings of the National Academy of Sciences, USA* **89**: 1428–1432.

Golumbek PT, Lazenby AJ, Levitsky HI et al (1991) Treatment of established renal cancer by tumor cells engineered to secrete interleukin-4. *Science* **254**: 713–716.

Gutierrez AA, Lemoine NR & Sikora K (1992) Gene therapy for cancer. *Lancet* **339**: 715–721.

Hock H, Dorsch M, Diamanstein T & Blankenstein T (1991) Interleukin 7 induces CD4+ T cell-dependent tumor rejection. *Journal of Experimental Medicine* **174**: 1291–1298.

Jung S & Schluesner HJ (1991) Human T lymphocytes recognize a peptide of single point-mutated, oncogenic ras proteins. *Journal of Experimental Medicine* **173**: 273–276.

Karp SE, Hwu, P, Farber A et al (1992) In vivo activity of tumor necrosis factor (TNF) mutants. Secretory but not membrane-bound TNF mediates the regression of retrovirally transduced tumor. *Journal of Immunology* **149**: 2076–2081.

Leimig T, Foreman NK, Rill DR et al (1993) Immunomodulatory effects of IL-2 transduced human neuroblastoma. (Unpublished data).

Ley V, Langlade-Demoyen P, Kourilsky P & Larsson-Sciard E-L (1991) Interleukin 2-dependent activation of tumor-specific cytotoxic T lymphocytes in vivo. *European Journal of Immunology* **216:** 851–854.

Li W, Diamanstein T & Blankenstein T (1990) Lack of tumorigenicity of interleukin 4 autocrine growing cells seems related to the anti-tumor function of interleukin-4. *Molecular Immunology* **27:** 1331–1337.

Miller AD (1990) Progress towards human gene therapy. *Blood* **76:** 271–278.

Peace DJ, Chen W, Nelson H & Cheever MA (1991) T cell recognition of transforming proteins encoded by mutated ras proto-oncogenes. *Journal of Immunology* **146:** 2059–2065.

Platzer C, Richter G, Uberia K et al (1992) Interleukin-4-mediated tumor suppression in nude mice involves interferon-gamma. *European Journal of Immunology* **22:** 1729–1733.

Restifo NP, Spiess PJ, Karp SE et al (1992) A nonimmunogenic sarcoma transduced with the cDNA for interferon gamma elicits CD8+ T cells against the wild-type tumor: Correlation with antigen presentation capability. *Journal of Experimental Medicine* **175:** 1423–1431.

Rosenberg SA (1991) Immunotherapy and Gene Therapy of Cancer. *Cancer Research* **51** **(supplement):** 5074s–5079s.

Rosenberg SA (1992a) The immunotherapy and gene therapy of cancer. *Journal of Clinical Oncology* **10:** 180–199.

Rosenberg SA (1992b) Gene therapy for cancer. *Journal of the American Medical Association* **268:** 2416–2419.

Rosenberg SA, Spiess P & Lafreniere R (1986) A new approach to the adoptive immuno-therapy of cancer with tumor-infiltrating lymphocytes. *Science* **233:** 1318–1321.

Russell SJ (1990) Lymphokine gene therapy for cancer. *Immunology Today* **11.**

Russell SJ, Eccles SA, Flemming CL et al (1991) Decreased tumorigenicity of a transplantable rat sarcoma following transfer and expression of IL-2 cDNA. *International Journal of Cancer* **47:** 244–251.

Teng MN, Park BH, Koeppen HKW et al (1991) Long-term inhibition of tumor growth by tumor necrosis factor in the absence of cachexia or T-cell immunity. *Proceedings of the National Academy of Sciences, USA* **88:** 3535–3539.

Tepper RI, Pattengale PK & Leder P (1989) Murine interleukin-4 displays potent anti-tumor activity in vivo. *Cell* **57:** 503–512.

Tepper RI, Coffman RL & Leder P (1992) An eosinophil-dependent mechanism for the antitumor effect of interleukin-4. *Science* **257:** 548–551.

Torre-Amione G, Beauchamp RD, Koeppen H et al (1990) A highly immunogenic tumor transfected with a murine transforming growth factor type B1 cDNA escapes immune surveillance. *Proceedings of the National Academy of Sciences, USA* **87:** 1486–1490.

Townsend A & Bodmer H (1989) Antigen recognition by class I-restricted T lymphocytes. *Annual Reviews of Immunology* **7:** 601–624.

Townsend SE & Allison JP (1993) Tumor rejection after direct costimulation of CD8+ T cells by B7-transfected melanoma cells. *Science* **259:** 368–370.

Watanabe Y, Kuribayashi K, Miyatake S et al (1989) Exogenous expression of mouse interferon gamma cDNA in mouse neuroblastoma C1300 cells results in reduced tumorigenicity by augmented anti-tumor immunity. *Proceedings of the National Academy of Sciences, USA* **86:** 9456–9460.

Yamada G, Kitamura Y, Sonoda H et al (1987) Retroviral expression of the human IL-2 gene in a murine T cell line results in cell growth autonomy and tumorigenicity. *EMBO Journal* **6:** 2705–2709.

8

Down-regulation of cytokine action

PHILIP L. McCARTHY

Over the past several years, it has become apparent that there are diverse mechanisms that inhibit the effect of assorted cytokines (Kahan, 1989; Arend et al, 1991; Fernandez-Botran, 1991; Marsh et al, 1992; Riegel et al, 1992; Sher et al, 1992; Walsh et al, 1992) and that down-regulation may occur at the molecular, cellular and organ level. This chapter will focus on the proteins and glycoproteins released by cells that down-regulate or block the effects of cytokines, particularly on direct antagonists, soluble receptors and selected immunoregulatory cytokines.

Figure 1 depicts the regulation of cytokine effects which can occur at different sites of cytokine action. Cytokine release may be increased or decreased at the level of DNA transcription, RNA translation, mRNA stability, or cytokine secretion. Cytokine receptor expression on the target cells may be up-regulated or down-regulated by other cytokines or intracellular signals and down-regulation may also occur at a post-receptor level. Cell activation occurs when a cytokine binds to its receptor leading to intracellular signalling that often is associated with gene transcription and mRNA translation, resulting in the synthesis of proteins required for cellular activation (see Chapter 2). These intracellular events can be attenuated by agents that interfere with intracellular signalling or DNA and RNA processing. The action of cytokines can be blocked by soluble receptors that bind the cytokine and prevent cellular interaction. In addition, antibodies may be produced that will bind to the cytokine or to its receptor and prevent cytokine effects. Receptor antagonists have been isolated that are natural products of the immune system or can be generated by molecular manipulation in vitro. These antagonists bind to cellular receptors and block interaction with their respective cytokine, thus preventing cellular activation.

Analysis of cytokine down-regulation must take into account the participation of cytokines in cell differentiation and proliferation, cellular physiology and immune activation and inactivation (Arai et al, 1990; Goldring and Goldring, 1991; Neta et al, 1992). The complexity can be illustrated by describing the cytokines released following immune activation and showing how their multiplicity of potential actions can be circumscribed.

Baillière's Clinical Haematology—
Vol. 7, No. 1, March 1994
ISBN 0–7020–1819–8

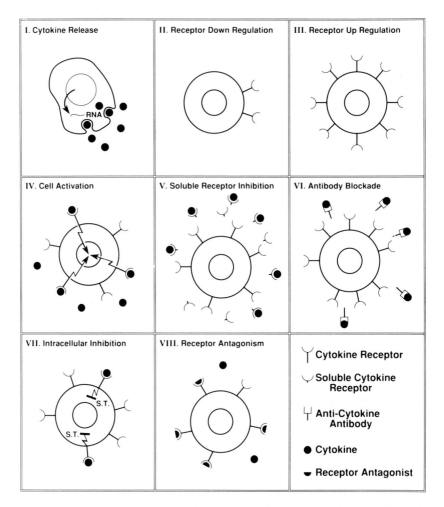

Figure 1. Regulation of cytokine action. Cytokine production may be modulated at the level of synthesis and secretion (I). The cytokine binds to the target cell causing cellular activation (IV). Regulation of cytokine action may occur at the level of receptor expression (II and III), intracellular signal transduction (VII), soluble receptor-cytokine binding (V), antibody blockade (VI), or receptor antagonism (VIII). See text for full details.

IMMUNE ACTIVATION

Many clinically important inflammatory processes are driven by immune activation and regulated by cytokines. The initial signalling of the immune system involves T-cell recognition of antigen with the participation of antigen-presenting cells or macrophages. The T-cell compartment is expanded, accompanied by the release of cytokines such as IL-1, IL-2, IL-3, IL-4, IL-7, IL-10, TNF-α and TNF-β, interferon-γ (IFN-γ), and granulocyte–macrophage colony-stimulating factor (GM-CSF). IL-2 is the primary cytokine that stimulates further T-cell proliferation. As will be described, a down-regulatory response also can occur which is mediated by the release and action of cytokines such as transforming growth factor-β (TGF-β), IL-4 and IL-10 which inhibit selected cellular function during immune activation (Sher et al, 1992). A secondary phase of the immune response is manifested by the action of effector cells activated by T cells. These effector cells include macrophages, natural killer (NK) cells and cytotoxic T cells. During this secondary phase of immune activation, there is further production and release of inflammatory cytokines. In particular, IL-1, TNF-α and -β, IL-6 and IL-8 are important mediators of the immune response amplification (Beutler and Cerami, 1988; Cerami, 1992; Dinarello and Wolfe, 1992; Matsushima et al, 1992). As inflammation is further modulated after the initial activation stimulus, cytokines including platelet derived growth factor (PDGF), basic fibroblast growth factor (bFGF), and TGF-β are released to assist in tissue repair and to regulate the inflammatory response.

Let us consider two of these cytokines, IL-1 and TNF, in more detail, and illustrate their activities and their control. Mononuclear cells and macrophages are the primary source of IL-1. It is secreted in two forms that are derived from separate genes: IL-1α and IL-1β. Both have similar mechanisms of action and biological activity. IL-1α is primarily an intracellular and membrane-associated molecule while IL-1β can be detected in the serum of patients who have profound inflammation. IL-1α binds both type I and type II IL-1 receptors with a stronger affinity than IL-1β, although IL-1β appears to be more involved as an effector molecule for cellular activation. The type I receptors are present on many cell types whereas type II receptors are expressed primarily on B cells and macrophages (Matsushima et al, 1986; Bomsztyk et al, 1989; Chizzonite et al, 1989; Sims et al, 1989). Recent work has demonstrated that the Type II IL-1 receptor appears to be an inhibitory receptor for the action of IL-1 and is regulated by the action of IL-4 (Colotta et al, 1993). IL-1α is secreted by epithelial and endothelial cells and may function as a mediator of endothelial cell participation in inflammation (Pober and Cotran, 1990; Mantovani et al, 1992).

TNF is also secreted in two forms: TNF-α (cachectin) and TNF-β (lymphotoxin). TNF-α originates from a variety of cellular sources including mononuclear and endothelial cells. TNF-β is produced primarily by activated lymphocytes. Both bind to the two types of TNF receptors (see below) and have indistinguishable biological activity.

IL-1 and TNF will cause peripheral blood mononuclear cell secretion of IL-6 and IL-8 (DeForge et al, 1992). IL-6 causes B-cell proliferation as well as modulation of inflammation and the release of acute-phase reactant proteins when injected into experimental animals. IL-8 is a leukocyte-activating factor that stimulates neutrophil chemotaxis, phagocytosis and superoxide generation during immune activation. Injection of IL-1, TNF-α, IL-6 or IL-8 causes inflammatory responses in animals, and large doses of IL-1 and TNF can induce lethal hypotension (Beutler et al, 1986; Le and Vilček, 1987; Beutler and Cerami, 1988; Dinarello, 1992; Dinarello and Wolfe, 1992).

Control of these cytokines is essential since their excessive activity plays a fundamental role in the pathogenesis of many inflammatory diseases, including sepsis, inflammatory bowel disease, vasculitis and rheumatoid arthritis. Solid organ and bone marrow allografts represent unique forms of generalized activation of the immune system related to histoincompatibility and many of the complications of these procedures, including rejection, graft-versus-host disease (GVHD), interstitial pneumonitis, hepatic veno-occlusive disease and microangiopathy may all be related to inadequately regulated cytokine production (Piquet et al, 1986; Holler et al, 1990; Imagawa et al, 1990; McCarthy et al, 1991).

In preclinical models and in preliminary clinical trials, down-regulation of these cytokines has decreased the deleterious effects of inflammation suggesting a clinical application for individual or combined inhibition of TNF and IL-1, IL-6 and IL-8. The following sections describe how down-regulation of these (and other cytokines) may be achieved.

ACHIEVING CYTOKINE DOWN-REGULATION

Immunosuppression

Immunosuppression has been the traditional form of cytokine down-regulation. Relatively non-specific agents such as glucocorticoids, cyclophosphamide, azathioprine, anti-T-cell antibodies and cyclosporin have been utilized in an attempt to control inflammation associated with auto-immune disorders and transplantation. All of these agents are directed primarily against the T-cell compartment and have more general, non-selective immunosuppressive effects. Glucocorticoids have direct impact on cell proliferation and inhibit cytokine production. Agents such as azathioprine and cyclophosphamide inhibit cell division and they disrupt DNA transcription and RNA translation resulting in decreased cytokine production. Anti-T-cell antibodies have anti-inflammatory properties due to a direct anti-lymphocyte effect which leads to increased clearance and decreased function of T lymphocytes. Immunophilin binding drugs such as cyclosporin, FK506, and rapamycin more selectively inhibit immune responses by interacting with a class of proteins that function as peptidyl-prolyl isomerases (Kahan, 1989; Walsh et al, 1992). Cyclosporin binds the protein group cyclophilins which are so named due to their affinity for cyclosporin. FK506 and rapamycin binds to a closely-related group of peptidylprolyl isomerases known as FK binding proteins. Both the cyclophilins and the FK binding proteins are members of the immunophilin class of proteins which are defined by their binding to these agents and their ability to down-regulate T-cell function. In turn, another intracellular protein, calcineurin which is a phosphatase 2B protein, is inhibited by binding to the cyclosporin–cyclophilin or FK506–FK binding protein complex. The complex of calcineurin, immunophilin, and immunophilin-binding drug appears to be important in the down-regulation of T-cell function. Calcineurin mediates a calcium-dependent activation pathway for DNA transcription of T-cell activation proteins. DNA transcription of IL-2 in particular, is decreased by immunophilin binding class of drugs leading to inhibition of T cell activation.

Blockade of signal transduction by IL-1 and TNF

The molecular signalling of cellular activation by TNF or IL-1 is complex. IL-1 induces the phosphorylation of cellular proteins in a manner independent of protein kinase C and A (PKC and PKA). Furthermore, it will cause intra-cellular stimulation of guanine nucleotide binding proteins (G-proteins) and increase levels of cyclic AMP (Dinarello, 1991). The phospholipase C (PLC) and phospholipase A2 (PLA2) enzymatic cascades are also activated by IL-1, leading to the release of arachidonic acid (Burch et al, 1988; Galella et al, 1992). IL-1β will activate the sphingomyelin signalling pathway which leads to ceramide-induced protein kinase activation and increased IL-2 production (Mathias et al, 1993). Many different cell types are activated by IL-1, leading to induction of phospholipase enzymatic cascades and demonstrating a shared mechanism of cellular activation by IL-1 (Kester et al, 1989). However, despite intensive investigation, a complete understanding of signal transduction in response to IL-1 remains to be determined.

TNF is another example of a cytokine that triggers a complex pattern of signal transduction. The PLC enzymatic cascade has been linked to cellular activation by TNF with a resultant increase in the nuclear transcription factor NF-κB (Hohmann et al, 1992; Schütze et al, 1992). The PLC, PKA, PLA2 and the G-protein cascades are activated by TNF binding to the cellular TNF receptor (Krönke et al, 1992). In addition, the tyrosine kinase (TK) enzymatic cascades are modulated by TNF and in turn affect the cellular response to further cytokine stimulation.

These complex signalling systems might be manipulated by the use of relatively specific enzymatic inhibitors that lead to a diminished response to cytokine activation and efforts are being directed at the development of drugs that will selectively block the production, secretion or action of cytokines. These agents may prove to be useful in a clinical setting. For example, PKC inhibitors such as staurosporin and H7 and the TK inhibitor herbimycin A, modulate the different cellular responses to IL-1 or TNF (Dornand et al, 1992; Iwasaki et al, 1992). Inhibitors of PKC decrease IL-1 secretion by mononuclear cells, but do not affect the intracellular cytokine production (Bakouche et al, 1992). If cytokines are not released from the cell, or if they are degraded due to intracellular accumulation, this would result in down-regulation of cytokine action.

Pentoxifylline is another agent that has been shown to inhibit TNF production in vitro. Pentoxifylline is a xanthine-derivative which acts as a phosphodiesterase inhibitor and elevates intracellular levels of cyclic AMP which in turn decreases cellular mRNA levels of TNF. For example, the normal response of mononuclear cells after exposure to stimulatory agents such as lipopolysaccharide is to increase production of TNF. This increase is blocked by pentoxifylline, resulting in decreased production and secretion of TNF. Pentoxifylline is being investigated as a potential inhibitor of HIV replication since this process may be enhanced by TNF production (Fazely et al, 1991). The drug has also been used in clinical bone marrow transplantation to prevent inflammatory complications of BMT—including mucositis, GVHD, hepatic veno-occlusive disease and renal failure—with initially encouraging results (Bianco et al, 1991). However, these results have not been confirmed in prospective randomized studies (Attal et al, 1993).

Another agent with the capacity to modulate inflammatory cytokine production is adenosine triphosphate-magnesium chloride (ATP-MgCl$_2$). Magnesium deficiency will increase plasma levels of IL-1, IL-6 and TNF-α in experimental rodent models of magnesium deficiency (Weglicki et al, 1992). Furthermore, administration of ATP-MgCl$_2$ will decrease plasma levels of TNF and IL-6 and increase survival following the induction of experimental trauma, suggesting that increasing circulating cellular magnesium levels will inhibit the production of inflammatory cytokines (Wang et al, 1992). Intravenous administration of magnesium chloride may prove to be a simple means for down-regulation of inflammatory cytokine production.

Cytokine receptors and receptor antagonists

Soluble receptors have been described for several interleukins and cytokines. In considering the mechanisms of cytokine action and strategies for down-regulation of cytokine action, investigators have categorized different families of cytokine receptors on the basis of shared protein homology and enzymatic function (Fernandez-Botran, 1991; Kaczmarski and Mufti, 1991; Taga and Kishimoto, 1992). The cytokine receptors can be grouped into distinct categories with some degree of overlap (Table 1):

Table 1. The seven cytokine receptor families are categorized on the basis of sequence homology of the extracellular and intracellular domains as well as functional tyrosine kinase activity.

1. *Immunoglobulin-like superfamily* IL-1 receptor PDGF receptor M-CSF receptor	4. *Tyrosine kinase receptor superfamily* Stem-cell factor receptor NGF receptor EGF receptor Insulin and IGF-I receptor bFGF receptor
2. *Haematopoietic cytokine receptor superfamily* IL-2 receptor IL-3 receptor IL-4 receptor IL-5 receptor IL-7 receptor IL-9 receptor EPO receptor GM-CSF receptor factor	5. *Tyrosine kinase and immunoglobulin receptor superfamily* PDGF receptor M-CSF receptor 6. *Tumour necrosis factor/nerve growth factor receptor family* TNF receptor NGF receptor CD40 CD27
3. *Haematopoietic cytokine and immunoglobulin-like superfamily* G-CSF receptor IL-6 receptor LIF receptor Ciliary neurotrophic factor receptor	7. *Interferon receptor family* IFN-α/β receptor IFN-γ receptor

1. The immunoglobulin-like superfamily with extracellular domains having immunoglobulin homology.
2. The haematopoietic cytokine receptor superfamily with extracellular domains that have a shared amino acid sequence near the extracellular surface, consisting of a Trp–Ser–X–Trp–Ser amino acid motif which will impair cytokine signalling and binding if disrupted.
3. The receptors having both cytokine superfamily and immunoglobulin-like superfamily features.
4. The tyrosine kinase receptor family with intracellular tyrosine kinase activity.
5. The receptors with both intracellular tyrosine kinase activity and extracellular immunoglobulin-like family features.
6. The TNF-NGF receptor family with shared extracellular homology.
7. The interferon receptor family with shared extracellular homology.

Because of shared homology among the members of many of these cytokine superfamilies, blocking cytokine action by antibody would require identification of a unique epitope for each receptor.

An alternative approach to blockade is to compete with the receptors themselves. Soluble receptors have been described for several interleukins and cytokines (Table 2). Soluble forms of the receptors for IL-1, IL-2, IL-4, IL-5, IL-6, IL-7, IL-9, TNF, IFN-γ, LIF, EGF, IGF, NGF, CD27 ligand, CD40 ligand, G-CSF, GM-CSF, growth hormone and thyrotropin have been identified and cloned. Each receptor binds its respective cytokine and usually will block the action of the cytokine on the target cells, although soluble receptors for IL-6 and LIF may be up regulators of cytokine action and will be discussed below.

Table 2. List of the cytokines for which native soluble receptors have been isolated and purified.

IL-1 (type I and Type II receptors)	EGF
IL-2 (α and β chains)	IGF-I
IL-4	NGF
IL-5	G-CSF
IL-6	GM-CSF
IL-7	Growth hormone
IL-9	Thyrotropin
TNF (p55 and p70 receptors)	CD27 ligand
IFN-γ	CD40 ligand
LIF	

EFFECTS OF SPECIFIC SOLUBLE RECEPTORS OR RECEPTOR ANTAGONISTS

Soluble IL-1 receptors

Since IL-1 is produced in response to inflammatory stimuli and is responsible for initiating many of the manifestations of inflammatory processes, blocking the effects of IL-1α and IL-1β may have potential therapeutic benefits in modulating and decreasing the severity of clinical complications associated with inflammatory illnesses. There are two forms of the IL-1 receptor: type I which is expressed preferentially on T cells, fibroblasts and other cell types and type II which is expressed primarily on bone marrow cells, B cells, neutrophils and macrophages (Matsushima et al, 1986; Bomsztyk et al, 1989; Chizzonite et al, 1989; Sims et al, 1989). Despite a preferential expression of each receptor type on specific cell populations, there is considerable overlap of receptor expression among all cells. While the type I receptor appears to be the primary binding site for IL-1-induced activation, cells will often express both receptors, suggesting a complex signalling system. The type II receptor may function primarily as an inhibitory molecule for the action of IL-1 by binding IL-1 and preventing its interaction with the type I receptor (Colotta et al, 1993). Soluble forms of the type I IL-1 receptor have been detected in the human serum and soluble forms of the type II IL-1 receptor have been isolated from human serum and other body fluids (CA Jacobs, personal communication; Symons et al, 1991). The biological function of both soluble IL-1 receptors is not well understood but there is potential for their use as pharmacological agents. In preclinical animal models, the type I soluble IL-1 receptor will inhibit inflammation associated with cardiac allograft rejection, allograft lymph node hyperplasia, allergic encephalomyelitis, and IL-1-induced ocular inflammation (Fanslow et al, 1990; Jacobs et al, 1991a; Rosenbaum and Boney, 1992). A phase I study of soluble type I IL-1 receptor has been completed without significant toxic effects. Clinical trials are currently underway to determine the utility of soluble IL-1 receptor in the modulation of cutaneous hypersensitivity responses and as a possible therapeutic agent in sepsis and GVHD. A phase I study of soluble IL-1 receptor in severe GVHD has been completed without toxicity (McCarthy et al, 1993). Therapeutic benefit was seen in patients treated at higher dose levels but this observation will require further confirmation in phase II and III levels.

IL-1 stimulates the growth of myeloid leukaemic cell lines and fresh isolates of acute myelogenous leukaemia cells from patients (Rambaldi et al, 1991). IL-1 has been shown to stimulate chronic myelogenous leukaemia (CML) colony growth, and incubating CML cells with inhibitors and antagonists of IL-1 prevents leukaemic colony formation (Estrov et al, 1991). Trials utilizing inhibitors of IL-1 in CML are in progress to determine if these agents will have significant clinical effects in the treatment of this haematological malignancy.

IL-1 receptor antagonists

The interleukin-1 receptor antagonist (IL-1ra) is one of a group of proteins produced by mononuclear cells in response to IL-1 secretion and inflammation. IL-1ra and its related proteins were isolated from the urine of patients with acute myelomonocytic leukaemia and shown to inhibit the action of IL-1. IL-1ra was purified, cloned, and found to bind to both type I and type II IL-1 receptors and prevent cellular activation (Hannum et al,

1990; Eisenberg et al, 1990). Only a small percentage (10%) of the cellular IL-1 receptors need to interact with IL-1 for cellular activation, so that IL-1ra must bind to nearly 100% of the cell's membrane IL-1 receptors to prevent the action of IL-1. Therefore, IL-1ra would need to be present in quantities that are over 1000-fold higher than IL-1 to completely block the action of IL-1. This is confirmed by the in vivo observation that serum concentrations of IL-1ra are raised to levels three logs or greater than serum levels of IL-1 after endotoxin administration (Granowitz et al, 1991b).

IL-1ra competes with IL-1 for binding to both IL-1 receptors and has no agonist activity (Eisenberg et al, 1990; Hannum et al, 1990; Granowitz et al, 1991a). It has been shown to block IL-1-induced cellular activation and in experimental animal models, it blunts the deleterious inflammatory effects of arthritis, sepsis and GVHD (Ohlsson et al, 1990; McCarthy et al, 1991; McIntyre et al, 1991; Schwab et al, 1991). There has been no appreciable toxicity from IL-1ra in phase I clinical trials and further trials are underway to investigate the utility of IL-1ra as a treatment for sepsis, GVHD and rheumatoid arthritis. IL-1ra inhibits myeloid leukaemia cell growth in vitro as has been demonstrated with the soluble IL-1 receptor (Estrov et al, 1991; Rambaldi et al, 1991). Therefore, this agent may be useful for the treatment of myeloid leukaemia and it is undergoing evaluation in clinical trials.

Soluble TNF receptors

TNF-α and -β are cytokines with pleiomorphic functions ranging from the up regulation of inflammation to effects on haematopoiesis (Old, 1985; Beutler and Cerami, 1988). TNF-α and -β have identical biological effects and the genes for each molecule are located next to each other within the human histocompatibility locus. As with IL-1, TNF expression is increased by many stimuli including lipopolysaccharide and other bacterial cell wall components as well as cytokines, including IL-1, GM-CSF, IL-2 and TNF itself. IL-1, IL-2, IL-4, IL-6, IL-8, TGF-β, IFN-γ, GM-CSF and PDGF are some of the cytokines that are modulated by TNF (Neta et al, 1992). Clinical use of TNF as an anti-tumour agent has been limited due to the inability to escalate the TNF dose because of inflammatory side-effects due to cytokine release and direct TNF toxicity.

Most cell types express TNF receptors; exceptions include red cells, resting lymphocytes and some B-cell subsets (Schall et al, 1990; Pfizenmaier et al, 1992). Soluble TNF receptors have been isolated from human urine and from the serum of patients with cancer or inflammatory illnesses such as sepsis (Gatanaga et al, 1990; Engelmann et al, 1990). There are two distinct receptors; 55–60 and 70–80 kDa molecular mass. Both receptors are present in transmembranous and soluble forms with the 70 kDa form thought to mediate cytotoxicity and systemic inflammatory effects and the 55 kDa form responsible for increased cellular transcription through activation of NF-κB (Heller et al, 1992; Kruppa et al, 1992). Molecular mutations of TNF have been derived that are unable to bind the 70 kDa membrane receptor but retain affinity for the 55 kDa receptor and induce cytotoxicity (Van Ostade et al, 1993). Selective binding to the 55 kDa receptor may lead to decreased

systemic inflammation associated with TNF and may have clinical application for selective tumour killing without major systemic inflammation.

Soluble TNF receptors derived from both the 55 and 70 kDa receptors bind
TNF and prevent its interaction with cellular receptors (Seckinger and Dayer,
1992). The binding of TNF to the soluble TNF receptor generates a stable
complex that is eliminated without cellular interaction. Unlike most soluble
receptors that are generated by DNA alternative splicing, the soluble TNF
receptors are derived by proteolytic cleavage (Pfizenmaier et al, 1992).
Inhibition of TNF effects by soluble TNF receptors has been demonstrated in
a number of experimental systems of inflammation including lethal
bacteraemia in primate models of sepsis (Seckinger et al, 1990; Van Zee et al,
1992). In our laboratory we have demonstrated that chemotherapy-induced
endothelial cell death is enhanced by TNF-α and inhibited by soluble TNF
receptors and that this effect may be selective for non-malignant cells
(McCarthy et al, 1992). Soluble TNF receptors will attenuate the clinical
manifestations of TNF release suggesting that these molecules may be useful
in the management of severe inflammatory states such as sepsis, GVHD,
chemotherapy-induced toxicity and inflammatory bowel disease.

It is important to note, however, that recent in vitro data indicate that *low*
concentrations of soluble TNF receptors may actually stabilize the TNF
molecule and preserve bioactivity (Aderka et al, 1992). This implies that
there are different dose-dependent effects of soluble TNF receptor. An
analogous situation may be true for TNF itself. At high concentrations, TNF
suppresses the development of diabetes in non-obese diabetic mice possibly
through immune regulation (Satoh et al, 1989; Jacob et al, 1990). However,
when TNF-α is given to strains of obese diabetic mice and rats, it promotes
the development of obesity (Hotamisligil et al, 1993). The insulin resistance
that develops in these obese, diabetic animals can be blocked by a soluble
TNF receptor, suggesting a new role for TNF in endocrinological regulation.
Close monitoring of the clinical utilization of soluble TNF receptors at
different dose levels should yield valuable clinical data.

Because TNF inhibits the growth of some cancers, the use of TNF blocking
agents in patients with malignancies will require careful observation to
ascertain if soluble TNF receptors promote tumour growth as well as diminish
the unwanted adverse effects of the cytokine. The wide spectrum of TNF's
biological effects, ranging from cachexia to radiation protection, provide a
challenge for investigators who aim to discover the precise therapeutic role
for inhibition of TNF-α and TNF-β. Whatever the ultimate importance of
TNF inhibition, the therapeutic effects of the approach may be enhanced
when it is combined with other anti-inflammatory agents such as soluble IL-1
receptor or IL-1ra.

Soluble IL-2 receptors

The IL-2 receptor is expressed primarily on T cells and NK cells, the primary
target cells for IL-2 activation, and on B cells and macrophages/monocytes.
There are three forms of the IL-2 receptor, each of which has lower affinity
for IL-2 than a complex of all three receptors. Resting T cells express a

transmembrane receptor that is a 75 kDa molecule (IL-2Rβ), and a 70 kDa γ chain. This βγ complex can transduce signals, and is termed the intermediate affinity receptor. Once activated, T cells up regulate the expression of a 55 kDa protein (IL-2Rα or Tac) the low affinity receptor that associates with the 70 kDa molecule and forms a high affinity receptor for IL-2. IL-2 binds to either membrane-associated IL-2Rα or IL-2Rβ receptor with a lower affinity than the IL-2Rα/β complex (Fung and Greene, 1990; Taniguchi, 1992). Malignant T-cell tumours and activated T cells secrete soluble IL-2Rα receptors that can be detected in human serum or in culture (Treiger et al, 1986). The significance of these soluble IL-2 receptors as modulators of inflammation is not known. At present, the level of soluble IL-2Rα is useful as an indicator of the degree of inflammation or infection that is present. It also is useful as a clinical marker to follow the progression or response to therapy of malignant T-cell tumours that secrete soluble IL-2Rα. The soluble IL-2Rα will bind IL-2 with the same affinity as the isolated membrane form but has a lower affinity than the membrane α/β complex (Josimovi-Alasevic et al, 1988).

The IL-2Rβ chain is also expressed in a soluble form but binds IL-2 with a much lower affinity than the membrane form (Tsudo et al, 1990). There has been no evidence for the existence of a soluble α/β complex. Therefore, owing to the low affinity of each receptor alone for IL-2 as compared with the α/β complex, in vitro inhibition of T-cell activation by IL-2 requires over a 1000-fold concentration of soluble IL-2R (Kondo et al, 1988). Thus, soluble forms of the α and β chains of the IL-2 receptor would need to be given in large quantities to affect T cell function in vivo. A hybrid soluble α/β molecule would need to be developed that will bind IL-2 with an affinity that is similar to the IL-2 receptor membrane complex.

Soluble IL-4 receptors

IL-4 participates in a variety of haematopoietic and immunological responses, including the regulation of immunoglobulin synthesis, B-cell proliferation, T-cell and macrophage function and haematopoietic differentiation (Beckmann et al, 1992). IL-4 is capable of enhancing or suppressing B- and T-cell function. It increases B-cell production of the immunoglobulin classes IgE and IgG_1 while decreasing the production of IgG_2 and IgG_3. IL-4 stimulates T-cell proliferation but will inhibit the generation of cytolytic T cells; it acts with IL-10 to suppress selected T-cell helper activity (see IL-4 and IL-10 cytokine sections). Because of its pleiomorphic effects, the clinical consequences of down-regulation of the action of IL-4 will need to be carefully considered. The IL-4 receptor is expressed on many haematopoietic cells including B cells, T cells, and macrophages and transmembrane and natural soluble receptors for IL-4 have been isolated and cloned (Mosley et al, 1989; Idzerda et al, 1990). The soluble IL-4 receptor binds IL-4 with an affinity similar to the transmembranous receptor and will block the biological effects of IL-4 (Garrone et al, 1991; Jacobs et al, 1991b). The role of the receptor in vivo remains to be determined. It has been suggested that it may act as a transport protein for IL-4 and also increases the bioavailability of the cytokine (Fernandez-Botran and Vitetta, 1991). However, soluble IL-4 receptor will inhibit immune alloreactivity in vitro and in vivo in an experimental cardiac allograft model demonstrating that the soluble receptor will block IL-4 activity (Fanslow et al, 1991; Maliszewski et al, 1992). Ultimately, soluble IL-4R may be useful for down-regulating selected T-cell function, in particular in bone marrow and solid organ transplants.

Soluble IL-5 receptors

IL-5 is a haematopoietic growth factor that is involved in haematopoietic proliferation, in particular the proliferation and differentiation of eosinophil and B-cell precursors (McKenzie and Sanderson, 1992). The receptor for IL-5 is a complex structure composed of two chains: one molecule is an IL-5-specific receptor protein designated IL-5Rα and the other molecule is identical to the β chain of the GM-CSF receptor and the IL-3 receptor (Takaki et al, 1990; Kitamura et al, 1991; Tavernier et al, 1991). Unlike most other soluble receptors that are derived from alternative DNA splicing of the transmembrane form, the two soluble forms of the IL-5 receptor are derived without splicing, whereas the transmembrane form of the IL-5 receptor is derived from alternative splicing (Tavernier et al, 1992). The potential biological function and clinical utility of the soluble IL-5 receptor remains to be determined.

Soluble IL-6 receptors

IL-6 is a cytokine with pleiotrophic effects primarily related to B-cell proliferation and differentiation, haematopoiesis and inflammation (Hirano, 1992). Elevation of IL-6 has been associated with inflammatory states such as sepsis, rheumatoid arthritis, thyroiditis and AIDS. Serum and cellular IL-6 levels are elevated in association with certain B-cell tumours, in particular, multiple myeloma. The receptor for IL-6 consists of two molecules: IL-6 receptor α (IL-6Rα) which binds IL-6, and a second, larger molecule, gp130 that is thought to transduce the IL-6 binding signal (Taga et al, 1992). This complex of two receptors with one common receptor shared with other cytokine receptors is analogous to the two receptor complexes for IL-3, GM-CSF and IL-5. Recent evidence suggests that gp130 also functions to convert the leukaemia inhibitory factor (LIF) receptor to a high affinity receptor for LIF and another cytokine, oncostatin M (Gearing et al, 1992) which—as its name suggests—inhibits selected tumour cell growth. The LIF receptor and gp130 are part of a tripartite receptor complex for ciliary neutrotrophic factor (CNTF) (Davis et al, 1993). This complex interaction of IL-6, LIF, oncostatin M and CNTF receptor molecules further demonstrates the intricate network connecting cytokines and their receptors.

The biological role of soluble IL-6Rα may not be that of an inhibitor of IL-6 action. There is evidence that it enhances the action of IL-6, possibly as a carrier protein that facilitates interaction with the gp130 signal transducer (Mackiewicz et al, 1992; Novick et al, 1992; Taga et al, 1992). Further preclinical testing with isolated soluble IL-6Rα will be required to determine its precise biological function and therapeutic potential.

Soluble LIF receptors

Leukaemia inhibitory factor (LIF) is a cytokine with marked pleiotrophic effects including the differentiation and suppression of myeloid leukaemia cells, the inhibition of differentiation of primitive embryonal stem cells and the differentiation of neuronal cells (Hilton and Gough, 1991; Yamamori, 1992). It is detected in the serum of patients in septic shock and with various inflammatory diseases but its biological role in inflammatory illness is not determined (Waring et al, 1992). A soluble receptor for LIF has been isolated from serum and will inhibit the action of LIF in vitro (Layton et al, 1992). Owing to the complex interaction among the receptors for LIF, IL-6, oncostatin M and CNTF, the biological role for the soluble LIF receptor will need to be determined in the context of other cytokines with which it shares common receptor proteins.

Soluble IL-7, IL-9 and IL-12 receptors

IL-7 is a growth factor with proliferative effects on early B- and T-cell progenitors (Arai et al, 1990). IL-7 will potentiate the effects of cytokines in particular, IL-1, IL-2 and IL-4. A soluble IL-7 receptor (IL-7R) has been cloned along with the transmembrane receptor (Goodwin et al, 1990). The soluble IL-7R will inhibit the in vitro effects of IL-7 but the in vivo biological activity of the soluble IL-7R has not been elucidated.

IL-9 is a cytokine with T-cell and mast cell growth factor properties and enhances erythroid colony formation in the presence of erythropoietin (Uyttenhove et al, 1988; Donahue et al, 1990; Hultner et al, 1990). The IL-9 transmembrane receptor recently has been isolated along with a natural soluble form (Renauld et al, 1992). The biological role of the soluble form remains to be determined.

IL-12 induces a variety of cellular actions including the regulation of immunoglobulin synthesis and T and NK cell proliferation and differentiation (Gately et al, 1991; Naume et al, 1992; Podalaski et al, 1992). The membrane IL-12 receptor has been isolated. The DNA sequence suggests that a soluble IL-12 receptor exists as well as the transmembrane form (Podalaski et al, 1992).

Other soluble receptors

The isolation of natural soluble binding proteins related to their respective transmembrane receptors have been described for EGF (Nieto-Sampedro, 1988; Flickinger et al, 1992), IGF (Clemmons, 1991), NGF (Welcher et al, 1991), CD27 ligand (Hintzen et al, 1991), CD40 ligand (Fanslow et al, 1992), G-CSF (Fukunaga et al, 1990), GM-CSF (Raines et al, 1991; Sasaki et al, 1992), IFN-γ (Novick et al, 1989), growth hormone (Leung et al, 1987) and thyrotropin (Graves et al, 1992). These soluble receptors will bind their respective cytokine in vitro and may block cytokine interaction with the cellular transmembrane receptor and modulate cellular function in vivo.

OTHER MECHANISMS OF CYTOKINE DOWN-REGULATION

Cytokine conversion to receptor antagonist

Cytokines can be changed to receptor antagonists by single amino acid substitutions that will convert active cytokines into antagonist proteins. An example is the alteration of IL-4 into an antagonist protein by substitution of a tyrosine for aspartic acid at position 124 (Kruse et al, 1992). This molecule binds to the IL-4 receptor without agonist activity in a manner reminiscent of the natural IL-1 receptor antagonist which binds to the IL-1 receptor. Similar mutations with variable biological activity have been constructed from the TNF molecule (Lin, 1992). Molecular engineering of cytokines may provide a new source of antagonist proteins for the down-regulation and modification of cytokine action.

Anti-cytokine and anti-receptor antibodies

Naturally occurring autoantibodies against IL-1α, IFN-α, IFN-γ, TNF-α, NGF and IL-6 have been isolated from the serum of normal individuals and patients with inflammatory illness (Bendtzen et al, 1990; Hansen et al, 1991; Viani et al, 1991). Their biological significance is uncertain because they are present in low titres and are only erratically detected in inflammatory disease. Antibody formation against IFN-α occurs in patients who receive IFN-α injections and has been reported in patients with autoimmune disease (Prummer et al, 1989; Ronnblom et al, 1992). The anti-IFN-α antibodies typically do not interfere with IFN-α therapy and usually can be overwhelmed if clinically significant by increasing the IFN-α dose. In general then, the presence of naturally occurring antibodies to cytokines is of uncertain physiological significance and their role in immune regulation is unclear.

Monoclonal antibodies (Mabs) have been developed against cytokines and cytokine receptors in an attempt to block cytokine action. Anti-IL-2 receptor therapy has been utilized to treat selected T-cell lymphomas but without absolute clinical efficacy due to the inability to completely eliminate disease (Waldmann, 1992). Anti-receptor antibody therapy may be more effective in combination with other receptor antibodies, after conjugation with potent cellular toxins, or with chemotherapy. Much attention has focused on the inhibition of inflammatory cytokines such as TNF and IL-1 because of their participation in lethal inflammatory events such as sepsis. While anti-TNF antibodies will protect against the morbid effects of endotoxin in animal models, timing of treatment is important in inhibiting the lethal effects of endotoxin or related agents (Beutler et al, 1986). If anti-TNF treatment is delayed, the inhibitory effect can be lost. This may be due to the early expression of TNF that initiates immune activation after endotoxin challenge.

Two antibodies against bacterial cell wall products have been utilized in clinical trials with moderate success (Bone, 1991). Early trials with anti-TNF antibodies in the treatment of septic shock and GVHD have generated mixed results. Murine monoclonal anti-TNF antibody treatment of patients with severe GVHD had some clinical efficacy but after discontinuation of treatment, GVHD recurred in most patients (Herve et al, 1992). In a pilot study of patients with septic shock, the administration of murine anti-TNF Mab led to improved left ventricular function but these effects were temporary (Vincent et al, 1992). Murine anti-TNF Mab has also been used in patients with hairy cell leukaemia (HCL) because of evidence suggesting the cytokine contributed to tumour cell growth. The patients had a modest reduction in tumour burden after anti-TNF antibody treatment, but a major limiting factor was the development of anti-murine antibodies and serum sickness after prolonged treatment (Huang et al, 1992). A similar problem has developed in some patients who have received prolonged courses of the murine monoclonal anti-endotoxin antibodies.

Monoclonal antibody directed against cytokines can have unwanted effects. In experimental models of infection, treatment of animals infected with *Listeria monocytogenes* or *Mycobacterium species* with anti-IFN-γ or anti-TNF antibodies will cause worsening of the respective infection (Kaufmann and Flesch, 1990). The application of anti-cytokine or anti-cytokine receptor antibodies designed to block the action of inflammation will need to be monitored for immunosuppressive effects that may cause an increased frequency of opportunistic infections.

α_2-Macroglobulin

α_2-Macroglobulin (α_2M) is a relatively non-specific, multifunctional binding plasma protein that modulates the effects of diverse proteins and serves as a proteinase inhibitor, carrier protein and potential modulator of cytokine function (James, 1990; Borth, 1992; Gonias, 1992). It will bind to a variety of cytokines including TNF, TGF-β, PDGF, IL-6, NGF, bFGF and IL-1 (LaMarre et al, 1991). Binding to the native α_2M molecule does not affect cytokine action in vitro but after proteolytic cleavage, α_2M may act as an inhibitor of cytokines. Generating specificity at the cellular level or at the level of the α_2M molecule may provide a means for selective inhibition of cytokine function.

CYTOKINE DOWN-REGULATION OF IMMUNE FUNCTION

Transforming growth factor β

TGF-β is a member of a family of closely-related cytokines with marked pleiomorphic effects, ranging from enhancement of wound healing and fibrosis, to inhibition of epithelial cell and haematopoietic proliferation. TGF-β has been documented to inhibit oncogene expression and selected tumour cell growth (Keller et al, 1992; Massague et al, 1992; Matrisian et al,

1992). It is secreted by many different cell types, but primarily by platelets and endothelial cells. TGF-β has anti-inflammatory effects that are related to the decreased production of inflammatory cytokines. Cellular production of IL-1, TNF-α and IFN-γ mRNA is inhibited by TGF-β (Espevik et al, 1987). In animal models, TGF-β inhibits the development of collagen-induced arthritis, allergic encephalomyelitis, rheumatoid arthritis and multiple sclerosis (Kuruvilla et al, 1991). In numerous models of inflammatory disease, TNF and TGF-β have antagonistic effects on their cellular targets, suggesting that they regulate each other's action through intracellular signalling and transcription regulation. Mice homozygous for a mutation that results in no expression of TGF-β, develop a wasting syndrome shortly after birth manifested by raised tissue levels of inflammatory cytokines including TNF-α, IL-1β, IFN-γ and macrophage inflammatory protein 1α (Shull et al, 1992). Histopathological analysis of these animals revealed inflammatory cell infiltration and tissue necrosis in multiple organs. Mice homozygous for this mutation in TGF-β expression demonstrate the profound regulatory effect of this molecule on inflammation.

TGF-β does not only down-regulate other cytokines; it has been demonstrated to increase IL-6 production by monocytes, but will also inhibit release of further amounts to IL-6 in response to activation cytokines such as IL-2 (Turner et al, 1990; Musso et al, 1992). TGF-β will stimulate the production of IL-1ra from mononuclear cells, demonstrating another mechanism for the down-regulation of cytokine-mediated inflammation (Turner et al, 1991).

The interplay of TGF-β and inflammatory cytokines is illustrated by the events which follow severe hepatic inflammation. This phenomenon is down-regulated through the production of anti-inflammatory mediators such as TGF-β. As a consequence of the inhibition of inflammation, hepatic lipocytes (Ito cells) then participate in the formation of hepatic fibrosis, which is accompanied by the deposition of extracellular collagen and other matrix glycoproteins. Intracellular collagen synthesis by Ito cells is up-regulated at the level of DNA transcription by TGF-β whereas TNF-α inhibits collagen DNA transcription and will antagonize the effect of TGF-β (Armendariz-Borunda et al, 1992). Treatment of these cells with IL-1β has no effect on the DNA transcription or mRNA levels of collagen, but through a post-transcriptional event, IL-1β decreases the synthesis of collagen protein. The interplay of TNF, TGF-β and IL-1 is an integral component of the modulation of hepatic inflammation and development of fibrosis.

TGF-β may be effective as short-term therapy of inflammation, but since TGF-β receptors are expressed on many different cell types, long-term down-regulation of the action of TNF by TGF-β could be accompanied by deleterious effects on other aspects of immune, haematopoietic or endocrine function.

Interleukin-4

IL-4 has a wide range of effects on the cells that express the IL-4 receptor. IL-4 will down-regulate the production of IFN-γ by mononuclear cells

(Peleman et al, 1989). It will increase production of IL-10, a cytokine inhibitory factor, by CD4+ T-helper (Th2) cells (see below), increase the proliferation of CD8+ cytotoxic T cells and decrease the number of CD4+ helper T cells, NK cells and IL-2 activated killer cells (Jansen et al, 1990; Paul, 1991). While IL-4 has immunomodulatory effects that down-regulate selected monocyte and T-cell function, it is a stimulator of T-cell proliferation and enhances allograft rejection. Use of IL-4 as an immunosuppressive agent will require careful preclinical study and attention to its many diverse effects.

Interleukin-10

IL-10 is a lymphokine produced primarily by a selected subset of T-helper cells (Th2 cells), macrophages and Ly-1 + B cells (Howard and O'Garra, 1992). It was originally described as cytokine synthesis inhibition factor (CSIF) due to its ability to suppress the production of lymphokines by a subpopulation of T-helper cells designated Th1 (Fiorentino et al, 1989). Th1 cells generate cytotoxic and inflammatory reactions while Th2 cells stimulate immunoglobulin synthesis and help down-regulate Th1 cytokine secretion via IL-10 (Street and Mosmann, 1991; Sher et al, 1992). The lymphokines produced by stimulated Th1 cells include IL-2, IL-3, GM-CSF, and the inflammatory cytokines TNF-β and IFN-γ. In addition to IL-10, Th2 cells secrete IL-4, IL-5 and IL-6.

IL-10 also inhibits certain macrophage functions such as antigen presentation to Th1 cells, up-regulation of major histocompatibility complex (MHC) class II expression, and production of TNF-α, IL-1α, IL-1β, IL-6 and IL-8 (de Waal Malefyt et al, 1991a). It also increases the expression of IL-1ra, an inhibitor of IL-1 (Howard and O'Garra, 1992). This emphasizes the multipotent ability of IL-10 to down-regulate the inflammatory response at the T-cell and macrophage level.

While down-regulating selected inflammatory responses of the T-cell compartment, IL-10 participates in the up-regulation of B-cell function. IL-10 is a stimulant of B cell proliferation, differentiation and immunoglobulin synthesis, especially when combined with IL-4 (Rousset et al, 1992). Mice treated with anti-IL-10 antibody which blocked the action of IL-10, developed decreased immunoglobulin M levels, had a decreased ability to mount antibody responses to selected antigens and were depleted of a subpopulation of B cells with the surface marker Ly-1.

The response of the host to infectious agents is modulated by IL-10. *Schistosoma mansoni*, a helminthic parasite, causes an up-regulation of Th2 cells and an increased production of IL-10 (Sher et al, 1991). IL-10 inhibits macrophage cytotoxicity against helminthic infection suggesting that the parasite may evade host elimination through down-regulation of the host inflammatory response (Oswald et al, 1992). IL-10 has extensive sequence homology and shared biological properties with a product of the Epstein–Barr virus (EBV) genome, BZRF1, that has been designated viral IL-10 (v-IL-10) (de Waal Malefyt et al, 1991b). The production of viral IL-10 may play a role in the pathogenesis of EBV and other viral infections.

The participation of IL-10 in immune down-regulation by infectious agents may cause immune suppression and opportunistic infection as has been seen with other immunosuppressive agents such as anti-lymphocyte globulin, glucocorticoids or cyclosporin.

SUMMARY

The study of cytokines that regulate all areas of cellular communication has expanded over the past few years. The control and modulation of the complex network of cytokine action remains an area of intense interest. Agents that will modulate cytokine signal transduction at the cellular level will assist in the understanding of the molecular basis of cytokine cellular activation and in the design of drugs for the management of clinical disease. Recent work has demonstrated the existence of complex mechanisms of negative regulation of cytokine action. New methods utilizing isolated protein products that participate in immunomodulation may prove useful for clinical regulation of the host response to cytokine up-regulation. Currently, most interest in soluble cytokine receptors, natural cytokine inhibitors, genetically engineered cytokine antagonists and single or combinations of anti-inflammatory cytokines has focused on the possibility that they may become standard pharmacological agents for the treatment of inflammatory complications of clinical disease. Specifically, TNF and IL-1 inhibitors and the cytokines IL-10 and TGF-β, alone or in combination may be effective for the inhibition of severe clinical inflammation. Soluble receptors for other cytokines such as IL-6 may prove to be carrier proteins that enhance cytokine action and will require cautious investigation. Because most cytokines are pleiomorphic in their activities, down-regulation through the utilization of direct inhibitors or anti-inflammatory cytokines may cause immunosuppression, making the host susceptible to opportunistic infection. Selective and short-term inhibition of inflammatory cytokine action may be necessary to prevent unwanted clinical side-effects.

Acknowledgements

The careful reading and editing by Dr Michael Kroll and Ms Jane McCarthy is gratefully appreciated. Supported in part by a grant from the Methodist Foundation, Houston TX.

REFERENCES

Aderka D, Engelmann H, Maor Y et al (1992) Stabilization of the bioactivity of tumor necrosis factor by its soluble receptors. *Journal of Experimental Medicine* **175:** 323–329.
Arai K, Lee F, Miyajima A et al (1990) Cytokines: coordinators of immune and inflammatory responses. *Annual Reviews of Biochemistry* **59:** 783–836.
Arend WP, Malyak M, Bigler CF et al (1991) The biological role of naturally-occurring cytokine inhibitors. *British Journal of Rheumatology* **30 (supplement 2):** 49–52.
Armendariz-Borunda J, Katayama K & Seyer JM (1992) Transcriptional mechanisms of type I collagen gene expression are differentially regulated by interleukin-1 β, tumor necrosis factor α, and transforming growth factor β in Ito cells. *Journal of Biological Chemistry* **267:** 14316–14321.

Attal M, Huguet F, Rubie H et al (1993) Prevention of regimen-related toxicities after bone marrow transplantation by pentoxifylline: a prospective, randomized trial. *Blood* **82**: 732–736.

Bakouche O, Moreau JL & Lachman LB (1992) Secretion of IL-1: role of protein kinase C. *Journal of Immunology* **148**: 84–91.

Beckmann MP, Casman D, Fanslow W et al (1992) The interleukin-4 receptor: structure, function, and signal transduction. *Chemical Immunology* **51**: 107–134.

Bendtzen K, Svenson M, Jønsson V & Hippe E (1990) Autoantibodies to cytokines—friends or foes? *Immunology Today* **11**: 167–169.

Beutler B & Cerami A (1988) Tumor necrosis, cachexia, shock and inflammation: a common mediator. *Annual Reviews of Biochemistry* **57**: 505–518.

Beutler B, Milsark IW & Cerami AC (1986) Passive immunization against cachectin/tumor necrosis factor protects mice from lethal effect of endotoxin. *Science* **229**: 869–871.

Bianco JA, Appelbaum FR, Nemunaitis J et al (1991) Phase I–II trial of pentoxifylline for the prevention of transplant-related toxicities following bone marrow transplantation. *Blood* **78**: 1205–1211.

Bomsztyk K, Sims JE, Stanton TH et al (1989) Evidence for different IL-1 receptors in T and B cell lines. *Proceedings of the National Academy of Sciences, USA* **86**: 8034–8038.

Bone RC (1991) A critical evaluation of new agents for the treatment of sepsis. *Journal of the American Medical Association* **266**: 1686–1691.

Borth W (1992) α_2-Macroglobulin, a multifunctional binding protein with targeting characteristics. *FASEB Journal* **6**: 3345–3353.

Burch RM, Connor JR & Axelrod J (1988) Interleukin-1 amplifies receptor-mediated activation of phospholipase A2 in 3T3 fibroblasts. *Proceedings of the National Academy of Sciences, USA* **85**: 6306–6309.

Cerami A (1992) Inflammatory cytokines. *Clinical Immunology and Immunopathology* **62**: (1 Pt 2) P S3–S10.

Chizzonite R, Truit T, Kilian PL et al (1989) Two high affinity interleukin-1 receptors represent separate gene products. *Proceedings of the National Academy of Sciences, USA* **86**: 8029–8033.

Clemmons DR (1991) Insulin-like growth factor binding proteins: roles in regulating IGF physiology. *Journal of Developmental Physiology* **15**: 105–110.

Colotta F, Re F, Muzio M et al (1993) Interleukin-1 type II receptor: a decoy target for IL-1 that is regulated by IL-4. *Science* **261**: 472–475.

Davis S, Aldrich TH, Stahl N et al (1993) LIFR beta and gp130 as heterodimerizing signal transducers of the tripartite CNTF receptor. *Science* **260**: 1805–1808.

de Waal Malefyt R, Abrams J, Bennett B et al (1991a) Interleukin 10 (IL-10) inhibits cytokine synthesis by human monocytes: an autoregulatory role of IL-10 produced by monocytes. *Journal of Experimental Medicine* **174**: 1209–1220.

de Waal Malefyt R, Haanen J, Spits H et al (1991b) Interleukin 10 and viral IL-10 strongly reduce antigen-specific human T cell proliferation by diminishing the antigen-presenting capacity of monocytes via downregulation of class II major histocompatibility complex expression. *Journal of Experimental Medicine* **174**: 915–924.

DeForge LE, Kenney JS, Jones ML et al (1992) Biphasic production of IL-8 in lipopolysaccharide (LPS)-stimulated human whole blood. Separation of LPS- and cytokine-stimulated components using anti-tumor necrosis factor and anti-IL-1 antibodies. *Journal of Immunology* **148**: 2133–2141.

Dinarello CA (1991) Interleukin-1 and interleukin-1 antagonism. *Blood* **77**: 1627–1652.

Dinarello CA (1992) Interleukin-1 in infectious diseases. *Immunological Reviews* **127**: 119–146.

Dinarello CA & Wolf SM (1992) The role of interleukin-1 in disease. *New England Journal of Medicine* **328**: 106–113.

Donhue RE, Yang YC & Clark SC (1990) Human P40 T-cell growth factor (interleukin-9) supports erythroid colony formation. *Blood* **75**: 2271–2275.

Dornand J, Bouaboula M, dAngeac AD et al (1992) Contrasting effects of the protein kinase C inhibitor staurosporine on the interleukin-1 and phorbol ester activation pathways in the EL4-6.1 thymoma cell line. *Journal of Cellular Physiology* **151**: 71–80.

Eisenberg SP, Evans RJ, Arend WP et al (1990) Primary structure and functional expression from complementary DNA of a human interleukin-1 receptor antagonist. *Nature* **343**: 341–346.

Engelmann HD, Aderka M, Rubenstein M et al (1990) A tumor necrosis factor-binding protein purified to homogeneity from human urine protects cells from tumor necrosis factor toxicity. *Journal of Biological Chemistry* **264**: 11974–11980.

Espevik T, Figari IS, Shalaby MR et al (1987) Inhibition of cytokine production by cyclosporin A and transforming growth factor beta. *Journal of Experimental Medicine* **166**: 571–576.

Estrov Z, Kurzrock R, Wetzler M et al (1991) Suppression of chronic myelogenous leukemia colony growth by interleukin-1 (IL-1) receptor antagonist and soluble IL-1 receptors: a novel application for inhibitors of IL-1 activity. *Blood* **78**: 1476–1484.

Fanslow WC, Sims JE, Sassenfeld H et al (1990) Regulation of alloreactivity in vivo by a soluble form of the interleukin-1 receptor. *Science* **248**: 739–742.

Fanslow WC, Clifford KN & Park LS (1991) Regulation of alloreactivity in vivo by IL-4 and the soluble IL-4 receptor. *Journal of Immunology* **147**: 535–540.

Fanslow WC, Anderson DM, Grabstein KH et al (1992) Soluble forms of CD40 inhibit biologic responses of human B cells. *Journal of Immunology* **149**: 655–660.

Fazely F, Dezube BJ, Allen-Ryan et al (1991) Pentoxifylline (Trental) decreases the replication of the human immunodeficiency virus type 1 in human peripheral blood mononuclear cells and in cultured T cells. *Blood* **77**: 1653–1656.

Fernandez-Botran R (1991) Soluble cytokine receptors: their role in immunoregulation. *FASEB Journal* **5**: 2567–2574.

Fernandez-Botran R & Vitetta ES (1991) Evidence that natural murine soluble interleukin 4 receptors may act as transport proteins. *Journal of Experimental Medicine* **174**: 673–681.

Fiorentino DF, Bond MW & Mosmann TR (1989) Two types of mouse T helper cell. IV. Th2 clones secrete a factor that inhibits cytokine production by Th1 clones. *Journal of Experimental Medicine* **170**: 2081–2095.

Flickinger TW, Maihle NJ & Kung HJ (1992) An alternatively processed mRNA from the avian c-erbB gene encodes a soluble truncated form of the receptor that can block ligand-dependent transformation. *Molecular and Cellular Biology* **12**: 883–893.

Fukunaga R, Seto Y, Mizushima S & Nagata S (1990) Three different mRNAs encoding human granulocyte colony stimulating factor receptor. *Proceedings of the National Academy of Sciences, USA* **87**: 8702–8706.

Fung MR & Greene WC (1990) The human interleukin-2 receptor: insights into subunit structure and growth signal transduction. *Seminars in Immunology* **2**: 119–128.

Galella G, Medini L, Stragliotto E et al (1992) In human monocytes interleukin-1 stimulates a phospholipase C active on phosphatidylcholine and inactive on phosphatidylinositol. *Biochemical Pharmacology* **44**: 715–720.

Garrone P, Djossou O, Galizzi JP & Banchereau J (1991) A recombinant extracellular domain of the human interleukin 4 receptor inhibits the biological effects of interleukin 4 on T and B lymphocytes. *European Journal of Immunology* **21**: 1365–1369.

Gatanaga T, Lentz R, Masunaka I et al (1990) Identification of TNF-LT blocking factor(s) in the serum and ultrafiltrates of human cancer patients. *Lymphokine Research* **9**: 225–229.

Gately MK, Desai BB, Wolitzky AG et al (1991) Regulation of human lymphocyte proliferation by a heterodimeric cytokine, IL-12 (cytotoxic lymphocyte maturation factor). *Journal of Immunology* **147**: 874–882.

Gearing DP, Comeau MR, Friend DJ et al (1992) The IL-6 signal transducer, gp130: an oncostatin M receptor and affinity converter for the LIF receptor. *Science* **255**: 1435–1437.

Goldring MB & Goldring SR (1991) Cytokines and cell growth control. *Critical Reviews in Eukaryotic Gene Expression* **1**: 301–326.

Gonias SL (1992) α_2-Macroglobulin: a protein at the interface of fibrinolysis and cellular growth regulation. *Experimental Hematology* **20**: 302–311.

Goodwin RG, Friend D, Ziegler SF et al (1990) Cloning of the human and murine interleukin-7 receptors: demonstration of a soluble form and homology to a new receptor superfamily. *Cell* **60**: 941–951.

Granowitz EV, Clark BD, Mancilla J & Dinarello CA (1991a) Interleukin-1 receptor antagonist competitively inhibits the binding of interleukin-1 to the type II interleukin-1 receptor. *Journal of Biological Chemistry* **266**: 14147–14150.

Granowitz EV, Santos AA, Poutsiaka DD et al (1991b) Production of interleukin-1 receptor antagonist during experimental endotoxemia. *Lancet* **338**: 1423–1424.

Graves PN, Tomer Y & Davies TF (1992) Cloning and sequencing of a 1.3 KB variant of human thyrotropin receptor RNA lacking the transmembrane domain. *Biochemical and Biophysical Research Communications* **187**: 1135–1143.

Hannum CH, Wilcox, Arend WP et al (1990) Interleukin-1 receptor antagonist activity of a human interleukin-1 inhibitor. *Nature* **343**: 336–340.

Hansen MB, Svenson M, Diamant M & Bendtzen K (1991) Anti-interleukin-6 antibodies in normal human serum. *Scandinavian Journal of Immunology* **33**: 777–781.

Heller RA, Song K, Fan N & Chang D (1992) The p70 Tumor necrosis factor receptor mediates cytotoxicity. *Cell* **70**: 47–56.

Herve P, Flesch M, Tiberghien P et al (1992) Phase I–II trial of a monoclonal anti-tumor necrosis factor alpha antibody for the treatment of refractory severe acute graft-versus-host disease. *Blood* **79**: 3362–3368.

Hilton DJ & Gough NM (1991) Leukemia inhibitory factor: a biological perspective. *Journal of Cellular Biochemistry* **46**: 21–26.

Hintzen RQ, de Jong R, Hack CE et al (1991) A soluble form of the human T cell differentiation antigen CD27 is released after triggering of the TCR/CD3 complex. *Journal of Immunology* **147**: 29–35.

Hirano T (1992) The biology of interleukin-6. *Chemical Immunology* **51**: 153–180.

Hohmann HP, Remy R, Aigner L et al (1992) Protein kinases negatively affect nuclear factor-kappa B activation by tumor necrosis factor-alpha at two different stages in promyelocytic HL60 cells. *Journal of Biological Chemistry* **267**: 2065–2072.

Holler E, Kolb HJ, Moller A et al (1990) Increased levels serum levels of tumor necrosis factor alpha precede major complications of bone marrow transplantation. *Blood* **75**: 1011–1016.

Hotamisligil GS, Shargill NS & Spiegelman BM (1993) Adipose expression of tumor necrosis factor-α: direct role in obesity-linked insulin resistance. *Science* **259**: 87–91.

Howard M & O'Garra A (1992) Biological properties of interleukin 10. *Immunology Today* **13**: 198–200.

Huang D, Reittie JE, Stephens S et al (1992) Effects of anti-TNF monoclonal antibody infusion in patients with hairy cell leukemia. *British Journal of Haematology* **81**: 231–234.

Hultner L, Druez C & Moeller J (1990) Mast cell growth-enhancing activity (MEA) is structurally related and functionally identical to the novel mouse T cell growth factor P40/TCGFIII (interleukin-9). *European Journal of Immunology* **20**: 1413–1416.

Idzerda RL, March CJ, Mosley B et al (1990) Human interleukin 4 receptor confers biological responsiveness and defines a novel receptor superfamily. *Journal of Experimental Medicine* **171**: 861–873.

Imagawa DK, Millis JM, Olthoff KM et al (1990) The role of tumor necrosis factor in allograft rejection. *Transplantation* **50**: 189–193.

Iwasaki T, Uehara Y, Graves L et al (1992) Herbimycin A blocks IL-1-induced NF-kappa B DNA-binding activity in lymphoid cell lines. *FEBS Letters* **198**: 240–244.

Jacobs CA, Baker PE, Roux ER et al (1991a) Experimental autoimmune encephalomyelitis is exacerbated by IL-1 alpha and suppressed by soluble IL-1 receptor. *Journal of Immunology* **146**: 2983–2989.

Jacobs CA, Lynch DH, Roux ER et al (1991b) Characterization and pharmokinetic parameters of recombinant soluble interleukin-4 receptor. *Blood* **77**: 2396–2403.

Jacob CO, Aiso S, Michie SA et al (1990) Prevention of diabetes in non-obese diabetic mice by tumor necrosis factor: similarities between TNF α and IL-1. *Proceedings of the National Academy of Sciences, USA* **87**: 968–972.

James K (1990) Interactions between cytokines and α_2-Macroglobulin. *Immunology Today* **11**: 163–166.

Jansen JH, Fibbe WE, Willemze R & Kluin-Nelemans JC (1990) Interleukin-4, a regulatory protein. *Blut* **60**: 269–274.

Josimovi-Alasevic O, Herrmann T & Diamantstein T (1988) Demonstrations of two distinct forms of released low-affinity type interleukin 2 receptors. *European Journal of Immunology* **18**: 1855–1857.

Kaczmarski RS & Mufti GJ (1991) The cytokine receptor superfamily. *Blood Reviews* **5**: 193–203.

Kahan BD (1989) Cyclosporine. *New England Journal of Medicine* **321**: 1725–1738.

Kaufmann SH & Flesch IE (1990) Cytokines in antibacterial resistance: possible applications for immunomodulation. *Lung* **168 (supplement)**: 1025–1032.

Keller JR, Jacobsen SE, Dubois CM et al (1992) Transforming growth factor beta: a bi-directional regulator of hematopoietic cell growth. *International Journal of Cell Cloning* **10**: 2–11.

Kester M, Simonson MS, Mene P & Sedor JR (1989) Interleukin-1 generates transmembrane signals from phospholipids through novel pathways in cultured rat mesangial cells. *Journal of Clinical Investigation* **83**: 718–723.

Kitamura T, Sato N, Arai K & Miyajima A (1991) Expression cloning of the human IL-3 receptor cDNA reveals a shared β subunit for the human IL-3 and GM-CSF receptors. *Cell* **66**: 1165–1174.

Kondo N, Kondo S, Shimuzu A et al (1988) A soluble 'anchor minus' interleukin 2 receptor suppresses in vitro interleukin 2-mediated immune responses. *Immunology Letters* **19**: 299–308.

Krönke M, Schütze, Scheurich P & Pfizenmaier K (1992) TNF signal transduction and TNF-responsive genes. *Immunology Series* **56**: 189–216.

Kruppa G, Thoma B, Machleidt T et al (1992) Inhibition of tumor necrosis factor (TNF)-mediated NF-κB activation by selective blockade of the human 55-kD TNF receptor. *Journal of Immunology* **148**: 3152–3157.

Kruse N, Tony HP & Sebald W (1992) Conversion of human interleukin-4 into a high affinity antagonist by a single amino acid substitution. *EMBO Journal* **11**: 3237–3244.

Kuruvilla AP, Shah R, Hochwald GM et al (1991) Protective effect of transforming growth factor β1 on experimental autoimmune diseases in mice. *Proceedings of the National Academy of Sciences, USA* **88**: 2918–2921.

Lamarre J, Wollenberg GK, Gonias SL & Hayes MA (1991) Cytokine binding and clearance properties of proteinase-activated alpha 2-macroglobulins. *Laboratory Investigation* **65**: 3–14.

Layon MJ, Cross BA, Metcalf D et al (1992) A major binding protein for leukemia inhibitory factor in normal mouse serum: identification as a soluble form of the cellular receptor. *Proceedings of the National Academy of Sciences, USA* **89**: 8616–8620.

Le J & Vilček J (1987) Tumor necrosis factor and interleukin 1: cytokines with multiple overlapping biological activities. *Laboratory Investigation* **56**: 234–248.

Leung DW, Spencer SA, Cachianes G et al (1987) Growth hormone receptor and serum binding protein: purification, cloning and expression. *Nature* **330**: 537–543.

Lin LS (1992) TNF muteins. In Beutler B (ed.) *Tumor Necrosis Factors*, pp 33–48. New York: Raven Press.

McCarthy PL Jr, Abhyankar S, Neben S et al (1991) Inhibition of interleukin-1 by an interleukin-1 receptor antagonist prevents graft-versus-host disease. *Blood* **78**: 1915–1918.

McCarthy PL Jr, Nolasco L, Nolasco N et al (1992) Inhibition of dacarbazine (DTIC)-induced endothelial cell (EC) death by inflammatory cytokine inhibitors. *Blood* **80**: 477a.

McCarthy PL Jr, Williams L, Harris-Bacile M et al (1993) Phase I/II clinical study of soluble interleukin-1 receptor (sIL-1R) in steroid-resistant graft versus host disease (GVHD). *Blood* **82**: 215a.

McIntyre KW, Stepan GJ, Kolinsky KD et al (1991) Inhibition of interleukin 1 (IL-1) binding and bioactivity in vitro and modulation of acute inflammation in vivo by IL-1 receptor antagonist and anti-IL-1 receptor monoclonal antibody. *Journal of Experimental Medicine* **173**: 931–939.

McKenzie ANJ & Sanderson CJ (1992) Interleukin-5. *Chemical Immunology* **51**: 181–204.

Mackiewicz A, Schooltink H, Heinrich PC & Rose-John S (1992) Complex of soluble human IL-6-receptor/IL-6 up-regulates expression of acute-phase proteins. *Journal of Immunology* **149**: 2021–2027.

Maliszewski CR, Morrissey PJ, Fanslow WC et al (1992) Delayed allograft rejection in mice transgenic for a soluble form of the IL-4 receptor. *Cellular Immunology* **143**: 434–448.

Mantovani A, Bussolino F & Dejana E (1992) Cytokine regulation of endothelial function. *FASEB Journal* **6**: 2591–2599.

Marsh JW, Vehe KL & White HM (1992) Immunosuppressants. *Gastroenterology Clinics of North America* **21**: 679–693.

Massague J, Cheifetz S, Laiho M et al (1992) Transforming growth factor-beta. *Cancer Surveys* **12**: 81–103.

Mathias S, Younes A, Kan CC et al (1993) Activation of the sphingomyelin signaling pathway in intact EL4 cells and in a cell-free system by IL-1β. *Science* **259**: 519–522.

Matrisian LM, Ganser GL, Kerr LD et al (1992) Negative regulation of gene expression by TGF-beta. *Molecular Reproduction and Development* **32**: 111–120.

Matsushima K, Akahoshi T, Yamada M et al (1986) Properties of a specific interleukin-1 receptor on human Epstein–Barr virus transformed B lymphocytes: Identity of the receptors for IL-1α and IL-1β. *Journal of Immunology* **136**: 4496–4508.

Matsushima K, Baldwin ET & Mukaida N (1992) Interleukin-8 and MCAF: novel leukocyte recruitment and activating cytokines. *Chemical Immunology* **51**: 236–265.

Mosley B, Beckmann MP, March CJ et al (1989) The murine interleukin-4 receptor: molecular cloning and characterization of secreted and membrane bound forms. *Cell* **59**: 335–348.

Musso T, Espinoza-Delgado I, Pulkki K et al (1992) IL-2 induces IL-6 production in human monocytes. *Journal of Immunology* **148**: 795–800.

Naume B, Gately M & Espevik T (1992) A comparative study of IL-12 (cytotoxic lymphocyte maturation factor), IL-2-, and IL-7-induced effects on immunomagnetically purified CD56+ NK cells. *Journal of Immunology* **148**: 2429–2436.

Neta R, Sayers TJ & Oppenheim JJ (1992) Relationship of TNF to interleukins. *Immunology Series* **56**: 499–566.

Nieto-Sampedro M (1988) Astrocyte mitogen inhibitor related to epidermal growth factor receptor. *Science* **240**: 1784–1786.

Novick D, Engelmann H, Wallach D & Rubinstein M (1989) Soluble cytokine receptors are present in normal human urine. *Journal of Experimental Medicine* **170**: 1409–1414.

Novick D, Shulman LM, Chen L & Revel M (1992) Enhancement of interleukin 6 cytostatic effect on human breast carcinoma cells by soluble IL-6 receptor from urine and reversion by monoclonal antibody. *Cytokine* **4**: 6–11.

Ohlsson K, Bjork P, Bergenfeldt M et al (1990) Interleukin-1 receptor antagonist reduces mortality from endotoxin shock. *Nature* **348**: 550–552.

Old LJ (1985) Tumor necrosis factor (TNF). *Science* **230**: 630–632.

Oswald IP, Wynn TA, Sher A & James SL (1992) Interleukin 10 inhibits macrophage microbicidal activity by blocking the endogenous production of tumor necrosis factor required as a costimulatory factor for interferon gamma-induced activation. *Proceedings of the National Academy of Sciences, USA* **89**: 8676–8680.

Paul WE (1991) Interleukin-4: a prototypic immunoregulatory lymphokine. *Blood* **77**: 1859–1870.

Peleman R, Wu J, Fargeas C & Delespesse G (1989) Recombinant interleukin 4 suppresses the production of interferon gamma by human mononuclear cells. *Journal of Experimental Medicine* **170**: 1751–1756.

Pfizenmaier K, Himmler A, Schütze S et al (1992) TNF receptors and TNF signal transduction. In Beutler B (ed.) *Tumor Necrosis Factors*, pp 439–472. New York: Raven Press.

Piguet PF, Grau GE, Allet B & Vassalli P (1986) Tumor necrosis factor/cachectin is an effector of skin and gut lesions of the acute phase of the graft-vs-host disease. *Journal of Experimental Medicine* **166**: 1280–1289.

Pober JS & Cotran RS (1990) The role of endothelial cells in inflammation. *Transplantation* **50**: 537–544.

Podalaski FJ, Nanduri BV, Hulmes JD et al (1992) Molecular characterization of interleukin 12. *Archives of Biochemistry and Biophysics* **294**: 230–237.

Prummer O, Seyfarth C, Scherbaum WA et al (1989) Interferon-alpha antibodies in autoimmune diseases. *Journal of Interferon Research* **9 (supplement 1)**: S64–S67.

Raines MA, Liu L, Quan SG et al (1991) Identification and molecular cloning of a soluble human granulocyte-macrophage colony stimulating factor receptor. *Proceedings of the National Academy of Sciences, USA* **88**: 8203–8207.

Rambaldi A, Torcia M, Bettone S et al (1991) Modulation of cell proliferation and cytokine production in acute myeloblastic leukemia by interleukin-1 receptor antagonist and lack of its expression by leukemic cells. *Blood* **78**: 3248–3253.

Renauld JC, Druez C, Kermouni A et al (1992) Expression cloning of the murine and human interleukin 9 receptor cDNAs. *Proceedings of the National Academy of Sciences, USA* **89**: 5690–5694.

Riegel JS, Corthesy B, Flanagan WM & Crabtree GR (1992) Regulation of the interleukin-2 gene. *Chemical Immunology* **51**: 266–298.

Ronnblom LE, Janson ET, Perers A et al (1992) Characterization of anti-interferon-alpha antibodies appearing during recombinant interferon-alpha 2a treatment. *Clinical and Experimental Immunology* **89**: 330–335.

Rosenbaum JT & Boney RS (1992) Use of soluble interleukin-1 receptor to inhibit ocular inflammation. *Current Eye Research* **10**: 1137–1139.

Roussett F, Garcia E, Defrance T et al (1992) Interleukin 10 is a potent growth and differentiation factor for activated human B lymphocytes. *Proceedings of the National Academy of Sciences, USA* **89**: 1890–1893.

Sasaki K, Chiba S, Mano H et al (1992) Identification of a soluble GM-CSF binding protein in the supernatant of a human choriocarcinoma cell line. *Biochemical and Biophysical Research Communications* **183**: 252–257.

Satoh J, Seino H, Abo T et al (1989) Recombinant tumor necrosis factor α suppresses autoimmune diabetes in nonobese diabetic mice. *Journal of Clinical Investigation* **84**: 1345–1348.

Schall TJ, Lewis M, Koller KJ et al (1990) Molecular cloning and expression of a receptor for human tumor necrosis factor. *Cell* **61**: 361–370.

Schütze S, Potthoff K, Machleidt T et al (1992) TNF activates NF-κB by phosphatidylcholine-specific phospholipase C-induced 'acidic' sphingomyelin breakdown. *Cell* **71**: 767–776.

Schwab JH, Anderle SK, Brown RR et al (1991) Pro- and anti-inflammatory roles of interleukin-1 in recurrence of bacterial cell wall-induced arthritis in rats. *Infection and Immunity* **59**: 4436–4442.

Seckinger P & Dayer JM (1992) Natural inhibitors of TNF. *Immunology Series* **56**: 217–236.

Seckinger P, Zhang JH, Hauptmann B & Dayer JM (1990) Characterization of a tumor necrosis factor-α (TNF-α) inhibitor: evidence of immunological cross-reactivity with the TNF receptor. *Proceedings of the National Academy of Sciences, USA* **87**: 5188–5192.

Sher A, Fiorentino D, Caspar P et al (1991) Production of IL-10 by CD4+ T lymphocytes correlates with down-regulation of Th1 cytokine synthesis in helminth infection. *Journal of Immunology* **147**: 2713–2716.

Sher A, Gazzinelli RT, Oswald IP et al (1992) Role of T-cell derived cytokines in the downregulation of immune responses in parasitic and retroviral infection. *Immunological Reviews* **127**: 183–204.

Shull MM, Ormsby I, Kier A et al (1992) Targeted disruption of the mouse transforming growth factor-β1 gene results in multifocal inflammatory disease. *Nature* **359**: 693–699.

Sims JE, Acres RB, Grubin CE et al (1989) Cloning of the interleukin-1 receptor from human T-cells. *Proceedings of the National Academy of Sciences, USA* **86**: 8946–8950.

Street NE & Mosmann TR (1991) Functional diversity of T lymphocytes due to secretion of different cytokine patterns. *FASEB Journal* **5**: 171–177.

Symons JA, Eastgate JA & Duff GW (1991) Purification and characterization of a novel soluble receptor for interleukin 1. *Journal of Experimental Medicine* **174**: 1251–1254.

Taga T & Kishimoto T (1992) Cytokine receptors and signal transduction. *FASEB Journal* **6**: 3387–3396.

Taga T, Hibi M, Murakami M et al (1992) Interleukin-6 receptor and signals. *Chemical Immunology* **51**: 181–204.

Takaki S, Tominaga A, Hitoshi Y et al (1990) Molecular cloning and expression of the murine interleukin-5 receptor. *EMBO Journal* **9**: 4367–4374.

Taniguchi T (1992) Structure and function of IL-2 and IL-2 receptors. *Behring Institute Mitteilungen* **91**: 87–95.

Tavernier J, Devos R, Cornelis S et al (1991) A human high affinity interleukin-5 receptor (IL5R) is composed of an IL5-specific alpha chain and a beta chain shared with the receptor for GM-CSF. *Cell* **66**: 1175–1184.

Tavernier J, Tuypens T, Plaetinck G et al (1992) Molecular basis of the membrane-anchored and two soluble isoforms of the human interleukin 5 receptor alpha subunit. *Proceedings of the National Academy of Sciences, USA* **89**: 7041–7045.

Treiger BF, Leonard WJ, Svetlik P et al (1986) A secreted form of the human interleukin-2 receptor encoded by an 'anchor minus' cDNA. *Journal of Immunology* **136**: 4099–4105.

Tsudo M, Katasuyama H, Kitamura F et al (1990) The IL-2 receptor beta-chain (p70). Ligand binding ability of the cDNA-encoding membrane and secreted forms. *Journal of Immunology* **145**: 599–606.

Turner M, Chantry D & Feldmann M (1990) Transforming growth factor β induces the production of interleukin 6 by human peripheral blood mononuclear cells. *Cytokine* **2**: 211–216.

Turner M, Chantry D, Katsikis P et al (1991) Induction of the interleukin 1 receptor antagonist protein by transforming growth factor β. *European Journal of Immunology* **21:** 1635–1639.

Uyttenhove C, Simpson RJ & Van Snick J (1988) Functional and structural characterization of P40, a mouse glycoprotein with T cell growth factor activity. *Proceedings of the National Academy of Sciences, USA* **85:** 6834–6938.

Van Ostade X, Vandenabelle P, Everaerdt B et al (1993) Human TNF mutants with selective activity on the p55 receptor. *Nature* **361:** 266–269.

Van Zee KJ, Kohno T, Fischer E et al (1992) Tumor necrosis factor soluble receptors circulate during experimental and clinical inflammation and can protect against excessive tumor necrosis factor alpha in vitro and in vivo. *Proceedings of the National Academy of Sciences, USA* **89:** 4845–4849.

Viani E, Flamminio G, Caruso A et al (1991) Purification of natural human IFN-gamma antibodies. *Immunology Letters* **30:** 53–58.

Vincent JL, Bakker J, Marecaux G et al (1992) Administration of anti-TNF antibody improves left ventricular function in septic shock patients. Results of a pilot study. *Chest* **101:** 810–815.

Waldmann TA (1992) Immune receptors: targets for therapy of leukemia/lymphoma. *Annual Review of Immunology* **10:** 675–704.

Walsh CT, Zydowsky LD & McKeon FD (1992) Cyclosporin A, the cyclophilin class of peptidylprolyl isomerases, and blockade of T cell signal transduction. *Journal of Biological Chemistry* **267:** 13115–13118.

Wang P, Ba ZF, Morrison MH et al (1992) Mechanism of the beneficial effects of ATP-$MgCl_2$ following trauma-hemorrhage and resuscitation: downregulation of inflammatory cytokine (TNF, IL-6) release. *Journal of Surgical Research* **52:** 364–371.

Waring P, Wycherley K, Cary D et al (1992) Leukemia inhibitory factor levels are elevated in septic shock and various inflammatory body fluids. *Journal of Clinical Investigation* **90:** 2031–2037.

Weglicki WB, Phillips TM, Freedman AM et al (1992) Magnesium-deficiency elevates circulating levels of inflammatory cytokines and endothelin. *Molecular and Cellular Biochemistry* **110:** 169–173.

Welcher AA, Bitler CM, Radeke MJ & Shooter EM (1991) Nerve growth factor binding domain of the nerve growth factor receptor. *Proceedings of the National Academy of Sciences, USA* **88:** 159–163.

Yamamori T (1992) Molecular mechanisms for generation of neural diversity and specificity: roles of polypeptide factors in development of postmitotic neurons. *Neuroscience Research* **12:** 545–582.

Index

Note: Page numbers of article titles are in **bold** type.